Jenny Jones

JENNY JONES

my story

with Patsi Bale Cox

**Andrews McMeel
Publishing**

Kansas City

www.andrewsmcmeel.com

Library of Congress Cataloging-in-Publication Data

Jones, Jenny, 1946–
    Jenny Jones : my story / Jenny Jones with Patsi Bale Cox.
      p.   cm.
    ISBN 0-8362-3729-3 (hc)
    1. Jones, Jenny, 1946–   . 2. Television personalities—
United States—Biography. I. Cox, Patsi Bale. II. Title.
PN1992.4.J66A3   1997
791.45'028'092—dc21
[B]   97-39596
                                            CIP

I dedicate this book to my mother.

Contents

Acknowledgments

Denis, you are the love of my life, my rock. Without you there would be no book, for you are the one who convinced me that I had a story worth telling. Patsi Cox, you helped me gain much insight into my relationships, and this is a better book because of it. And for all the details I couldn't remember, Dana Lasker, my executive assistant, thanks for helping bring them all back with your meticulous memory. Liz, for the hours you spent poring through your old diaries, I am very grateful, and Roula, thanks for always being available to verify the slightest detail.

I owe a lot to Warner Bros., for believing in me in the first place, and for sticking by me when the road was rough. And I owe a special thanks to Jim Paratore, Alan Perris, and Barbara Brogliatti for their support with this book. As for Debby and Ed Glavin, my executive producers, thanks for helping lighten my workload so I could have the time I needed to write. Thanks also to Leigh Ann Dwyer, director of research at *Jenny Jones*, for helping with this project.

The people most affected by the hectic schedule I had to keep in preparing this book were the ones I work closely with. Again Dana, thanks for always being there, and Brian L'Heureux, my personal assistant, thanks for all the late nights and emotional support.

As for the striking cover of this book, a serious thanks to the brilliant design and supervision of Tim Lynch, and for the styling services of Earl Nicholson. Styling services? Let's see, Earl did my makeup, picked my clothes, dressed me up, picked the furniture, and with Brian's help put together a great cover photo. And it was a good hair day, thanks to Marisa Stevoff and Dorota Kiszkiel.

And Ken Bank, the photographer who has taken all my studio

photos for the past seven years, I should only look as good as you make me look. You are gifted.

Thanks also to Mel Berger, agent extraordinaire, and Chris Schillig, my dedicated (and very patient) editor.

Prologue

I've been arrested four times in my life. The first was for shoplifting an iron when I was an eleven-year-old runaway living on my own in Canada. The second arrest was at the hands of the Immigration Department, when I was a twenty-one-year-old illegal alien playing in the United States with a band called the Swingin' Dolls. The following year I was busted for attempting to break into a haunted house in Reno, Nevada, with my band, the Cover Girls. And the last time, in 1984, when I was thirty-eight years old, I was arrested for carrying a handgun at the airport in Newark, New Jersey.

I've always tended to defy authority, but it's not something I regret, since my fierce need for independence has brought me many successes. It's brought me even more failures, but I don't regret those either. In fact, the desire to control my destiny has been the single force that has driven me throughout my life.

My father was a dominating, self-absorbed man who expected me to fail at every turn unless I did things his way. I showed myself as unworthy of his respect early on and spent the rest of my life trying to earn it back. My mother didn't measure up in his eyes, and for the rest of her life she dealt with it her way, by turning to alcohol.

In books and magazine articles I've read, the characteristics shared by children raised by an alcoholic parent are marked, and a psychologist might say I'm a textbook example of an alcoholic's child. Since we had no control over our surroundings as children, we try to make up for it as adults, grabbing hold of the reins and hanging on ferociously. We're not particularly trusting people, having lived through innumerable disappointments and broken promises.

Some of us compensate by becoming serious and responsible, others by being cheerfully irresponsible. I've been on both sides of the fence there. Four arrests before I turned forty should tell you that I've often acted recklessly, yet today I am scrupulously reliable. We also tend to bury our emotions deep down, where no one can detect the hurt and disappointment.

Sammy Davis Jr. once told me I was a dichotomy, and maybe I am. While I sometimes act fearless and confident, I'm often scared and insecure. I constantly seek approval, yet I entered professions where I was vulnerable to the disapproval of many. Did I say "disapproval"? Try direct, aim-for-the-heart shots. But I've kept on going, and while the shots did sting, I survived their impact.

I think a lot of us are scared and insecure; these past seven years of hosting a talk show have taught me that I'm not unique in my fears. So I'm writing this book for every person who's ever felt unqualified and inadequate: the people who wake up in the middle of the night, terrified that they've just had their last opportunity, and have blown it, and are about to be exposed for the imposters they really are. That's how I've lived most of my life. I'm going to throw my story out on the table, including all the personal disappointments, the professional setbacks, and the missteps. I hope somebody out there will read this, shake his or her head, and say, "Well, if she can do it, maybe I can too."

There's another thing you may learn from this book. People are always asking, "Where in the world do you get those talk show guests?" Where do we find the people who appear on shows like Out of Control Teens, Sibling Rivalry, Devastated by an Affair, I Survived an Attack, or Sexual Harassment? Once you read *My Story*, you'll see where many of the guests could have come from—my family.

Jenny Jones

1

Love and War

On September 1, 1939, the invading German army roared across Poland in tanks, crushing everything in its path, including the Polish army. They called it *Blitzkrieg*, a lightning attack that marked the beginning of World War II. My father, Jan Stronski, a twenty-four-year-old corporal in the Polish army, was taken captive on the front lines. Years later he decided to write a personal memoir, and in this work he told of the experience, a defining event in his life and one that would affect everyone close to him:

They pushed us and herded us like cattle into a Polish Catholic church. The church had no toilet facilities, and being pressed so closely together, it was impossible to sit down. If we had to go to the bathroom, we could only loosen our belts and let our pants drop to the floor. We urinated on each other and defecated on the floor. At night, we tried to sleep standing on our feet, resting our heads on one another's shoulders, a great mass of human bodies, just hanging together.

The first day we received nothing to eat. The second day we were given soup at noontime. At approximately 4 A.M. that morning, we were taken outside, fifteen at a time, and allowed to go to the toilet in a field nearby. The opening and closing of the door provided some ventilation, but it did not eliminate the terrible stench of human waste. This situation lasted two days and three nights before we were moved to a nearby warehouse. I truly believe that if we had had to remain in the church any longer, we would all have died.

At night, when I could not sleep, I listened to the guards giving the command to march to the field, the "Stop!" and "Sit!" Then came the command to "Stand up!" I noted that it took approximately fifteen minutes from the time one group returned to the warehouse until another arrived at the field, and I began to plan my escape.

I observed that the light was dim, a darkish gray, and it was foggy. It was September, and the potato plants in the nearby field were at their full height. The foliage was about a foot and a half tall, and it might provide a little cover. Just beyond the potato field were the hills, which might provide safe refuge.

At 4 A.M. we were ordered to form a column in groups of three and march to the field. The guard stationed himself at the rear of the column, holding a machine gun to our backs. The commands started: "Stop!" then "Sit!" and finally "Stand up!" I dropped to the ground on my stomach. Holding a cross in my left hand, I crossed myself with my right hand and prayed to God, in his kindness, to keep me from being shot. My body was frozen and numb. Every second I thought would be the last. I waited, thinking, Now he will pull the trigger. He will shoot me now, between the rows of potatoes. But the guard did not see me. The prayer kept me alive.

When the guard commanded our column to return to the warehouse, I knew he would return with a new group in fifteen minutes, and I determined to see how far I could get in that time. My hands were shaking and my knees were numb from the wet, cold ground. I began crawling on my stomach, pulling myself along by my elbows between the rows. I was still hidden by the foliage, the dim light, and the fog.

I had no sooner reached the hill when suddenly, from another direction, came the command "Stop!" Then someone cried out in Polish, "Please don't shoot!" I heard a shot. I began to run. About a quarter mile ahead I spotted a Pol-

ish farmhouse. There was a scarecrow in the garden, and the farmer willingly gave me its clothing, urging me to leave as quickly as possible. I hurriedly removed my army uniform and dressed in the scarecrow suit. Now I could pass as a Polish farmer.

I continued walking east, careful to walk on the main road so as not to arouse the suspicions of the Germans, who were using the highway, leading columns of prisoners to the west. I was practically rubbing elbows with the German guards, who were walking or riding their horses alongside the columns of prisoners. I sang and whistled as I walked, and carried a walking stick as if I was just another farmer from a nearby village.

Thus began a decade of disenfranchisement, for the Stronskis and for millions of other Europeans. Father later said he learned two important lessons during the war and the years immediately following it: First, it often takes enormous willpower just to survive; second, count on no one but yourself. He never forgot those lessons, not in his work, his marriage, or his childrearing.

When Father finally made it back to his home in rural Poland, he hesitated before going inside, concerned about his appearance. That was typical. For my father, image was everything. He was a handsome, muscular man who'd always been a sharp dresser; his army uniforms were custom made and neatly pressed. He always had coins to jingle in his pocket. Now he would face his mother in filthy rags. But as subsequent events would show, his clothing was the least of his worries.

Father had been in the military since 1936, when he was drafted into the infantry at the age of twenty-one. Now that he had escaped and was living incognito with his family, he knew no other way to make a living, so he established a black-market business, smuggling pork in his horse cart to nearby villages. Ironically, when the Soviet army defeated the Germans in the area and took control of his village, it was not these black-market activities that led to his arrest. It was the young woman who would become my mother.

One day, while in the city of Drohobycz, I saw a long line of people waiting in front of a store. In this crowd of people, I spotted a girl with a very sad but beautiful face. She had light blond hair and a creamy complexion, and she was very feminine in dress. I walked over to her and introduced myself. She told me her name was Zosia, a nickname for the more formal name of Zoska. I learned she had been waiting in line to buy bread since five o'clock in the morning. It was then nine o'clock. During our conversation, she told me her father had been arrested by the Bolsheviks and deported to Siberia. I asked what he had done. She replied, "His crime was only that he was a prison guard in Poland before the war."

Zosia told me she was living with her mother and younger brother, with no income, no job, and only temporary free shelter provided by friends. She allowed me to accompany her home and meet her family. Her mother embraced me like a friend, and I could see that they were lonely, poor, and helpless. I had been exposed to human tragedy and wished to give them the benefit of my strength and experience. I visited them every day. And every day I fell deeper and deeper in love with Zosia.

Mother was sixteen years old. Before Father could make any formal arrangements to marry her, both my father and Zosia's family were arrested for having ties to a former prison guard. Father was separated from the family and transported by train to the Russian state of Kazakhstan to a northern village inhabited primarily by Mongolian farmers, where he was put to work as a laborer. This is where he first learned the Bolshevik tenet *Seho dnia robotajesz, seho dnia kuszajesz:* Work today, eat today.

I guess when survival is all that drives you, it's hard to think past the end of the day. If you're still alive, you're satisfied. His survival instinct ultimately enabled him to make a better life, but, like the Soviet creed, it always seemed to be a day-to-day thing. He had to work today to eat today. My father was a controlling yet distant parent. I've always explained his emotional absence to myself by saying it took all his effort just to survive and he had no time left for his family.

After some months, Father received word from his mother that Zosia and her family had been taken to a village nearly six hundred miles from Kazakhstan. He was able to convince the Soviets to give him work unloading farm tools and other equipment at the train station in nearby Aktyubinsk. He was not under close supervision, and when the job was finished he used every bit of his considerable charm to convince a female conductor to allow him to board a train headed in the direction of the village where the family was living.

When he arrived he immediately proposed marriage to the startled Zosia. There was no church in the village, but the couple was told that in times of great turmoil, such as war, the Catholic church would sanction vows made before five witnesses. With Zosia's family and friends standing about them, my parents were married that day for the first of three times. My father later said he told Mother that the one thing she must never do was commit adultery. If she did, he said, he would break two of her ribs and dig out one of her eyes.

Before the two could leave the village, Father was arrested again. This time his crime was more serious: Not only had he left his farm labor post, he had done so to marry the daughter of a former prison guard. And this time his treatment was more severe. He was taken to a holding area with a hundred or so other men, stripped naked, and shaved, right down to his pubic hair; he recalled that the six Russian women who did the shaving often jerked the men into line by grabbing their penises. Then he was transferred to a prison on the Asian side of the Ural Mountains. Seven hundred miles of desert and mountains lay between the newlyweds.

Father was convinced he would never leave that prison. He was not allowed out of his cell, and he became so lonely he looked forward to seeing the ants that sometimes crawled on his windowsill. He contemplated suicide, wondering if he could use his shirt to hang himself from the cell bars or the light fixture. Fearing he might simply fall and become a helpless cripple, he began to starve himself to death. After he refused food for a week, a commissar interrogated him, asking detailed questions about his childhood, his service in the Polish army, and his escape from the Germans. Finally, the commissar told him he would be released, not because they believed he hadn't committed a crime but as a "special privilege."

The price he was to pay, as it turned out, was to return to Zosia's village as a spy for the Communists. Chosen because he could converse in both Polish and Russian, he was supposed to report any Poles or Ukrainians who were sympathetic to the Third Reich. Although he refused the espionage position, the Soviets believed he could be coerced once they allowed him to leave and he was reunited with his wife. He began making his way across the desert and the mountains.

Father was in a weakened physical condition and had no money, so at one point he got food by passing himself off as a Hungarian gypsy who could tell fortunes. He told his first customer that her husband had either already been arrested or soon would be — a fairly safe guess because under Stalin's regime hundreds, including this woman's husband, were arrested daily. The woman not only fed him, she told her friends about this marvelous gypsy mystic, and they gave him food as well. Another time during that trip, a Soviet official and his wife befriended him on a train and shared their lunch: dark bread spread with pigs' lard, a few sardines, and some salt pork. The food tasted so good he began to cry.

Without a Soviet-sanctioned ceremony, my parents were not considered married. So when he finally got back to my mother, they held a second wedding ceremony, which consisted of vows read from Soviet-prepared Communist marriage documents. My mother began working as a seamstress for the government, and my father was offered a job in a bakery.

He had learned that the best way to stay out of trouble was to keep his mouth shut, so he did. He remembered men being imprisoned for commenting on the size of Stalin's mustache or the number of airplanes flying over the village. The only public statements my parents made occurred at political rallies, when they shouted Communist slogans aloud and prayed silently that they would not be considered enemies of the people. But the Soviets were determined to use him to gather information about certain locals, and sidestepping his spying assignment was precarious.

> *Every week I reported to the Soviets, but empty-handed, giving different reasons for not having the information that they had instructed me to bring them. And every time, before I would leave, Zosia and I would cling to one another and kiss as though it was our last good-bye. As the weeks went on she grew more and more frightened, pleading with me, "If you don't cooperate with them, something will happen to you. You must tell them something, even if you have to fabricate it."*
>
> *And so I began to make up reports. I would give the Soviets a first or last name, claiming I had forgotten the other part, so no harm could come to the individual. Every week I had the feeling it would be my last week of freedom.*

Circumstances changed markedly when Germany attacked the Soviet Union in July of 1941. Soviet military officials soon came to Father with an offer to once again serve in the Polish army under their command. To rejoice in his good fortune, father brought home what he considered a traditional Russian celebration feast: dark bread, raw onions, pork lard, salt, and a bottle of vodka. Together with a group of his male friends, father passed a shot glass and the bottle of vodka around the table. Tradition called for each to take one shot of vodka and hand it to the next. When the bottle was passed to Mother, she quickly poured three shots in succession and downed them with gusto. Father was horrified. What might happen if she drank that amount with men who were not his friends, when he was not around?

"You are young and pretty," he later advised her. "It would be more appropriate for you to have taken just half a shot." He was right to be concerned about Mother's fondness for liquor.

2

Life Goes on,
and We Are Only Human

After many delays involving citizenship papers and government red tape, Father was inducted back into the Polish army. But he couldn't apply for military benefits for Mother because the Poles didn't recognize the couple's Communist marriage ceremony. They solved the dilemma by getting both earlier marriages annulled by a priest, who then married them in a Catholic ceremony.

Zosia was sent to Persia with a group of military wives and there gave birth to their first child, a son she named Roman. When Father got back to Teheran from a campaign at the front, he immediately went to the office where they kept records of Polish civilian families to find where his wife was living. There he was surprised to learn that Zosia was working. He knew she must have had the baby by this time, so why would she have taken a job? Anxious, he rushed to the address he'd been given. As soon as they embraced, he asked Zosia why she was working and who was keeping the child.

"Oh, I'm so sorry," she mumbled. "He looked like you, but he is dead."

My father remembered being in a state of shock as Mother led him through the streets of Teheran to a little Persian cemetery. There, he saw a small painted plywood cross inscribed *Here lies Roman Stronski. May he rest in peace.*

The baby had lived two months and then developed a stomach disorder and began bleeding from the bowels. Years later, when I was a baby, I too developed this condition. Father always said he was the one who saved me from death, and he believed he could have saved little Roman too. There were many things for which he never forgave my mother. Roman's death was the first.

When he learned that many of the military wives were being sent to South Africa, Father convinced the Polish army to accept Zosia as a recruit and the couple was sent to Palestine, where Father could visit Mother between campaigns. The first night he was in Jaffa, Father had a disturbing dream. He saw Mother lying at the bottom of a deep well. She was dressed in her military uniform and had her hands crossed on her chest. Her wedding ring was cracked through the middle. Father's response to this dream was very typical of his stern, unbending disposition.

> I was very angry with her, thinking, "What a foolish woman. She fell into the well and killed herself."

It's interesting that his reaction was one of anger, not compassion for the woman he loved and who appeared to be dead.

His iron-fisted nature is perhaps best seen in his disciplinary tactics regarding the soldiers who served under his wartime command:

> We were far into the desert. There was no place to go and nothing to do. I wanted to have Zosia with me, and I became very lonely. This gave me extra time to enforce discipline. I left no stone unturned. I inspected boxes, belt buckles, buttons, marching abilities, line formation, knowledge of weapons, and even singing. There was also a platoon of women at the camp, and while inspecting their tents I was most particular about their mess kits. Most of the time, when I took a toothpick and ran it around the cracks and crevices, I found dirt. I said to them, "You are supposed to be an example of motherhood and cleanliness. Look at this dirt! You must do better!" Soon, they too were in the best of shape.

In 1944, at age twenty-one, Mother gave birth to my sister, Helena Elizabeth, in Jaffa. On one trip home, Father decided to move his family out of the military compound and into what he considered more normal family living conditions, so he secured a room in a former Russian Orthodox monastery (now available for military wives) and moved Mother and Elizabeth there. He brought a large dog back with him so she and the baby would have extra protection. And he hired a teenage Muslim boy he'd recently met to care for the dog and look in on Mother and Elizabeth from time to time. Then he returned to the front.

Months went by before he could return to Jaffa. When he finally secured a leave, he found Mother's living quarters in disarray and infested with lice, bedbugs, and ticks. Mother had lost a great amount of weight and seemed distant toward him. He tried to locate Ebrahim, the young Muslim, to ask him why he had allowed this to happen, but when the boy saw him he ran away. A few days later, after Father had burned the bedclothes and cleaned out the infestation, Ebrahim appeared at their door and invited the family to attend a film. Ebrahim picked up little Elizabeth with such familiarity that Father felt jealous and a bit like an interloper. The film Ebrahim took them to see was an Arabian tale of a tragic lost love.

A few days later, when my father was visiting one of his military friends, he was shocked when his friend told him what had caused the change in my mother's behavior toward him. She was having an affair. My father cursed the war that had left her to face such temptation, all the while envisioning her in the arms of a handsome young Polish officer:

> I demanded to know who the man was. Reluctantly, my friend replied, "It is the young boy you asked to take care of your dog." Ignoring his request to remain calm, I became enraged. "No! This is not true! You are nothing but an old gossip!" My friend looked at me with pity in his eyes. "Go home and ask your wife."

When I reached home I addressed my wife in a stern and serious voice. "Zoska," I said, "come here."

I had never used this name to address her before. Consequently, she knew immediately there was a problem and that her tower of life was crumbling.

"Do you remember when I married you the first time in Siberia, I told you that if you ever wanted your freedom all you had to do was tell me?" I asked. "For all creatures must be free on this earth. But I said if you ever committed adultery or lied to me I would break two of your ribs and dig out one of your eyes. Now I am here to take back what I said." I then asked, "Did you have anything to do with Ebrahim?" She devastated me by saying, "Yes, I did."

Circumstances would have been much different if the affair had been with a Polish officer, a man my father considered his peer. That it was a Muslim street boy was unthinkable, and to make matters worse, Mother had given Father a venereal disease. Father got an extension of two weeks on his military leave and dealt with Mother in his usual orderly fashion. He explained that, although he had lost all respect for her as a wife, he would care for her out of love for his daughter, Elizabeth. He promised that after the war he would take them away from Palestine and find them a permanent home where Elizabeth could go to school and have some security. He would help Zosia find work. And then he would divorce her.

The war did end soon after that, and Father moved them to Jerusalem, where Mother began earning a living as a dressmaker. Father rented her a sewing machine and purchased used clothes to cut apart and make patterns. Father had not quite lost interest in Mother, because while living in Jerusalem she became pregnant by him again. As he explained in his memoir, "Life goes on, and we are only human after all." On learning of the pregnancy, Father insisted Mother do whatever she had to do to get rid of the baby, but she knew of no way to do this. By the time I was born, Father was resigned to having a second child but had no plans to care much for it.

When Mother went into labor, Father rushed to the home of a midwife who lived three blocks away; by the time the two of them returned, they heard the cries of an infant. Mother gave birth to me, quickly and alone, on June 7, 1946. Despite his feelings toward Mother and this pregnancy, Father decided to keep me.

> *When I first looked at this baby my spirit immediately changed. I forgot about Zoska, who she was and what she was, as I looked at this beautiful child. This child whom I hated before she was born and now loved dearly. So deep was my love for this baby, I wanted to name her after me. Being a girl, she was baptized with the name Janina, after my name in Polish, Jan. Now this new baby, so unwanted before birth, captured my heart. I was spending much more time with her than Elizabeth. Janina was so happy, always smiling and laughing. Then, after a few weeks, we found blood in her diaper. My heart sank. Not again. Not this bleeding again.*

I had developed the same stomach disorder that caused Roman's death, and I was hospitalized immediately. Day after day Father came to the hospital, only to find I had made no progress, was losing more weight, and was developing rashes on my body. I remained there for two months with no improvement, and finally Father approached hospital officials to ask that I be released in his care. But when he returned home and told my mother that the two of them would have to sign legal papers relieving the hospital of any responsibility, Mother merely shrugged and said, "In my opinion, she is already dead. If you bring her home it will only be for her funeral."

The next morning they brought me home anyway. According to my father, I looked like a skinned rabbit, bony and covered with a rash. For the next several months, Father nursed me back to health, all the while believing he could have done the same for Roman. He consulted an Arab doctor, who suggested a diet of cooked rice meal and lukewarm tea, adding mashed bananas after two weeks. When that appeared to be helping, Father added chicken, chewing the meat himself before feeding it to me. Although it was slow, I did recover completely. And so my mother's prediction was wrong. I did not come home for my own funeral.

Looking for the promised land

Once I was on the road to recovery, Father could again concern himself with another road, one that would lead us to a permanent home. My parents' citizenship was always in question since national boundaries were in flux. Mother was born in Lodz. Father was born in the Ukraine. By this time the Soviets controlled Poland, and neither of my parents could face returning to a Communist-controlled country. They had been through far too much under the Soviet regime. So, fearing that we would be deported from Palestine, my father moved us to Italy and we settled in Rome.

My parents didn't take to Italy at first. For one thing, Italian food was distasteful to them. They were used to eating noodles served with honey and sugar. The first time they sat down to an Italian meal of spaghetti with tomato sauce and cheese, both Mother and Father hated it. They thought it smelled rotten. And they found the Italian customs of loud conversation and animated gestures disturbing. I can just imagine them ducking every time a gesture was made, fearing for their safety. But it didn't take long for them to understand that they wouldn't be harmed.

Mother again started a dressmaking business, and in her spare time she made matching dresses for Liz and me. She dressed us alike until we went to school, at which time we wore matching uniforms anyway. Because Mother left Liz and me with a local woman, Italian became my first language, the language we spoke when we played games such as *Giro giro tondo*, Ring Around the Rosy. But we spoke only Polish at home. (Later, when we moved to Canada, I learned some English from my parents, complete with a Polish accent, but I didn't learn proper English until I started school.)

Even though Italy had allowed them to settle there, Father knew it was not a permanent solution to their refugee status. There was a problem. During his stay in Russia, Father had done what thousands of Poles had done and registered as a member of the Communist Party. It didn't matter that he'd done it as an act of self-preservation, it put him under suspicion with the Italians. Father wanted to find a home where he was beyond such suspicions, where he could become a citizen and begin a real life.

This new life he dreamed about did not include Mother. He no longer wanted to be married to her, but he hesitated to leave his two young daughters alone with her in Europe, where he believed females, young and old, were treated badly. He finally decided to take us to Canada, where he'd heard women were held in somewhat higher esteem. Once he was sure his wife and children could survive without a man, he planned to file for divorce.

One of the first things Father did when he arrived in Rome was to contact the International Red Cross and attempt to find out about his mother, who was still in Poland; his brother, who had been taken prisoner by the Germans during the war; and an aunt who had moved to Canada.

He took a job with the Vatican, managing a dormitory for displaced persons. He also had a little black-market cigarette and fabric business going on the side, so he soon built up enough of a nest egg to try to emigrate. Father's first choice was Argentina, but when a letter arrived from a relative in Canada, he booked passage on a boat to the port of Halifax. I was two years old.

The waters were rough on the Atlantic. People were sick and throwing up all day and all night, and father feared Liz and I would never make it to our new home alive. We survived the ocean voyage, but more turbulent waters awaited us in Canada.

3

The New World

We arrived in Halifax, Nova Scotia, in 1948, with no money or possessions other than our clothes, Mother's sewing machine, and several bolts of fine black-market Italian silk. We went directly to London, Ontario, where Father's aunt and uncle were living.

With a loan from his uncle, Father made a down payment on a house on Sackville Street and, since the dwelling had several sleeping rooms, started taking in boarders while Mother did alterations at home. The house seemed enormous, with stairs and halls and rooms that seemed to go on forever. A few years ago I drove past that "huge" house on Sackville Street, and it turned out to be a very modest dwelling. And the "gigantic" yard that I used to play in with my sister seemed barely large enough for a sandbox.

I've been back to London many times, and if you'll forgive me for bragging about my beautiful hometown, it truly is a lovely city. I spent many weekends at Springbank Park as a child, playing in a little round wading pool and riding a miniature train through the grounds. The park is alongside a river called the Thames, just like in England. My favorite thing to do was walk through Storybook Gardens, a wonderful little zoo based on children's stories. There, the Three Little Pigs display really had three little pigs. And while you wouldn't expect to see mice at a zoo, at the Hickory Dickory Dock exhibit the mouse did run up a clock, a pretty exciting sight for a small child. I think my favorite time of year to visit the park was autumn, when the foliage was breathtaking.

London is also the home of the University of Western Ontario, one of the most prestigious educational institutions in all of Canada. People come from all over the country to attend this highly respected school. It is where my father always hoped I would study, but I had other plans, one of which was show business. After all, London was not without its own world-renowned celebrity: Guy Lombardo!

As humble as our new home really was, to a refugee family fleeing post-war Europe it seemed like a palace. But it was not a happy home, because my father was not a happy man. Every time he looked at Mother he was reminded of her affair with a street boy and how she had disgraced him.

I was too young to realize at the time just how disrespectful his treatment of her was, but Liz remembers a particularly sad incident. One evening, some men were sitting at the kitchen table talking to my father, and Mother was standing over the sink. Liz says Father took his foot and raised the back of her skirt up and let all the men have a look. To him, she was little better than a woman he could buy on the street.

The first memory I have from the Sackville Street house was a traumatic one. I was about four years old and saw my father pick up the kitchen table and throw it at my mother. Then he spit on her and called her a tramp. It's odd that I don't remember if the table hit her or not, but I do remember seeing the spit in her hair as she lay cringing on the floor. It would be many years before Liz and I learned where Father's rage toward Mother had originated.

Just as Father's vision of himself did not include being saddled with a disreputable wife, his career ambitions did not include renting out rooms for a living. Wanting something more substantial, he sold the house for a four-thousand-dollar profit and used the money to open a shop.

When we first came to Canada, he had heard someone say that Canadian women spent a lot of money on clothing. So he rented a building on Richmond Street and went into the women's clothing business, specializing in bridal gowns. Even though he had no respect for Mother, he named the shop "Sophie's," which is English for Zosia. After all, as he said, "Zosia had the talent, and I had the money."

Father knew very little about the dress business, so he worked hard to learn. He studied fashion, fabric, design, color, and marketing. For her part, Mother was not only an excellent dressmaker but an economical one as well. One of her finest creations, as far as I was concerned, was a ballerina costume she made for me to wear to school on Halloween. She must have collected bits and pieces of fabric from her bridesmaid designs, and the result was a work of art. It was pink tulle, as fine a ballerina dress as could be purchased anywhere. I stood for hours, looking at myself in the mirror and imagining being on a stage with people applauding.

I didn't have much interest in Mother's dressmaking, but when I got older, she taught me the basics of sewing. Years later, when I started playing in bands and doing stand-up comedy, I made all my stage costumes, which not only offered me a creative outlet but saved a lot of money as well.

In 1952, when I was six years old, we moved into a tiny apartment above an Italian deli on Richmond Street, right across the street from the shop. It was so close that I could lean out the window and yell above the traffic noise to get Dad's attention. I can't imagine what the neighbors' thoughts were when they heard a small child screaming out the window, "Daddy! Daddy!" I'm surprised they didn't summon the police and fire departments to save me, when all I wanted was permission to have some ice cream.

Liz and I enrolled in dance classes, studying ballet and tap. I went each week with my little round ballet case, where I stored my shoes and leotards. When the lid was opened, there was a round mirror upon which I had pasted a picture of my favorite movie star, Marilyn Monroe. I used to fantasize what it would be like to be that glamorous and beautiful. I kept a scrapbook filled with photos of many glamorous movie stars. Marilyn was my favorite, but there were several others who were allowed to share scrapbook space with the icon. They included Liz Taylor, Jayne Mansfield, Yvonne De-Carlo, Ava Gardner, and Jane Russell.

Admiring these buxom women had quite an impact on how I felt about my own body, ultimately contributing to my having a series of breast implants, by far the worst decision I have ever made. But movie stars in the fifties had such mystique and glamour, how could I not be in awe? Some of the handsome men who also made the grade in my scrapbook were Rock Hudson, Jeff Chandler, Kirk Douglas, and Tony Curtis.

Liz and I both dreamed of being glamorous stars in movies or on the stage. We were always performing for anyone who would sit still long enough. We'd sing songs together, and after seeing some of the biblical epics that were so popular in the early fifties, we even had our own version of the Dance of the Seven Veils that Rita Hayworth did in *Salome*.

Our biggest form of entertainment was listening to the radio. Liz and I would sit on the floor with our ears almost pressed to the speaker, waiting when our favorite shows came on, *The Lone Ranger* and, my absolute favorite, *Inner Sanctum*, which always started with the sound of a creaking door. I would imagine something so horrifying and vile that I could barely go to sleep at night after listening to it. I think that was the beginning of my preoccupation with horror movies, which I watched constantly until they became too violent. (Now I don't like them at all.)

We went to a lot of movies when we were little, probably because we didn't have a television. And when we did get our first television set, there wasn't a remote control. If you had to actually get up and change the channel, you might as well go out to a movie.

Getting a television set back then was a really big deal, almost like getting a pool might be now. *The Honeymooners* was the first show I remember seeing, but we watched every show religiously, shows such as *I Love Lucy*, *My Little Margie*, *This Is Your Life*, and *The Life of Riley*. *The Lone Ranger* came on television, and although it was great to finally view the action, I think the imagination that radio stimulated was more exciting.

Wrestlemania

Our father's favorite form of entertainment was attending wrestling matches. He had always wanted to be a wrestler, and in 1950, he had even enrolled in a wrestling training program at the London YMCA. But because his size prohibited him from pursuing that particular dream, I think he became preoccupied with the sport. While we were small, his heroes were men such as Killer Kowalski and Gorgeous George. In later years he was obsessed with Hulk Hogan. In his mind, theirs were the ultimate success stories. They made millions of dollars a year, they lived in mansions, and they were surrounded by beautiful women.

My father wanted to be just like these huge men, and he began to live vicariously through them. So off to the matches he went, with his two daughters, ages six and eight, in tow. There are many things I might ask him now if he were still alive. One of them would be, Why in the world did you drag two small girls to these violent events, where unruly crowds of men hollered for blood (and usually got it—one wrestler even bit off another man's ear)?

I can't recall Mother ever going to the matches. It was just Liz and me trailing along behind our dad. Our household revolved around wrestling. If the match was in town, we went. If it was on television, we watched.

I hated going to the wrestling matches, and one night I balked. I twisted in my seat. I whined. I sulked. Not a word was said on the way home, but I knew I was in serious trouble. We went into the house, and I was instructed to lie down on the floor in the middle of the living room.

Mother and Liz watched in silence as Father paced around me in a circle, around and around. He talked to himself in Polish, contemplating my punishment. I watched his feet circle me again and again, not knowing what was going to happen to me for embarrassing him. Finally he took off his belt and started hitting me. I don't remember the actual blows; Liz is the one who remembers that part. For me the more fearful and humiliating time was the waiting. The belt was almost a relief.

Mother said nothing through any of this, but then she never said much, either to us or to him. I have some fond memories of her during that time, but not many. One rare recollection is of walking down Sackville Street with both Mother and Father. We were going for ice cream, and I wore a little matching coat and hat Mother had made. They each took one of my hands and swung me along between them. There were also nights when Mother sat beside our bed, playing a guitar and singing Polish folk songs until we drifted off to sleep. She did enjoy those weekends when we packed up sandwiches and Father drove our Nash Rambler to the beach at St. Thomas on Lake Ontario, or Fanshawe Dam. Mother loved sitting in the sun, watching Liz and me build sand castles or collect shells.

But those family times were rare. As I look back on those days, I picture Mother as living in a numbed state. She was just there. Part of her reclusive nature came from her Middle European upbringing, which taught that women did not question their husbands. But her affair with Ebrahim and Roman's mysterious death must also have played a part in her silence.

Our father felt he owned our mother, and she had allowed his son to die and betrayed her vows with a street boy. Blame became an integral part of their relationship, and a weapon he used against her with Liz and me.

"I was the one who saved you when you were a baby," he'd say to me. "Your mother didn't nurse you back to health. She refused to get up every two hours all through the night to feed you." He also took credit for seeing that I slept on dry sheets. I was a bed wetter throughout childhood. "Your mother wouldn't get up to change the sheets when you wet the bed," he'd say. "I was the one who had to awaken and care for you." The doctors told my parents the cause was emotional, not physical. That shouldn't have been a surprise, considering the tension in our house.

Excuse me, is that a kielbasa on your head?

In 1954 we moved to a duplex on Tecumseh Avenue in London's suburbs, quite an upgrade from the rooms on Richmond Street. Soon after we moved there I remember begging my father to let me have a pet rabbit. He finally gave in, and I used to take Sniffles out for rides in a buggy. When I tired of the novelty of my new pet, my father cooked Sniffles for dinner.

I was bothered by it, but our dietary habits were different. Sometimes when Father was driving and came across some roadkill, he'd say, "Too bad"—not for the unfortunate mishap but for the fact that we had no way to know how fresh the meat was.

Tecumseh Avenue was where I learned first-hand what it is to be a considered a refugee and an outsider. My parents were still very much tied to Poland, and we were constantly packing boxes of goods to send to our European relatives. I not only spoke broken English, but Mother made our clothing, and it wasn't always the most fashionable look. I think that's one reason we didn't fit in, and why the gangs of children in the neighborhood started calling us "D.P.s," in reference to our status as "displaced persons." (I took quickly to Canadian games, though. My favorites were dodge ball, tag, and "Mother, May I?")

Clothing wasn't the only way we were different from many of the other children. Some of our meals were hardly typical. We ate sugar sandwiches—on white bread, of course. My parents had never seen anything like white bread! Some of our other delicacies included pigs' feet in aspic and blood sausage. The first time I ever ate anything from a can was when a friend's mother served me Campbell's vegetable soup. And we colored Easter eggs by boiling the eggs with onion skins until the egg shells turned red.

So many of my parents' beliefs were rooted in Old World thinking. They thought putting a drop of kerosene on a sugar cube and making children eat it would cure a cold. We swallowed those cubes and burped up kerosene and got just as sick as any other kids. I can still remember the taste of kerosene in my mouth.

My hair was another problem. It was thin and fine, and Dad

believed the way to make it grow in thick was to shave it all off. So I hung out in the neighborhood with a bald head, never questioning Father's action, since his authority was irrefutable. And I didn't know how strange I looked until the children started pointing at me and laughing.

My hair finally grew back, just as thin and fine as ever. Then Mother styled it by rolling it up at the top and pinning it into a long roll from front to back. I looked like I had a kielbasa on my head. It might have been the style in Poland, but not in London, Ontario. But that's how they sent me from the house, and that's how I went out among the Canadian kids. Once again, they pointed and laughed.

One time I nearly became an insider. We had a spelling bee at school, and I came within a breath of winning. Though I spoke broken English, I prided myself on spelling the language correctly. I wanted to win that spelling bee, and I correctly spelled every long and difficult word they gave me. During the last round I was asked to spell *area*, probably the easiest word I'd been given that day. I thought, *I've got this!* and without thinking I beamed at the teacher and spelled it out: "a-r-i-a." Wrong! I returned to my seat, red-faced at having made such a simple mistake. Still a little immigrant, after all.

Our being D.P.s didn't seem to hurt Sophie's bridal shop, though, and with hard work the business grew. My parents hired an additional seamstress, a hand finisher, a cutter, an office girl, a fitting specialist, and two saleswomen. They had four sewing machines and fifty showroom samples. Within a few years Father had a permanent home, and he finally became the success he'd dreamed of being. Still, he was not a happy man. He remembered it this way in his memoirs:

> *I had no personal life and no love. I was like a rose in the sand with no roots. It was a situation I wouldn't wish on my worst enemy, to be young and strong, full of energy, and yet to be lonely and hungry for love. But if my life was destined to be lonely, then I would not fight it, but take life every day as it came. I concentrated all my energy on the business.*

Liz and I didn't know that Father and Mother often talked of ending their marriage. Years later we learned that Mother frequently talked about wanting her freedom, explaining that she didn't need a man. Father agreed, and even offered to buy her a small house and set her up in her own dress shop. He never considered asking for custody of his two daughters, believing that girls needed their mother far more than their father. Though I don't know why, neither of them made a move to dissolve the marriage. Nor do I know how long this arrangement might have continued if the Black Witch hadn't come into our lives.

4

The Black Witch

When Father was a young man he went to a fortune-teller. The man told him he would soon win a fight for survival, he would marry in the East and have two children with that wife, and he would live to age seventy-four. But, the fortune-teller added, true happiness would evade him until he crossed the ocean and met a beautiful young brunette.

That woman walked into our store one afternoon in 1954. She was a beautiful nineteen-year-old girl with dark hair from the Greek town of Xylokastron. Her name was Roula Frangos, and she was looking for work. The moment Father saw her, he remembered the words of the European fortune-teller and began to think Fate had brought her to him. So he hired her to work in the store.

She spoke Greek and a little Italian, and Father spoke Polish, some English, some Russian, and a very little Italian. So the two communicated in broken Italian. Father didn't tell Roula about his feelings for some time, believing she was "too young, too pretty and single" whereas he wasn't even divorced yet. Roula says she had no indication that his feelings for her were growing. And even if she had, I think she would have had to ask herself some hard questions when he fired her within a few weeks of her employment.

Father's personality shows itself well in his explanation of Roula's firing:

*I was intrigued with her fascinating personality, as
well as her beauty, but my main concern was making the
dollar and being successful. Despite the fact that I was attracted to Roula, I was unhappy with the quality of her work
and told her she needed more experience in the North American way of doing things. "You are not fast enough. You do
not produce enough. You need to learn more and then come
back."*

"I guess this means I'm fired," Roula said.
"It looks like it," Father answered.
Fate had brought Father his true love, and he'd fired her for
being unproductive.
Several days later, he saw Roula staring through the window
into his store and went out to talk to her. This time, he saw yet another possession.

*The closer I came to her the more beautiful she was in
my eyes. As I walked toward her suddenly it became very
clear. She is the one! I have now traveled across the ocean,
and she is the brunette who will bring me happiness. She
belongs to me.*

He offered to put her back on the payroll and give her simpler
duties. Father said later he believed she was attracted to him in the
beginning, too. But Roula says it wasn't so. "Your family seemed
very happy, very normal," she now says. "You two children were so
polite and well mannered, and Sophie and John were cordial. I had
no idea their marriage was already over, and when he first approached me I was furious. I told him he was just trying to take advantage of a young girl out on her own."
If Roula didn't know my parents' marriage was unhappy, certainly many others in London did. Although he didn't discuss it with
Liz and me, we later learned that Father told the story of Mother's
affair with a Palestinian street boy to many of his friends. Of course,

he omitted the fact that because of the affair he had contracted a venereal disease. That would have been too embarrassing.

Liz and I only learned about the affair and how it had damaged our parents' marriage when we were in our early teens. It would have been much better if we'd known what was going on when our parents divorced. As it was, we considered Roula a home-wrecker, and we dubbed her the Black Witch.

In 1955 Father sent Mother and Liz and me to a tobacco farm for the summer. It sounds very strange now, but when I was a child in Canada, going to a tobacco farm was a bit like going off to summer camp. In some ways, the farm was like a dude ranch. We learned how to work in the fields, chopping the tobacco and hanging it to dry in barns.

Liz and I had fun at the farm, and I even bested my big sister once. I asked one of the hands to show me how to start up the tractor, and he did. Then I approached Liz and arrogantly said I knew how to start the tractor. She took the bait and bet me I couldn't. So I climbed on the machine, started it up, and took her quarter.

Our being gone allowed Father to see Roula more frequently, and just before Mother and Liz and I were to return, they set off on an outing to a nearby lake. It didn't become quite the romantic interlude Father had planned, because while he was taking Roula on a romantic canoe ride, his back went out. Roula not only had to paddle back to shore, she also had to drive the thirty miles back to London. There was another problem: Roula didn't know how to drive. She remembers my nearly paralyzed Father telling her which pedals to push and when to speed up and slow down. Somehow she got them both home.

Mother didn't even question the trip, or how her husband had thrown out his back while vacationing with a young female employee. She just helped Roula carry Father to the bedroom on a makeshift stretcher. For months afterward, Liz and I helped Mother and Roula pull Father around the house on a piece of carpet.

While he was debilitated, Father gave a great deal of thought to his failed marriage and his love for Roula. He decided to ask Mother for a divorce. Maybe she was sick of being the Scarlet

Woman, or maybe she was just tired of dragging Father around the house, but Mother immediately agreed. She even told Roula that my father was a good man and would make her a good husband. I don't think she cared much one way or the other. I know now that she'd started drinking more, and I think her increased dependence on alcohol dulled her emotions.

5

The Next Best Thing
to Hollywood

We had never been to Montreal, so I don't know why Father decided it would be a good place for Mother to relocate. It's possible that he wanted her far enough away that she couldn't bother him, yet close enough that he could keep tabs on his daughters. Or it could be he believed she could find dressmaking opportunities in such a large city. Whatever the reason, in 1956, when I was nine years old, we moved to Montreal.

Liz and I didn't want to leave London, and to convince us to move, Father assured us that in Montreal we could be discovered and become movie stars. We'd wanted to be performers of some kind for as long as I could remember. As I mentioned, I collected photos from movie magazines and used to imagine my own picture in a magazine some day. In my case, those hopes were not about having money or being an actress. They had to do with feeling I was special.

Father explained that girls could get "discovered" in big cities; it would be almost like moving to New York. Of course, Father knew of no filmmakers producing movies in Montreal, but he convinced us it was the next best thing to Hollywood. By the time we left London, I believed a theatrical agent or some other important person was waiting in Montreal to make Jenny, as I was now called, special.

Father made down payments on a car and a duplex on Cavendish Boulevard in the district of Notre Dame de Grace and promised to establish Mother in a little dress shop. Not long after we moved, Father and Roula came to Montreal, bringing with them Roula's younger brother, Tom, recently arrived from Greece. Just a teenager, he was already a very accomplished carpenter who helped build cutting tables, sales counters, and work areas around the sewing machines. While Father set the wheels in motion to start the dress business, Mother and Roula went sightseeing in Montreal. They shopped together, discussed the current fashions in elegant store windows, and chatted like girlfriends. Roula says she always considered Mother a part of the family, even later, when Mother tried to stir up trouble between Father and his bride.

Roula's brother loved Montreal, and when Father and Roula left he begged to stay. After a conference with Mother, it was decided that Tom could share our part of the duplex. It's hard to believe that Mother welcomed Roula's brother into the family, but she did. European immigrants often had relatives and friends living with them. It was like a big family; if one member needed a place to stay, doors were immediately opened. Mother also saw Tom as a built-in baby-sitter, though I don't know why she thought she needed child care. She never dated or went out at night.

At the time, I guess I thought of Mother as the "older, scorned wife." Looking back, I realize she was a very attractive and desirable thirty-three-year-old woman. A couple of years ago I received a letter from an old friend who knew us in Montreal. In his note he said:

> I always thought that you had the best-looking mother of anyone I knew. Sophie was not just a good-looking, well-built woman, but I always thought she was one of the most elegant women I had ever seen. Maybe that's why I hung around you!

When the time came for the grand opening of Mother's shop, Father and Roula again came to Montreal. Naturally, they stayed with us in the duplex. This time they helped Mother coordinate an advertising campaign and stayed long enough to determine that the store had the potential to succeed. Father figured he had invested approximately $15,000 in Mother's new shop. He and Roula went back to London to begin their own life, leaving us to ours in Montreal.

Hands off! That ceramic chicken is mine!

We lived on the main floor of the duplex, and Mother rented out the second story to make her house payments. Since Tom lived with us, Liz and I shared a room. We kept it in a constant state of disarray, our closet floor piled high with a combination of clean and dirty clothes. I dreamed of a day when I had a room all to myself and could feel independent.

Mother didn't care much if we kept our bedroom clean, but she was pretty rigid about the rest of the house. One of my most vivid memories of Montreal is the smell of the paste wax Liz and I had to apply to the hardwood floors. First we cleaned the floors with steel wool, then we applied paste wax by hand, and finally we buffed the entire floor with an electric floor buffer. The cleaning process wasn't fun, but we took delight in seeing our Chihuahua, Cookie, run down the hall and try to make a left turn into the kitchen on that nice shiny floor.

It wasn't all work, though. Liz and I had a lot of fun when we first moved to Cavendish Boulevard. We loved playing board games such as Monopoly, Sorry, and Snakes and Ladders (the game known as Chutes and Ladders in the States). I had a little bicycle, which I painted in rainbow colors. We also invented a game called "lottery," in which we took items from throughout the house—vases, ashtrays, a ceramic chicken—and put them on the sofa. We numbered each item with a slip of paper and put identical numbers into a bowl. Next we drew numbers; whatever item we drew, we owned. Then we put everything back. Looking back on it, I wonder if we were trying to find things that were just "ours," if only temporarily.

Most of our family entertainment consisted of things to do for little or no money, such as going to the beach or to Montreal's

Granby Zoo. Speaking of animals, Mother did agree to let me have a pet squirrel monkey. Big mistake. Flying around the house, he terrorized us all. He lasted a week.

Another big form of entertainment was ice skating. Canada is full of ice skating rinks, and Liz and I used to skate every weekend. There were no shopping malls where we could hang out in those days, so skating rinks were our gathering places.

When I was nine years old I wanted to be either a nun or a concert pianist. I'd been taking piano lessons and even played for the school choir. But I was heading for nunhood until Liberace came on TV. Then, when I saw a movie called *The 5,000 Fingers of Dr. T.*, a fantasy film about a mad scientist forcing children to play piano, I became even more serious about my piano lessons, envisioning myself giving concerts on a big stage. (Another movie I'll never forget seeing was *House of Wax*, a 3-D horror film starring Vincent Price as a sculptor who made his creations by covering innocent victims with boiling wax. It was much too scary for my impressionable young mind.)

Mother's store was about two blocks from St. Monica's Catholic school, where we attended, so we walked back to the shop for lunch every day. It was always much the same meal: a Kaiser roll and a cup of coffee. I hated the coffee, so I loaded it with evaporated milk to help get it down. Maybe Mother thought the hot coffee was good for us on those cold days—and winters are *very* cold in Montreal. One day on my short walk to the store for lunch, the tip of my nose turned white with frostbite, and I was scared. Mother immediately put it in cool water, and it eventually thawed out, but after that my nose always got bright red in the cold. I was developing a large nose anyway, so it was a great source of embarrassment for me and a prime target for other kids' jokes. I was called everything from Hawk, Schnoz, Beak, and Rudolph to "the big nose from Winnetka." (I never did get past being self-conscious about my oversized nose and eventually had a rhinoplasty.)

Our school in Montreal was very strict. You had to attend church every week, and no matter how old you were you had to go to confession. I was too young to have any real sins on my head, but I felt a sense of obligation to the priest, who was surely expecting something. So I made things up. I didn't realize, of course, that in telling him these untruths I was actually committing the sin I so desperately needed for this confession in the first place. I wonder what the priest was thinking when a nine-year-old girl confessed in a darkened cubicle: "Bless me Father, for I have sinned. It's been one week since my last confession. I lied two hundred times. I cursed a hundred and fifty times, and I stole a hundred times." I think he understood, because he always let me off with a few Hail Mary's, and thanks to either a sense of humor or the sanctity of the confessional, he never called the police.

Trying to put the pieces together

There was a growing dark side to our home life, as Mother became even more bitter and withdrawn. It seemed that nothing, not her dressmaking and not her daughters, could make her happy, and I soon learned to keep my distance. One time, I ran across the carpet to give her an unannounced kiss, and when the static electricity gave her a shock she instinctively slapped me across the face. Once when I angered her, Liz says, Mother almost pulled my hair out.

Yet she didn't discipline us or get involved unless something affected her directly. Once Liz found a bunch of notes I'd written. They were almost in diary form, lists of people I liked and didn't like, little-girl secrets. Liz stole them and read them to kids in the neighborhood. I was sure Liz would be punished, but Mother shrugged it off, saying I shouldn't have put secrets on paper in the first place.

It took Mother a year to go broke, even though she had plenty of work. Father was sending her orders from Sophie's in London, and she had new customers in Montreal. But she never did seem able to control either her life or the shop. Once again, Father came to take charge. This time he checked over the books and the inventory and closed the business. But he still didn't want her back in London, so Mother started doing sewing and alterations from

the duplex, and we stayed on in Montreal. She advertised with flyers, which Liz and I distributed around the neighborhood.

I don't think Liz and I realized just how much Mother had started
to drink, and I'm now sure that her drinking played a role in her
losing the shop. But I don't think she ever wanted to be a businesswoman, and she never gave much thought to bookkeeping or inventory or cash flow. That was my father's domain.

She didn't give much thought to what her daughters were up
to, either. By the time I was ten years old I was boy crazy and starting to run wild. I wore makeup and made every attempt to look
older. I decided I was ready for my first kiss. His name was Mike
Mandel, and I met him at one of the local shops. I invited him over
and flirted with him like crazy, until he finally kissed me. The kiss
was not as enjoyable as knowing I was doing something I wasn't
supposed to be doing. My new boyfriend's religion was a very big
issue with Mother, who was anti-Semitic. One day she called him
by a racial slur, and he ran from our house and never returned. Both
Mother and Father were extremely prejudiced, but their views did
not become mine.

After Mother ran Mike off, I met a boy named Paul Russo and
started going out with him. We'd kiss, and Liz would time us to see
how long we could go without air. He was very clean–cut and responsible. He didn't smoke or drink or exhibit any of the delinquent
behavior I so admired. For years he was in and out of my life, and
I believed we were destined to be married.

Liz and I started skipping school and roaming the streets. We
would pick up guys anywhere—on the streets, at the movies, on
the bus—and I'd often go off necking with a nineteen- or twenty-
year-old-man. I was fearless, never considering the risks I was taking. So strong was my need to prove how tough I was, I even carved
my name in my forearm with a razor blade. Had I grown up in the
'90s, I'm sure I would have had body piercings and tattoos before
I hit my teens.

And I might have even posed for X-rated photos, because Liz

and I locked the bedroom door one night, got out the camera, and took what we deemed to be erotic photos of each other. What they really turned out to be were two silly-looking young girls trying to look sexy hiding their nakedness behind an open umbrella or under a large wraparound towel. I was trying to be Marilyn.

There were many gangs in Montreal at that time, and we hung out with several of them. They weren't the kind of gangs that terrorize the streets today; the most serious crimes committed by these Canadian kids were ditching school, drinking, and shoplifting. We sneaked into clubs and went to movies, lying about our ages when we had to. We hitchhiked all over Montreal, with no thought to the danger.

I began sneaking into the coat room at school dances and stealing wallets. It wasn't for the money, since kids our age seldom carried much cash; I collected pictures from my cache of stolen wallets. Any of those fourth-graders would have told you their wallet photos were more valuable than their small change.

Liz and I were rapidly turning into juvenile delinquents. Caught up in her own festering anger, Mother drank too much to deal with us on any workable level. About that time I started drinking myself. There were no drugs around, so smoking and drinking were our open signs of rebellion. Since Liz had already experimented with cigarettes, I decided it was time for me to take this important step into adulthood. I locked myself in the bathroom, put a cigarette in my mouth, struck a match, and went for it. Smoking didn't work for me. I gagged. I choked. I hated the smell. I never tried it again. On the other hand, drinking was easier. I sometimes threw up, but I didn't gag and choke. At one party I drank nine beers, a considerable amount of alcohol for anyone, let alone a preteen. Once on a train trip to London to visit Father, Liz and I picked up two guys and stayed up until 5 A.M. drinking, necking, and giggling. The other passengers complained because they couldn't sleep, but we didn't care.

I don't know why I started to turn rebellious. Maybe I wanted Mother to be forced to pay attention to me. Maybe I resented being shut out of her life, especially after being shut out of Father's, whom we rarely saw after the move to Montreal. Mother seemed to stop existing; maybe when I got drunk I no longer felt either her pain or mine. She never dated, and she had few friends. Completely without ambition, she had no goals and no dreams. That was probably the defining factor: She had no dreams. What life is worth living without a dream?

The only pleasures Mother seemed to have were doing jigsaw puzzles and listening to music. She always had a jigsaw puzzle in progress. I can remember so many nights when she sat at the kitchen table, seldom speaking to us, drink in hand, trying to put the pieces together.

She did instill her love of music in us, seeing to it we took piano lessons no matter how little money she might have. Mother had stacks of records that she'd brought from London, and she listened to them all the time. She loved many kinds of music: Jerry Vale, Dick Contino, Hawaiian music, classical music, Russian music. Sometimes she danced around while Dick Contino played "Lady of Spain" on the accordion. Was it the music that moved her or the alcohol?

Mother never tried to inspire me, but in her own way she did just that. I vowed I would always have dreams and I would never give them up, no matter what.

6

On My Own, and on the Run

Liz and I began talking about running away from home. I don't think anything specific prompted it, just our overwhelming unhappiness. We blamed Father for the divorce; and in the mid-fifties there was a substantial stigma attached to divorce. We didn't know anyone else who lived in a single-parent family. And of course there was Mother's alcoholism. We didn't recognize or understand her disease, but we were behaving like so many other children of alcoholics and looking for a way to get control of our lives.

Liz told her friend Lois about our plans, and Lois decided she wanted to come with us. I was eleven, Liz was thirteen, and Lois was sixteen. We'd get together in the evenings to plan our escape. Even though I was the youngest, I was very much a participant. We decided on the bus, since it was the cheapest form of transportation, and we agreed to head southwest, toward London. When the time came, Liz chickened out, but Lois and I packed up clothes, food, and everything else we thought we might need and hopped a bus. We went as far as our money would take us: Cornwall, Ontario.

We started learning the price of independence right away. A porter at the bus station helped us off the bus with our suitcases and boxes, and then he just stood there looking at us. Lois and I glanced at each other uneasily, wondering if we'd already been spotted as runaways. Finally he held out his hand.

"My quarter," he said.

I wasn't sure if he was telling us he wanted a quarter or was explaining that he was the porter. Not surprisingly, we had very little money with us, and we knew we'd have to pay for at least one night's lodging as well as a taxi ride. But we gave him twenty-five cents and scooted off to the newsstand to look through the classifieds. We located an inexpensive rooming house and piled our belongings into a taxicab that delivered us to our new home: a small room with one bed and bathroom privileges.

Lois looked older than her sixteen years, and with makeup I could pass for at least sixteen. No one questioned our ages.

Lois had never been on her own before, but she seemed to know all the angles. She said that working as waitresses would be the quickest way to get money. We might have to wait a week for our paychecks, but we'd get tips every day to keep us going. Working in restaurants also meant we could eat free. "If we were older we'd work as cocktail waitresses," Lois explained. "Then we'd really rake in the money."

We set out separately looking for jobs. Before I located a restaurant, I saw a movie theater with a sign in the window that read USHER WANTED. I went in and lied my way to a job interview. I wanted that job. Free movie viewing sounded almost as good as free food. The position also meant I'd be connected to the entertainment industry, and there was a growing feeling inside me that someday, somehow, I was going to get into show business. I reapplied my makeup, tried to look mature, and waited for the manager.

Within minutes, he called me into his office. He looked me up and down, sat back, and studied me carefully. He seemed very old.

"You're gonna hafta wear a short uniform," he said. "I'm gonna hafta see your legs."

Well, I didn't have any idea if that was standard procedure or not, so I pulled up my skirt a bit.

"Higher," he said. "I can't tell anything about your legs yet."

I pulled it higher and higher. He kept telling me to go farther. Finally I was up to the top of my thighs and almost showing my underpants.

"Go on," he said. "I gotta see all the way up so I can be sure."

I never questioned that showing my legs up to my underpants

was part of the interview. The reason I didn't go on with the skin show had nothing to do with modesty or morals. It had to do with me having my period.

"Uh, I can't pull my skirt up anymore," I stammered. "I'm wearing a sanitary pad."

That seemed to cool him off. He said not to bother showing him anymore. I didn't get the job.

I found work at a nearby café where the application process didn't require pulling up your dress. I quickly learned how to make coffee and operate the hot chocolate machine. And I learned that if you flirted with the guys who came in to eat, you got bigger tips, so I flirted like crazy. If anyone suspected I wasn't even a teenager yet, they didn't say anything.

At the end of our first day as working girls, Lois and I reconnoitered back at the rooming house, pooled our money, and patted ourselves on the backs. Then we ran out and picked up some guys and partied. We got drunk and we necked with the boys. We didn't have any idea who they were. We didn't have any idea who any of the guys were that we partied with over the next few weeks. Yes, weeks: We kept up the charade for almost a month. Then we met a guy with the last name of Bean. I can't remember his first name. He was a little older than the boys we usually ran around with, and, as it turned out, he was more responsible too. Soon after we met him, the word on the street was that we'd been fingered as runaways and it was our friend Mr. Bean who'd done it.

We hurriedly packed up and took a bus to nearby Kingston. When we arrived we went through the same process: We looked through the paper and located a cheap rooming house, we hit the streets, and we were working as waitresses by the end of the day. It was a good thing we had earned some money in Cornwall, because this rooming house manager wanted a deposit.

We learned in Kingston that living the way we wanted to required more money than we could earn. So we started shoplifting. That's the euphemism. It's still stealing, and I'd been doing it ever since we moved to Montreal with Mother. I loved the frosted pale pink lipsticks that girls were starting to wear, and since we had no money, I stole lipsticks from the Woolworth's where Mother took us to shop. I had absolutely no scruples about it. It didn't seem like a moral or ethical problem. I just didn't want to get caught.

For as long as I could remember, my father had loved "getting a deal." This very often involved switching a price tag or stacking two items together so the salesperson would charge him for only one. If someone had done it at his store, he'd have prosecuted them. When *he* did it, he was "getting a deal." I stole whenever I could get away with it and got quite a few good deals myself.

Lois and I finally got caught, not for being runaways but for shoplifting. We'd been observed and reported for stealing an iron, but the police didn't arrest us on the spot. They must have suspected we had bigger secrets than an iron, because they followed us back to the rooming house and found our stash of stolen merchandise. I was scared, because I'd never been in trouble with the police before, and we faced serious charges. We finally told them who we were, and when they checked with the authorities in Montreal they learned that, indeed, two girls named Lois and Janina had been missing for almost a month. The Montreal police had just about given up on ever finding us. I've often wondered how long we could have stayed away if we'd not been caught shoplifting.

We were taken to the police station that night, but as minors we were too young to be held in a cell overnight. After a few hours we were transferred to a hospital and kept under guard until the following morning, when the detective who'd arrested us drove us back to Montreal in the company of his wife.

When we walked into the house, Mother gushed and told the detective about how relieved she was that I was unharmed. She explained that she'd hired cabs to take her throughout Montreal looking for me. She described how she had cried every day and even hired a psychic to try and find me. She thanked the detective and his wife profusely for having delivered us safely home.

The moment they left, she turned a cold eye on me and slapped my face. But I can't blame her for being angry.

Mother spent the rest of that day crying and threatening to kill herself. The next day, and with no explanation, she took me to the doctor. I sat on the examining table wearing nothing but a little cotton gown, having no idea what he was about to do. He instructed me to lie back, and he lifted my legs into metal stirrups. I was confused and didn't know what was going on. He inserted something cold and hard into my vagina, and I screamed with pain.

"I'm sorry," he said. "I didn't know you were a virgin."

I was never told what that test was for and why he had to do that to me. And I'm sure Mother was surprised when he told her I was still a virgin. She wouldn't have believed me, had she asked, but she would believe him.

I was so naive about sex that once, when I was around twelve, I actually thought I'd become pregnant from dancing too close with a boy. All right, let's call it what it was: grinding. Even though we were both fully clothed, when my stomach seemed slightly swollen shortly thereafter, I became convinced I was going to have a baby. I shared my apprehension with a friend, who assured me I could not get pregnant through my clothes.

I planned to kill my parents first

The Catholic school didn't want me back, so Liz and I had to take long bus trips daily to a French school across town. Many of the Catholic girls who had once been my friends were no longer allowed to associate with me. I decided that if they were going to treat me like a criminal, I was going to act like one. So I decided to run away again, and when I approached Lois, she too was up for it.

This time it was going to be different, because I planned to kill my parents first. No, that's not a typo. I actually had a friend, Paulette, who was equally unhappy at home, and we spent hours walking and talking about how we could rub out our parents.

We decided it would be more expedient if I murdered her parents and she murdered mine. We'd walk home from school together, deep in our plotting. Sometimes we debated whether to shoot them or stab them, but in the end we determined that both methods were too messy and most certainly too personal. Ultimately, we agreed to push them all out of windows. I don't know how I thought either Mother or Father would sustain any real damage from being pushed out of a first-floor window, but that was the plan.

I never got past the logistics stage in my quest to eliminate my parents, and my scheme to run away again was no more successful. One night Lois's parents got wind of our plans and came to our house for a meeting. The following day Mother told Liz and me that Lois was forever banned from our home. I don't know what would have become of me if I'd stayed in Montreal with Mother. I was saved from whatever that fate was because, for better or worse, at that point Father took back control.

Mother hadn't told him I had run away, and when he got a letter from Mother's brother explaining that I'd been missing almost three weeks, he decided to ask for custody of Liz and me. He wrote:

> One day I received a letter from Poland from Zoska's brother which read, "Jan, I know that you have divorced my sister, but I still have confidence in you. Things are not good with her. Janina has run away from home and no one knows where she is. I received a letter from my sister and that is what she told me. I am sure she has told you nothing."
>
> This news to me was as if someone had hit me on the head with a hammer. My baby Janina was only eleven years old! I decided to call Zoska and ask to speak to Janina. She began to fumble and make excuses and would not allow me to speak to her. Now I knew what her brother had written was true. I confronted her and she finally admitted that Janina had left home with one of her girlfriends and had been gone for three weeks. The police had not yet been able to find them. Zoska had even consulted a psychic, but to no avail. My first instinct was to go immediately to Montreal, but I

had to watch my business so it wouldn't collapse like the one in Montreal. I was also having problems with my feet and legs. What good would I be to my children with a failed business and bad health?

Fortunately, Janina was found just a few days later and returned home in good health. But now I knew that the children could no longer stay with their mother. I decided to discuss this with Roula, hoping it would not cause conflict between us. Much to my surprise, she said to bring the children back to London.

"What do you think the neighbors will say?" I asked. Roula said the neighbors were of no concern to her. And so I set about convincing the girls to leave their mother and come to London with me.

In order to persuade my daughters that life with me would be good, I promised them they would ride on a train and, once back in London, I would buy them a piano and give them piano lessons and dancing lessons. I also promised to have parties for them often and build them an indoor swimming pool.

Mother didn't want us to leave Montreal and, in fact, tried to put up a custody fight. She and Father went to court. In addition to my running away, Father dredged up the fact that Liz and I went to school dances, wore makeup, and went out with boys. He talked about our future and the importance of our learning the retail business from him. And he spoke of the rules he intended to establish once we were back in London. John Stronski's daughters would no longer have the bad reputations he assumed Sophie's girls had acquired in Montreal.

When we heard what Father had told the court, it infuriated Liz and me, and we wrote him a letter detailing all the reasons we wanted to stay in Montreal. We acknowledged the kindness of his desire for us to enter the family business but added that we didn't want to be forced into any profession. And we pointed out how Father's affair with Roula had affected us in the past and might affect us in the future:

> We would like to discuss the moving situation which we are now in. We fully understand that moving from Quebec is for our financial benefit. We realize now that having left us in Montreal and staying with Miss Roula in London, whom you loved better than your own family, you kept Mommy working endlessly for you and still not making enough money to support a family. Now you want us back so that we will work for you while you have a good time with Miss Roula.

We reminded him that girls our age often wore makeup and went out with boys and, despite what he thought, we were not the wildest girls in our school. And we addressed the idea of our "reputation."

> You're always talking about our reputation with boys. I hope you know what yours is for leaving Mommy and us here in Montreal and showing everybody that you like Miss Roula better than your own family.

Also included was a complaint about Roula's brother Tom:

> We don't like the idea of you putting Tom here as your spy to tell you everything Mommy and we are doing.

Then we went for the big finish:

> How do you know what girls our age feel? Just because you didn't have any excitement in your younger years, does that mean we must be the same? You're always saying when you were our age you never stayed on the phone long. Did you even have one? You never watched television late. We suppose you had one of those then.

The last line revealed the real reason we didn't want to leave Montreal:

> *We're sorry we can't write any more, but we have to do*
> *a few things for our party on Saturday.*

The letter was useless. Father won custody in 1959, and we were sent back to London. When Mother tearfully put us on the train, I wouldn't talk to her. Maybe I blamed her for losing custody of us, I don't know. But when we left, all I wanted was to defy her and flaunt my independence. So I invited Paul Russo to meet me at the station. I stood beside him on the platform, and when the engineer called "All aboard!" I kissed him on the mouth and jumped on the train without looking back at Mother.

Lucky Roula. We were coming to live with her.

· *Where are they now?* ·

The last I heard, Lois had become a prostitute.

7

Uprooted Again

I had a lot of reasons to be anxious about moving back to London. Being a bed wetter was one of them. I was going to have to sleep on the couch temporarily, and I was terrified of having an accident. I couldn't bring myself to tell Father and Roula that Mother always had plastic sheets protecting my mattress in Montreal. Luckily, I only stayed on the couch a few days, without embarrassing myself.

Our treatment of Roula was almost as shameful as Father's treatment of Mother. We tried never to speak to her or acknowledge her in any way. When forced to communicate with her, we addressed our stepmother as Miss Roula. We'd picked that up from Father's store, where the staff referred to him as Mr. John, since Stronski was difficult for some to pronounce. I even hated the sound of Roula's voice and criticized the way she spoke. She was in an unenviable position: only twenty-four years old and saddled with two teenage juvenile delinquents who thought of her as nothing more than a young hussy who'd lured their father away. Roula handled it very well, all things considered.

The times we hurt her most were probably during visits from her family. When her father or brother visited, Roula says we treated them as if they didn't exist. If they walked into a room, we left. If they spoke to us, we didn't respond. Roula later said it hurt her deeply. Treating her like the enemy was one thing, but being rude to her family was quite another. Still, she said nothing to Father.

Like our mother, she was a submissive woman. He never lived with an equal, just women who adored him and did his bidding.

His control extended even into the kitchen, a traditionally female domain. Since my father liked to cook, when they were in the kitchen Roula was assigned the thankless role of assistant. If he wanted to cook potatoes, she would peel them. If they boiled over, he blamed her. If they turned out great, he took the credit. If not, he blamed her. His ego would never allow him to admit a mistake. And his scapegoat was always his wife. He could be extremely insensitive and totally self-absorbed. Everything was focused on him.

Roula didn't complain much, because she came from the Old World, where men ruled the house. If she got tired of being bullied, she kept it to herself. For one thing, she wouldn't have humiliated herself in front of her family. Her Greek Orthodox father was very much against Roula's marrying my Roman Catholic father. Also, Father was fifteen years older than Roula. And when Roula's father first came to Canada from Greece, my father still hadn't divorced my mother.

After traveling to Montreal for a conference with Mother, Roula's father had agreed that Roula could marry Father as soon as the divorce was final. But his attitude with his daughter was: "If you have any problems, keep them to yourself. Don't come crying to us!" Roula's mother had a different slant on the impending marriage. "If you marry a man with two children and an ex-wife, the ex-wife is your family too," she said. "And Zoska has no one in this world but the two girls and John, and now you, Roula." Even with that chilling thought, Roula married my father and took two stepdaughters into her house.

Roula never attempted to win us over. She was pleasant to us, and even stayed up with me when I wanted company during scary late night movies. But she never tried to justify her position in the household or to portray our mother in a bad light. Liz recently observed how much our relationship with our stepmother has changed over the years. "Roula changed so much we can be friends now," was her analysis. It wasn't Roula who changed. It was the two of us.

Roula only stepped in as a disciplinarian when she saw no other option. One of those times involved my lack of personal hygiene. Mother had been strict when it came to keeping the house clean, but she must not have taught us much about personal cleanliness. Of course, back then, many Europeans didn't bathe as regularly as North Americans. Neither Mother nor Father had access to water for hot baths each night while they traveled through war-ravaged countries in the 1940s. Jumping in the shower each morning was not part of our daily ritual. Nor was taking scrupulous care of our clothes.

Not long after we moved back to London with Father and Roula, she was putting away some of my clean laundry and got a shock. When she opened my drawer, there were clean clothes mixed in with dirty socks and underwear. She removed the dirty things and took them to the laundry basket.

"Jenny, you shouldn't keep dirty clothes in your drawer," she explained. "The clean clothes go into the drawer. The dirty ones go into a hamper."

"You're not my mother!" I said, and stormed out of the room.

Roula's personal hygiene lessons didn't take, and later my reluctance to bathe and wear clean clothes caused me a great deal of embarrassment. Once, while I was in high school, I told a classmate that I had a run in one of my stockings. "Maybe it's just a clean spot," she answered, without hesitation. I must have been very hardheaded about taking personal advice, because even that pointed comment didn't do the trick. When I was out on the road working as a rock musician in my late teens, one of the other band members handed me some Right Guard and suggested I use it. I had never known anyone who used deodorant before.

We may not have listened to Roula, but Father was a different story. There was no way to avoid listening to him. Father laid down his rules immediately. First, we would work at his store every day after school. We were no longer allowed to wear makeup, and our miniskirts went in the trash. We had weekly meetings to discuss appropriate behavior with the opposite sex. Oh, how Liz and I dreaded these Friday-night harangues! At dinner Father would announce the time and place. Liz and I would sneak glances at each other, and when he looked away she'd roll her eyes.

Father's lectures were easier to take than his ridiculing me because of my flat chest. I was in a family of big-busted women. My mother, Roula, and Liz all had more than ample bosoms. I had nothing. I wore falsies, as did all flat-chested girls back then. In fact, it was pretty much expected, because if you weren't big-busted, you were somehow less than a woman. I remember anxiously waiting for the delivery of the Mark Eden Bust Developer I'd ordered from an ad in the back of a magazine. Father used to give me special exercises to enlarge my bustline, and many times he suggested I put ice water on my chest, which I guess he believed would stimulate growth. At least he didn't pinch my nipples and make a honking sound, which was Mother's way of embarrassing me.

Liz held both our parents in disdain, referring to them as the "Old Man" and the "Old Doll." Once, Father told her if she turned out to be a tramp, he would slit her throat and then his own. She shrugged off the threat as easily as if he'd told her she'd have to stand in the corner for an hour.

Neither of us paid any heed to his weekly lectures. They usually took place at the kitchen table, and it was always about the same thing. He would begin by explaining that boys only wanted one thing from girls. And if the girls did that one thing, they would pay for it the rest of their lives. "You will be nothing but tramps," he said. "Have any of these boys touched you? Have they tried to do anything to you?" We solemnly shook our heads, hoping he would tire of his tirade and leave us alone.

Father even lectured at mealtime, monopolizing every conversation. Every Sunday dinner began with the retelling of his hardships in Europe. We heard the story of how he had been captured and had escaped so many times I thought if I ever heard it again I would lie down and die. And he started telling stories about Mother. He told us that, in Europe, Mother had been a drug addict, and her addiction was the reason she drank so much coffee now. He said she was an alcoholic raised in a family of drunks; Mother's father and brother had died from alcohol-related illnesses. And we learned she had slept with the Palestinian boy he had paid to watch his dog. Yet Father said Mother was a sexually frigid woman. We learned much more than we wanted to know.

I suspected Father was right about Mother's drinking problems. I started thinking about all the times I saw burn marks on her arms. They were from the iron she used in dressmaking, and I guess I had thought the burns were an occupational hazard. I began to understand that Mother had been drunk much of the time, both when she worked and when she was trying to take care of her daughters.

Father threatened to send us to boarding school, but he eventually settled on public high school in London. It was my first experience with a coed classroom, and it didn't take long for me to know I was not going to be one of the popular girls. The only social activity I'd done with boys was necking, and I had no idea how to act within the confines of the classroom. My appearance didn't help. I thought I was ugly, with my oversized nose and thin, stringy hair. My skin started to break out. As I mentioned earlier, I don't think I was very clean. And my homemade wardrobe was the cause of much snickering.

I hated everything about this new life, and my self-worth sank to zero. I seldom did my homework, unsuccessfully trying to bluff my way through when the teachers called on me. I got so many penalties for bad behavior that the school's principal called Father and threatened to expel me.

The Canadian courts did not take divorce lightly in the fifties, especially when children were involved, and we were paid regular visits by representatives of the Children's Aid Society. I remember that we were all on our best behavior during these visits. I always knew that if I even hinted that we were not being properly cared for, I could get my father in trouble. I liked that feeling of power.

The smell of gin makes me queasy

Not long after Liz and I arrived back in London, Mother also returned. She phoned Father from Montreal in late 1960 and told him she had no work and couldn't meet her financial obligations. Father told her to sell the house, the car, and whatever equipment she had left from the store. Including his original $15,000 investment, Father lost about $25,000 on Mother's sale and her subsequent move back to London. Roula convinced Father to let Mother stay with us and to give her a job in the shop that bore her name. She hadn't proven to be a good businesswoman, but she was still an accomplished seamstress.

I doubt that many second wives would have been so bighearted. But Roula saw this bad situation in her typical Old World way. Roula's mother had already cautioned her about her responsibilities toward the ex-wife. But I don't think Roula resented Mother. They seemed to form a friendship of sorts, and to this day Roula gets somewhat defensive if Mother's character is questioned.

Mother hadn't been back at the shop long when she started sneaking a bottle to work in her purse and sipping at it all day. Father soon caught on. Mother seldom dealt directly with the customers, but she did work in the shop. Father knew if he could smell alcohol on her breath, those few customers she did speak to might know she was drinking. He wasn't about to allow his drunken ex-wife to put off any of his clientele, so he moved her into rooms above the store for a time. There she could work and drink out of the customers' view. I remember going up to see her one afternoon and finding her naked and passed out in the bathtub. I wasn't angry at Mother, or even disgusted. I just felt sorry for her, and I wasn't even sure why.

Liz and I hated Mother's drinking, yet we were also getting drunk on a regular basis. I spent a lot of time and energy creating a fake ID so I could buy my own gin. One day Roula was looking through things in my room when she discovered a drawer full of empty gin bottles. I often skipped school to get drunk on gin and tonic. I drank so much one afternoon that I got violently ill, and to this day the smell of gin makes me queasy.

Roula confronted me about her discovery, but I don't think she believed I actually drank the liquor, since there were twenty or thirty bottles. Instead of admitting or denying my drinking, I turned the tables on her.

"What were you doing looking through my dresser?" I said.

It turned out she was looking for matches and saw nothing wrong in taking ones from the souvenir matchbooks I'd collected from various locations. But in any case, I was busted. Roula told Father, who demanded to know what those empty gin bottles were doing in my room, and although I somehow convinced him they belonged to friends of mine, I knew I should have thrown them away. I think I saw them as trophies of a sort, notches in my belt.

Still, I looked upon my drinking as a lark and Mother's as a problem.

Mother finally bought a small house and began isolating herself from others more and more. Father sent her work from the store, but with no one to wake her up after a night of drinking, Mother soon fell behind. Since she was making no money, Father suggested she at least get a roommate to help with her expenses. She refused, and he speculated that the reason she wanted no one around was because another person might interfere with her bingeing. My father was a man with selective morals. While he wasn't an alcoholic, we'd certainly seen him intoxicated. Once he was so drunk he sat at the kitchen table talking to himself and saluting himself in the mirror. The sight of it scared me so badly I called Roula at the store and asked her to come home.

Finally, Mother came back to Father and Roula again. She was penniless and in danger of losing the house. Father said he wasn't even angry by this time, just full of pity for her lost life. He made her an offer: If she sold the house she was living in and invested the money in Sophie's, he would pay her a "dividend" each month.

He feared if she sold the house and kept the money, she would drink it up within a few years. Mother agreed, moved into a rented apartment, and began getting a hundred-dollar check from Father and Roula each month. She claimed it was all she needed to exist.

I give my father credit for that. He always took care of Mother. He made sure she had a place to live and food to eat. On the other hand, it had been Mother's dressmaking talents that allowed him to start his business. So he wasn't being magnanimous. I don't think he ever really acknowledged her contribution to his business.

8

Sick and Tired of the Whole Family Mess

It's frustrating to try and explain what Father was like. In spite of his self-centered ways, he wanted to be a good parent. He loved us and tried to keep us safe and happy. But we who surrounded him were intimidated. No one would ever have said, "John, could you possibly focus on someone else's feelings for just one minute?" And if anyone had ever confronted him in that manner, he would have either tuned him out or written him off. He did that with a lot of people. If they crossed him, they were history. For example, twenty years ago he completely severed his relationship with his brother for what turned out to be an unfounded rumor. When I finally left home, he wrote me off for a long time.

Liz and I were constantly being pulled between Mother and Father. We knew she had fought for custody, and we frequently reminded him that he'd taken us away from our "mommy." Father would just shake his head and say he was sick and tired of the whole family mess. "If you had been living with me, you would never have run away like you did, Janina," he told me time after time. So to prove him wrong, I decided to run away again, and this time Liz was coming too!

It was 1961. I was fourteen and Liz was sixteen. This time Liz didn't chicken out, and this time we left notes. We somehow felt responsible for the continuing dissension between our parents. Liz told Father that with us out of the way, both he and Mother could get on with their lives. He would have more time for Roula, and maybe Mother would remarry. Liz, like Father, seemed preoccupied with public opinion:

> *I would appreciate it if you would tell people that we are away in school. That will be best. Remember that I love you and that everything will turn out well. So far, no one knows about this.*

My letter shows confusion, frustration, and pain:

Dear Dad,
    I hope you'll understand me and what I did. I don't think anyone can choose between two people she loves. No matter how much you tell me against Mom, I still love her. And I love you more than anything else, but I know you won't believe me. The reason we left is like you said: I'm sick and tired of the whole family mess. I won't choose between you and Mom. I wish you wouldn't worry because I'm still going to school and I won't lose my education. I know I'm very young, but I'm old enough to know that this time I did not make a mistake. I think if I leave for a while, things will cool down. I'm not "running away from home," but I am running away from a problem. I honestly think it will be better.
    Please tell Roula that I love her too. I'm sorry, very sorry, for the awful way I treated her. We will phone you in three or four weeks. Remember, Dad, I love you more than the world, and I never want to hurt you.

I typed the note, then added in script at the bottom: *I love you very much, Dad. Please forgive me.*
Neither Liz nor I left a note for Mother.

We rode the bus for the twenty-four–hour ride to Montreal and ran wild for a couple of days. The first thing I did was call my old boyfriend, Paul Russo. And the first thing he did when he hung up the phone was call Father. As I said, Paul was a responsible boy. We went to all our old favorite clubs, and hung out on the streets, and picked up boys again. We were staying in a basement room at a boardinghouse when Father found us. I remember we had some boys over, and I was standing in the kitchen when Father walked in. Liz was mad, but I was relieved. I wanted to go home. I immediately hugged him, crying and thinking; *He really does love me. He must, if he came all the way to Montreal to save me.*

Liz thought I was a turncoat for saying "I love you" to our father. She refused to say it and often talked of how she hated him. I could never say I hated him, no matter how bad things got. And things were bad.

But I didn't really want to be on my own this time. Being in that rooming house brought back memories of the first time I ran away, when I hadn't been quite as tough as I pretended. I'd been scared, even if I didn't fully realize it at eleven. Independence, which had meant working hard as a waitress and still not having any money, wasn't all it was cracked up to be. I hadn't given a thought to the fact that independence meant being on your own, and that included paying for necessities like toilet paper.

I think all I really wanted was my father's attention. I was happy to go home, especially when I learned we'd be flying in an airplane for the first time. And I believed things would get better. Surely Father would pay more attention to me. If he didn't, I just might run away again. And then he would be sorry.

9

Sex Ed
the Hard Way

In his own way, Father tried to make us happy back in London. He kept his word and moved us into a big ranch-style house, complete with an indoor swimming pool and a recreation room in the basement. He filled the pool room with large tropical plants and installed a stereo system and wet bar. He was so proud of that pool. It was forty by twenty feet, and the inside was lined with ceramic tile. He reminded us frequently that the pool was heat controlled, so you could swim in winter or summer. There was just one small problem: Neither Liz nor I swam.

It was so like our father to decide to build a swimming pool for us, even though we had little interest in swimming. Everything was for show. The big house, the pool, the wet bar—proof to the world that he was a success. He even bought a horse to keep in the backyard barn. We knew the house had strapped him financially. He frequently talked about financial and business problems at the dinner table, and I was always afraid we would lose everything.

It was not a groundless fear. Not long after he bought the house, he lost the lease on his building and had to move the store, which put him in an even tighter cash-flow position. "I don't know what I'm going to do," he would say. "I can't pay my creditors." He didn't realize what an impact being privy to those daily laments would have on a young, already insecure child. I never felt secure.

Even today, no matter how much I have, I'm afraid it won't be enough.

I think that tenuousness he conveyed to us made me even more determined to be able to support myself. Years later I'd get very angry when my fellow musicians out on the road made comments about hoping "something" would happen for them. I knew you had to make your own success and then be careful not to let it slip through your fingers.

As soon as Liz was old enough to drive, Father bought her a Pontiac convertible. I know it was simply to prove to his fellow businessmen that he could afford to buy his daughter a flashy new car. But we loved riding around in it. It's funny that he constantly preached to us about the evils of running around with boys and then bought Liz a convertible to make it easier.

Liz and I both started modeling for Father's store. We would dress up in bridal gowns and stand there in the window, turning slowly so the gowns could be viewed from all angles. Sometimes we attracted a pretty big crowd, too. In many ways my father was a great retail innovator, and certainly the first person I'd ever heard of to use live mannequins in the window. But it wasn't long before I started asserting my independence. When I was fifteen, I quit my job at the store to work as a waitress. I was thrilled because now I really had my own money.

Liz and I wanted to be stars, so we started singing together in what we envisioned as a female Everly Brothers act. Not long before we moved back to London, Liz and I had won second prize in the New Talents of 1959 contest on CKVL radio in Verdun, Quebec, singing the Gene Vincent hit "Be Bop A Lula." Now that we were back in London, we decided to pursue our performing more seriously. We spent hours rehearsing. I played the piano, and we both sang two-part harmonies on songs like "Bye Bye Love" and "Let It Be Me." We decided to try some original material, too, and I even wrote a song about a friend of ours.

The lyrics went:

Paul Yorke, is a pretty good guy.
Man oh man, here's the reason why.
At a party he is really hep.
He's the guy always in step.
He's a lanky little creature (slightly cracked).
He's a devil for the teacher (talkin' back).
He goes through the town with a great big smile.
He never does a thing that is worthwhile.
Paul Yorke.

We were so positive it was a hit song we got Paul to sign an authorization form to use his name. Father thought it was worthy of a recording session and took us to a small studio, where we made a record for $30. Let's just say we didn't have to buy tickets to the Grammy Awards that year.

Our next big chance, and the one that led to the demise of the singing Stronski sisters, came through a young piano player named Garth Hudson. Garth was just a kid himself, but he already showed great promise. He arranged for us to play a show at the St. Barnabas Teen Town with him. He practiced with us until we were sure we could do it. After all, we'd won second place in the New Talents contest the previous year. We didn't stop to think that it had been a children's amateur show, and this time we'd be judged as professionals.

We bombed. I was so embarrassed, I wanted a chance to redeem myself, and right after we left the stage I begged Garth to let us go back out for a second chance. Garth said going back onstage wasn't a good idea.

That was the end of our singing act, but it was a good lesson, and one I'd like to pass along to anyone wanting to be in the entertainment business—or any business, for that matter. Be ready when your opportunities come. If you aren't ready, pass. Better to be overqualified than not ready.

Ousted for a hickey

I sometimes feel that Liz and I spent our entire time in high school necking with boys. I remember dating a boy named Wayne Cromwell, and all we did was neck. We necked at his house, at my house, in the backseat of his car, outside the school. And grinding. There was lots of grinding. I'd do just about anything except have sexual intercourse.

I didn't even know that boys ejaculated until my second year in high school. I was invited to the prom at a neighboring school, Clarke Road High. After dancing awhile, we went out to my date's car to neck. Before I knew it, he had unzipped his pants, grabbed my hand, and shoved it down on his penis. Then he masturbated, using his hand and mine. Suddenly he shook a little, groaned, and I felt something on my hand. With the exception of my pelvic exam and my father's tramp lectures, this was all the sex education I had.

One night when I was fourteen I came home with a hickey on my neck, and when Father noticed it he was furious. It wasn't as bad as it looked. My current boyfriend, Helmut, whom Father knew and liked, and I had been out with friends when one of them dared Helmut to put a hickey on my neck. Obligingly, he delivered on the dare. Father wouldn't let me explain and kept badgering me in his native tongue to identify the culprit.

"Who did this to you?" he shouted in Polish.

"Helmut," I said.

"What did he do to you?"

I was so scared. I spoke Polish, but I didn't know the word for "hickey." Since I didn't answer, Father thought I was being insolent, and that made him even angrier.

"Answer me!" he shouted again, his face turning a deep red.

"On mnie ugryz," I said, which translates to "He bit me." I was desperate for an answer, and that was the closest I could come.

Father banned Helmut from the house forever. Once my father had an idea in his head, there was no turning him around.

Mother was convinced I was having sex. When Mother was staying with Father and Roula, she would order me out to the car, point to the rear window, and ask, "Are those footprints? Have you had your feet up there doing things with boys?" Mother practically dusted the car windows for prints. I don't know why she thought I was sexually active, because she certainly hadn't explained sex to me. I remember starting my period, when I was ten years old and living in Montreal, and wondering what was going on. I stuck some Kleenex in my underwear and thought I was bleeding to death. I only learned what was happening to me when Mother found one of my tissues and asked me about it. I was relieved to know I wasn't seriously ill.

Liz and I always tried to pass ourselves off as worldly, but I was very naive about guys. One day when I was about fourteen, I went to a party with Liz and some of her friends at the beach. Some of the guys were Liz's age, but some were older, in their late teens or early twenties. Liz was off drinking when one of the older guys asked if anyone wanted to go with him on a beer run.

"Sure," I said, feeling very grown up.

We picked up the beer, and he drove out to a deserted area where cliffs overlooked the lake. He parked the car and asked me if I wanted to go down and look at the water.

"Sure," I repeated.

We went down a steep embankment and then walked along a

fallen tree trunk across a pool of water to the beach. Without a word of warning, he pushed me down and started trying to make out with me. I was used to boys kissing or necking, but this was obviously a more serious and aggressive action. I pushed him away.

"Stop it," I said.

"C'mon, we both know why you came here," he said.

"I just came along for the ride," I said, trying not to show my fear. "I'm a virgin."

"You won't be a virgin when you leave," he said.

"I'm only fourteen," I said, hoping that would scare him off.

He didn't buy it, since all the other girls at the party were at least sixteen. I thought I was going to be raped right there on the beach unless I could think of some way to get away from him. So I told him I had to go to the bathroom. As soon as I got behind the bush, I started running. I headed for the fallen tree, afraid to look back. About halfway across, I fell off the tree and into the water, making a big splash. I never looked back, even though he must have heard the noise. If he was right behind me, I didn't want to know about it. I got up and headed up the rocky cliff, grabbing branches to keep from slipping back down. I made it to the road and kept running for about two miles, fully expecting him to pull up alongside of me. Luckily for me he never did, and I made it to a farmhouse, where the owner agreed to return me to the party and to my sister. To my relief, the guy from the beach never did show up again.

I was lucky that times were so different, or I might have been a statistic that day, and many others.

Supermodel fantasies

One of the few real pleasures of my high school years was sports. I made the girls' volleyball, track, and tennis teams, and I was a good solid competitive player. I thought, as much as Father loved wrestling, he'd be excited to attend some of my sports events. During one track and field meet I ran the 440 relay, threw the shot, ran hurdles, and competed in the high jump. It hurt me that my parents didn't come.

In 1962 I was chosen to be the school's representative to a two-week athletic camp at Lake Couchiching, Ontario. I was proud of being a good athlete and, since I was not one of the top students, even prouder to have been chosen to represent my school. Girls from all over Ontario came to this camp, most of us by train.

It wasn't exactly what I expected, more like boot camp than a summer sports outing. We were awakened at dawn, and no matter what we were doing, there was always a counselor yelling, "Hustle! Hustle!" No matter where we were going, we never got there fast enough. Nevertheless, it was a positive experience in that I met a lot of sports-minded girls, participated in some good discussions about the importance of girls' athletics programs, and, in general, felt good about myself. And I finally learned how to swim.

That was one of my very few good high school experiences. I was so bored with the school that when I was sixteen I decided to try modeling after school. I'd look at pictures of the very together-looking high-fashion models in magazines and then stand in front of the mirror and look at myself, knowing I was a misfit. But I was determined to try. I did have some experience modeling gowns in Father's store window, and the glamour of it certainly appealed to me.

One day I read an ad for the Barbizon Modeling School in New York City. That, I thought, was my ticket out of town. I actually believed I might be able to make it as a runway model with the proper training, so I made an appointment, booked a flight, and headed to New York. My meeting was short, since I learned quickly that the training was expensive, and I'd have to move to New York. I don't know what I'd thought would happen. That they'd offer me a scholarship? I decided I'd settle for the modeling school in London, Ontario.

In the meantime, I had a night to kill in New York. I went out to a jazz club armed with my fake ID, and did what came naturally—I got so drunk I blacked out. One minute I was sitting alone, sipping a drink, and the next thing I knew I woke up in the morning in my hotel room bed. I still don't know how I got back there.

The next day I enrolled at what I believe was the only school of its kind in London, the Paula Bricklin Charm School. I didn't know anything about dressing properly, and I suspect many of the girls silently laughed at my attempts at sophistication.

One day when I was sitting in class, Paula began lecturing about the inappropriateness of wearing spike heels with a winter suit. Guess what yours truly was wearing? I wore those spike heels everywhere, even to high school classes, and I must have looked as out-of-place and foolish in Central High's classrooms as I did at modeling school.

Even though I stumbled through the course feeling clunky and awkward, I got my diploma and even got some modeling jobs as a result. My photo was on the wrapper for a bar of soap, and I appeared in a television ad once. I did a publicity stunt for a swimsuit company when topless bathing suits became popular. I modeled one wearing a wig long enough to cover up bosoms I didn't have. I assumed they chose me for that job because, if my breasts were accidentally exposed, nobody would care. But most of my jobs came from wholesalers who came to town to show their samples to local buyers. In fact, when I used to accompany my father to a hotel suite to look at samples for his store, he always whispered derogatory comments about the models to me. "See that girl?" he would say. "She's a tramp. That's all models really are—tramps."

You can imagine my father's reaction when I told him of my plans. He thought models were tramps, and I wanted to be one. He wanted me to stay in school, and I was ready to quit. He thought I was on a path headed straight to hell. I said I could handle myself, but I was just sixteen, and he knew I couldn't.

My sexual naiveté was obvious on several occasions. One salesman asked me to give him a neck rub between clients. I did, and it took years for me to understand how inappropriate it was for him to request the massage. Once, I was in a hotel lobby when a young businessman struck up a conversation with me. I had a lot of 1960s-style makeup on and I was wearing a fall, one of those hairpieces that were so popular. I'm sure he had no idea I was only sixteen years old. He asked me out and said we should stop by his room first. I really believed he just wanted to change his jacket or something. I did ask myself what he could possibly see in me. When we got in the elevator I realized people were staring. They knew something was up; I was so young, and certainly not in this expensively dressed man's league.

The moment we got to his room he started mauling me. I pushed him away and he reared back, looked incredulous, and said, "Why do you think I asked you up here?" I stupidly told him I thought he liked me and wanted to be friends. He laughed. "Friends? Why in God's name would I want to be friends with you?" He came back at me, and we tussled on the bed for several minutes. When I wouldn't put out, he backhanded me. Who knows, maybe the salesman thought I was a prostitute. I ran out of the room, took the elevator to the lobby, and raced from the hotel, the front desk clerk staring at me as I ran. When I got home I realized my hairpiece was gone. It must have come off on the bed.

I angrily picked up the telephone and called the hotel. He wasn't in his room, so I left a message: *Leave my hairpiece at the front desk.* When I went back to the hotel later that day, the desk clerk gave me a funny look and handed me a brown paper bag, carefully holding it upright as though he thought something might jump out of it. I carried that bag out of the lobby with as much dignity as I could muster, but I was humiliated.

10

Somebody Pinch Me!

I initially believed it was modeling that might help me get out of London and on my own, but not after Liz and I started hanging out with musicians. I was fascinated by the drums and asked a drummer we knew if I could try his set out. The very first time I picked up the sticks and the drummer showed me a simple beat, I played it. He seemed genuinely impressed and said, "People usually don't get it so quickly." I asked what kind of money a drummer could make. He said, "Seventy-five dollars a week on the road."

Wow! Somebody pinch me! The two things I wanted most in the world: money and leaving home!

The next day I bought a used drum set on credit, and by that evening it was set up in the basement and I was practicing. I bought the Beatles album *Beatlemania* and practiced with Ringo Starr every day. His style was simple, stylish, easy to follow, and in three months I got my first job.

Father's dream was that Liz and I would graduate from high school, go to college, and work with him in the store, eventually taking over the business. But Liz and I had other plans. She wanted to get married—and did—and I wanted to be a rock-and-roll drummer.

I don't remember the exact night I chose to tell my father that I was going to be a professional musician, but I think we played it out at the dinner table during one of his endless reminiscences about World War II and his escape from the Germans.

It's amazing that I ever found the nerve to give my father the following news briefs:

One: I was dropping out of high school.
Two: I would not be working at the store.
Three: I was going to become a professional musician.

Father stormed and threatened. He told me if I left to go out and play drums with a band, I could never come home again. But I was neither his Polish army recruit nor his wife.

What to do about Jenny? became the question of the day. I agitated the family even more by sleeping until noon every day and then practicing my drums long into the night. I'm sure if Father could have had me locked up somewhere he would have done it. He continually characterized women in show business as tramps and whores and warned me I'd be raped and murdered. I know that Roula was trying to calm him down, since she believed I'd inherited Father's hardheadedness and thought we'd be alienated from each other for all time. So she advised him to be very careful in how he dealt with me during those tense days.

Finally, one day he came down to the basement recreation room while I was practicing.

"Listen," he said. "You either go to work in the store or go to work someplace else or go back to school. If you don't do one of those things you can just get out of my house. I can't take any more of this stupid drumming business!"

I looked him in the eye for a moment and went to my bedroom to pack.

"You are going straight to hell," he said, stomping into my room.

I think he was angry for a number of reasons. First, he really did think that musicians were worthless and that any woman who went out on the road with them was a tramp. He worried about how it would look to people in London if they knew John Stronski's daughter was playing in bars and living in motels with a bunch of guys. Remember, he wrote in his memoirs that, before bringing Liz and me back to live with him, he asked Roula what the neighbors would think. Imagine caring what the neighbors would think of your children living in your home!

Image and public opinion were everything.

Father had a selective moral code. A woman who played music with bands was a tramp. But he sanctioned an affair between a young woman and a Greek Orthodox priest. They were friends of the family. We all knew they were having an affair, but they were always welcome in our home and were allowed to stay as late into the evening as they wanted to.

He also had some very real fears about the dangers for an under-age girl working in night clubs. I was the queen of fake IDs, but I hadn't shown much sense as far as knowing when to be cautious, whom to trust, and how to stay out of trouble. Father thought I would be running into a disreputable cast of characters out on the road, and he was right. But the main thing that got under Father's skin was the fact that he felt his control over me slipping away.

My motives for wanting to leave were divided, too. I obviously had a defiant nature. But I also knew I had to find my own happiness. Nobody in the Stronski household was going to do it for me.

Father relented, partly because Roula intervened on my behalf. He finally apologized and asked me to unpack. I didn't walk out that night, but I did quit school and stop working at the bridal shop. I took whatever modeling jobs I could get and started saving all my money, knowing I'd need equipment and costumes.

Getting my first job as a drummer proved easy. All I had to do was get a professional picture taken, in a costume Mother made for me, a black-fringed dress slit all the way up both sides. I took my first 8 by 10 to an agent.

"You'll work," he said, without asking to hear me play. After all, a girl drummer was a novelty act. There was only one other female drummer that I knew of in all of Canada, and she was in Quebec. Nobody cared if I was any good.

Independence Day

Soon after that, the agent called and said he had work for a combo he'd put together consisting of two guys playing bass and guitar and me playing drums. We didn't even rehearse before we left. We just accepted the gig and showed up.

I said nothing to Father and Roula about the job. I packed a few things and waited for the guys to pick me up. Father only learned of the plan when the car was waiting in the drive. He was livid. He grabbed my coat and hid it, thinking, I suppose, that if I didn't have a coat I couldn't leave. He should have known it would take a lot more than that to keep me from my dream.

"If you leave, don't ever come back." Those were to be the last words Father spoke to me for months.

Our first paying gig was in Sept-Îles, located far up in northeastern Quebec. It took two days to get there, although it was easy to know when you arrived, because the road ended. But I was just seventeen, and the end of that road was my beginning. I was finally on my own, with a two-week engagement that would pay $60 a week. Life was good.

The club was in a residence hotel where many people lived year-round and everyone knew everyone else. The manager was a dirty old man who smelled of booze and couldn't get it through his head that I wasn't interested in him. Every night he was in the club hitting on me, and every night I told him to leave me alone. Every night when the bar closed and I went upstairs to my room, he phoned me; sometimes he came up and knocked on my door. I'm surprised I had the sense to stay away from him, since liquor was free to band members, and I was drinking heavily.

One night I really abused the free liquor privilege and got blackout-stage drunk. The next morning, when I awakened, the last thing I remembered saying was, "I really have to get some sleep." I stumbled down to breakfast and an unfriendly group of people in the front lobby. What had I done? I couldn't imagine. I found my bandmates in the coffee shop, and they explained my drunken faux pas.

Sometime after I had staggered to my room, I called the front desk and said, "Please tell Mr. So-and-so not to bother me tonight. I really have to get some sleep."

The woman at the front desk that night was his wife.

We're not stupid—you're a lesbian!

It was easy to throw a band together, and the agent kept putting me with different groups that would fill the needs of his venues. I use the word *venues* loosely because I was working some rough nightclubs, mostly mining towns in northern Ontario like Sudbury, Timmins, Kirkland Lake, and Kapuskasing. When I didn't have a ride I took the train from job to job. If they wanted a four-piece rock-and-roll band or a three-piece country band, that's what they got. It was good experience, because playing with different groups made me a better drummer. Besides rehearsing every day in the clubs, I also practiced on my own with drumsticks in my hotel room. I took my job seriously and planned to become the best female drummer in Canada. I practiced for hours, listening to music and copying what I heard.

I played in a band with Bobby J. Newman, who'd released a single called "Baby's Gone Away," and his record label booked him to open for Roy Orbison in Chatham, Ontario. I played the show, and although I never got to meet Roy, I did meet his wife. She walked in the ladies' room while I was curling my eyelashes and said, "Oh, you should be careful doing that. One of my kids grabbed my arm while I was curling my lashes and I yanked them all out!"

I'd play anywhere. Once, the agent called and asked me to play in a revue that included a stripper. "It's easy and you can do it," he said. "The most important thing is that you watch her every move and accent it with your drums." I said, "Sure." A stripper and a female drummer dressed in hot pants in a mining town? That agent didn't need to tell me. It was an easy sell.

Our first night I think I did a respectable job backing the dancer. I watched her like a hawk and accented every one of her bumps. After the show two hulking miners approached me at the bar and said, "You're not fooling anyone. We're not stupid—you're a lesbian. We saw the way you were watching the dancer. You never took your eyes off her."

I must have been quite a disappointment to them; there were not a lot of women in these mining communities. What a shame to waste one who did come along. I didn't care one way or the other what they thought about my sexuality, though. I just wanted to be self-reliant, and music was allowing me that opportunity.

I was still naive. One night a guy in the audience came up to me during break and told me I'd been awarded the Beaver Shot of the Year Award. He handed me a card to commemorate the compliment, assuring me that it was a great honor. I thought it must have something to do with being a good drummer. I thanked him and kept the card for months before finding out what it really meant.

I continued playing with various groups—names like Jenny and the Guys or Jenny and Her Boyfriends—too many names to remember. Since there were few women on the circuit, newspapers always ran my picture. The first time I was asked for my full name for a newspaper ad, I said, "It's Jenny Stronski." The man said, "Well, you can't expect us to put that in the paper." During the early sixties everyone had a stage name, nothing complicated. He said, "We need to use another name. How about Jones?" "OK," I said. "Jenny Jones it is."

11

In Mother's Footsteps

Mother liked the idea of her daughter playing in a band. She helped make my stage clothes and started traveling all over Canada to see me play. She loved music, being on the road, and seeing me up on stage, but more importantly she loved being in bars. I always had to instruct the bartenders that when Mother ordered a vodka, she meant a double or even a triple. By doing that I forged a bond between us, but I also became an enabler in the drinking problem that stalked her for her entire life.

Even though Mother wasn't afraid for me to be on the road, she did worry that I was having sex. One night she saw a jar of Vaseline in my bathroom. Her eyes narrowed. "What do you use that for?" she asked sharply. I used Vaseline for lip gloss, but I don't think Mother believed it. Asking me if I had a jar of Vaseline was as close as she got to parenting. We were more like friends, or maybe close acquaintances, certainly not confidantes.

Though she was convinced that I was sexually active in my teens, I didn't lose my virginity until I was in my twenties. I credit my father for my abstinence, partly because of his lectures about not having sex and partly because he belittled my body to the point that I was too embarrassed to let anyone see me naked.

I was eighteen, playing with Jenny and the Up-Set, my first serious rhythm-and-blues and rock band. We used to play "Devil with the Blue Dress," "Land of a Thousand Dances," and all the James

Brown songs. I wanted to sing too, but I had no confidence. When I finally got up the nerve, I picked the easiest song I could find, "These Boots Were Made for Walkin'," which was recorded by Nancy Sinatra and had a four-note range. At that time, I was having serious feelings about Johnny, the sax player. I also had advanced from drinking to taking pills, uppers we called bennies. I had been awake for three days when I got behind the wheel of my mother's car to drive back to London between gigs. It was the middle of the day and I kept nodding off, but I didn't pull over. I guess I thought the pills would keep me awake. All of a sudden, the car rolled over three times and landed on all four wheels in the fast lane of the opposite side of the highway. Surprisingly, no bones were broken. I had the car towed and took the bus back to London. Mother didn't even reprimand me. She seemed genuinely proud, almost loving at times. I'm sure it infuriated Father when she'd go out on the road with his wayward daughter.

But he had other problems in 1965. Liz had gotten divorced and married a guy named Andy, and the two of them were enamored of everything we now relate to sixties youth. They were antiestablishment and antibusiness. Liz decided she wanted no part of the store, since a bridal shop more than qualified as "establishment." So Liz did macramé and they both did drugs.

Since the antiestablishment newlyweds had no place to live, Father bought the house next door and rented it to them. Father suspected Liz and Andy had become involved in the sixties drug culture, and that they were selling marijuana from their house. One day he approached Liz and asked her point-blank if she had any pot. She admitted that she did, wondering if he was going to have them evicted or turn her in to the police. He asked her for a joint, which he then smoked.

It was just another example of his selective moral code.

Father's attitude toward me began to change when I started sending my press clippings back to London. A girl drummer was a novelty, so the local papers almost always ran my photo. Between jobs on the road, I worked as an accounts payable clerk at a man-

ufacturing plant and lived in a motel. But Father's attitude hadn't
changed enough to invite me back home. I was still banned.

When he did see me, he said, "Jenny, wouldn't you be happy
just being a rich man's daughter?" Funny how he went from poor-
house to "rich man" so easily.

One day in the fall of 1965, I came home between gigs and
went to see everyone at the store. The moment I stepped through
the door, I started to cry uncontrollably. I think it was the culmination of being out on my own and at odds with my family. I had
a career, but my personal life wasn't coming together. Father decided I must either be having a nervous breakdown or be pregnant.
I knew I wasn't pregnant, and I didn't think I was having a nervous
breakdown. It could just have been a bout of typical teenage angst.

Once he found out I wasn't pregnant, Father tried a long shot.
Hoping I would decide to retire to the position of "rich man's
daughter," he suggested I take a trip to Europe to clear my head.
He must have believed that if I got away for a while I would surely
come to my senses and give up what he called "this drumming business." The trip sounded like a good idea to me too, but for a different reason. I hoped to find work with bands in Europe, and even
took some stage clothes with me. But it didn't take long to learn
that work was difficult to find, whereas guys were everywhere. I
mailed the stage clothes back home and stayed to have fun.

Armando — oh, those Italian men!

I started out in London, England, met a guy at the airport, and made
a date with him the next day. I went on to Paris and met two American soldiers, who took me all over France and invited me to a party
at the base. I met a Frenchman in Marseilles who took me to a romantic dinner. I felt very grown up when he said, "Can I order for
you, *ma chérie?*"

"Of course," I responded, doing my best impression of Grace
Kelly.

He ordered in French, and although I took French in school I wasn't sure what I was getting. When I saw my dinner I didn't know what to do. It was a combination of all the things I had refused to eat my whole life: seafood, scallops, clams.

Yuck!

But he was so good-looking I ate it. It was a good time to open my mind and palate to unfamiliar foods, just in case another good-looking Frenchman took me to dinner. (I'm proud to say I now enjoy all foods, including seafood.)

I quickly forgot about my Frenchman when I went on to Italy and met Armando. There *is* something about Italian men. We spent a week together as he drove me all over Italy. We picnicked, staying in the same hotel room but in different beds. He took me to meet his parents, and the day before I left he proposed. It lost a little in his translation, but it was still romantic. We were sitting in his car and he was saying how much he would miss me, and then he said, "Jenny, will you marriage with me?" I was crazy about Armando but not crazy enough to get married. I had a music career to pursue.

Hollywood and Vine

I returned from Europe ready to work. I knew nothing was going to happen for me traveling around the back roads of Canada playing bars, so I started thinking about going to the United States. I'd saved enough on the road to buy a red and white Corvair convertible, which allowed me to take jobs even farther away, like the USA. I had applied for a work permit and was told it could take two years, but I couldn't wait that long. So I started working clubs as an illegal alien in the United States, with the ultimate goal of working my way across the country to California. I just knew something good would happen for me in California. I even called ahead to an acting school I had seen advertised in a magazine, thinking that a career as a movie star awaited me if I could just get to LA.

Playing in American venues was a very different experience. I was used to some strict liquor laws in Canada; by comparison, what went on in American bars seemed like a wild, out-of-control free-for-all. People were standing up with drinks in their hands! People were ordering two drinks at once! In Canada it was illegal to stand with a drink in your hand. You had to be seated, and if you wanted to go talk to someone at a different table, you had to leave your drink behind or get a server to bring it over.

In the '60s, clubs in Canada were terribly discriminatory toward the female clientele. In some clubs women could not sit at the bar. There were clubs where women were not allowed in at all unless escorted by a man. These bars had two entrances, one marked GENTLEMEN and the other marked LADIES AND ESCORTS.

We took one look at the bar situation across the border and knew that America really was the land of the free. I started making plans to head west. I knew I would have to save some money, and I was determined not to ask my father for help. Unfortunately, I had to swallow my pride when my drums were stolen one night in Cleveland. I had finished a week's engagement at a club there and had just packed up my drums and loaded them into the backseat of my Corvair. I ran back in to get my paycheck, and when I returned to the car it was empty. My drums were gone, right down to the sticks, and with the drums went my livelihood. I had no choice but to call home. It was the first time since I left home at seventeen that I needed help.

"Those drums again," Father said. "I'll have to think about this and call you back later." Then he sat down and talked to Roula.

"Who knows what she's doing out there with all those men," he said. "Maybe if I don't give her the money she'll have to come home. She can't work without drums."

Roula took my side, convinced him that it was an emergency, and told him he shouldn't turn me down. (She probably didn't want me to move back home anymore than I wanted to do it!) He wired the money that afternoon. I continued to work, and with each job I headed farther west until we played Des Moines, Iowa. I gave the band one last chance to come with me, but they said no; it was too far from home. So on our last night the bar staff threw me a good luck party, complete with a cake, and the next morning I was on my way. I had no idea what awaited me in California, but whatever it was I was ready.

I arrived in California during the spring of 1967, when I was just a few months short of turning twenty-one. Los Angeles was exactly as I'd imagined it. I drove into the city, staring wide-eyed at all the palm trees and freeway signs. It was the biggest city I'd ever seen.

I rented a small furnished studio apartment in North Hollywood. The apartments all opened onto a courtyard, with palm trees and a swimming pool—everything California was supposed to be. The first thing I did was sign up at the musicians' union for work. The next thing I did was buy some postcards to send back to London. I couldn't wait to show off my new return address on Vineland Avenue in North Hollywood!

The people who managed the apartments had a son named Sal, a handsome Italian who I later found out was a Burbank police officer. He was gorgeous. I'll never forget the first time I saw him in his uniform. *Mama mia!* I was crazy about him, but he didn't appreciate my working in nightclubs. Maybe he knew my father. But I wasn't going to let him go and got to know his parents just to stay close to him.

While waiting for work as a drummer, I got a job at a strip club called the Pink Pussycat in Hollywood. The strippers only peeled down to pasties and G-strings, but it was pretty racy for 1967. The club had a three-piece combo with piano, bass, and drums. To this day I can remember the cheesy sound of that band playing music-to-strip-by.

I was hired as a hostess, which meant directing patrons to their tables and checking IDs at the front door. I was underage myself; if anyone could spot a false identification, it was the queen of fake IDs. The hostess wasn't expected to look as sexy as the strippers; still, I had to wear a skimpy costume. It was cold in the club, and wearing a skimpy outfit meant shivering all night. I asked if I could start wearing a sweater and they said no, so I lasted only a few weeks. I later heard that soon after I quit the club was raided, and several people were busted on drug and prostitution charges. I also heard that since I had come and gone so quickly, everybody thought I was a narc.

I went from checking IDs at the Pink Pussycat to taking tickets at the Ivar Theater in Hollywood. The theater had quite a history, from legitimate theater to strip club. But at that time it was showing *The Bubble* in 3D starring Deborah Walley. I must have seen the movie about thirty times while I worked there.

I wasn't making much money, but I did manage to save enough to pay my father back the $900 I'd borrowed to replace my drums. He was surprised and even tried to turn down the money. I told him I didn't want to owe anyone anything.

Mother drove to Los Angeles to live with me that summer. She had always traveled to see me play and she loved to drive; this was just a longer trip. I was looking forward to her coming, because I was a long way from home. It was one of the best times we ever had. It was good to have the company in a new environment. She was supportive of what I was trying to do, and I don't remember her drinking being a problem during her stay. She was very social, and as I started making friends, she quickly became a welcome part of the crowd. It's funny that I can't remember specifics about her during that stay. I guess it's easier to remember the bad times.

12

The Swingin' Dolls

After a short stint with a dance band at the beer bar in Santa Monica, I was approached about moving to Las Vegas to join an all-girl band named the Swingin' Dolls. I jumped at the chance. I didn't know much about Las Vegas, but I knew it was an entertainment capital; who knew, maybe that's where I'd make it as an entertainer.

My thinking had changed since I got to California, too. After spending my childhood dreaming about being a movie star, I was initially impressed that Los Angeles was the film capital of the world. I thought getting into the movies was the only way to be in show business, but I wasn't a musician then. After I got proficient on the drums, my thinking changed, and I realized that movie stardom was not the only avenue. I was becoming a good drummer with a flashy style. I could make it in music.

I'd heard that musicians could always find work in Vegas. The players there had more job security in the casinos than we did playing LA bars. And the money was reportedly good.

There were two things I had to address before heading for Vegas. One was Sal, but he agreed to come and see me there, even though he had never been to Vegas. As I said, he wasn't much on show business or gambling. The other problem was Mother, who had just recently moved in with me. She couldn't have afforded the rent at the apartment on Vineland, so I scouted around and helped her find a job as a live-in caretaker for an elderly gentleman.

Once Mother was settled in the new job, I quit the beer bar and started rehearsing with the Swingin' Dolls in Newport Beach, where the band leader, Marlane, lived. This was more rehearsing than I had ever done before, and a more professional organization than I was used to. The Swingin' Dolls had an agent, a manager, an elaborate wardrobe, and a one-year contract with the Del Webb Corporation, which included the Mint and Sahara hotels in Las Vegas and the Sahara-Tahoe.

I remember our first day of rehearsal at Marlane's house. I had never met the band before, and they were anxious to hear me play. I think they expected me to play girlie drums, but I'd come from hard-rock bands and I surprised them. There were four of us: Marlane on keyboards and vocals, Joyce on guitar and comedy, Dolores on bass and vocals, and me. I was fitted for my wardrobe; then I packed my Corvair and hit the road.

I drove through the desert all the way to Las Vegas in August. When I finally arrived and got out of the car I was shocked. Nobody had warned me about the unrelenting heat. It was 110 degrees! But the oppressive temperatures didn't lessen my enthusiasm. Driving into Las Vegas for the first time was an even bigger rush than seeing LA had been. I took a ton of pictures the first day I was in town. Milton Berle was appearing at Caesar's Palace; Tony Bennett and Count Basie were in the main showroom of the Sahara. (I could never have imagined that twenty years later I would be opening for Tony Bennett, and it wouldn't be playing the drums.) Everywhere I looked I saw bright lights and glitzy costumes. It was the epitome of glamour to me, and glamour is what I'd been seeking ever since I was a little girl playing with movie-star paper dolls. I was wild with excitement.

The Swingin' Dolls' first job was at the Sahara Hotel on the Las Vegas Strip on the midnight to 5 A.M. shift. We alternated with other bands; in fact, we did so in all the casinos, usually coming across the same groups more than once. Some of the performers we worked with were Lee Greenwood, the Hager Twins, the Kings Four, Expression, and the Leland Four. My big solo every night was in a song called "Watermelon Man." Between sets I cruised the casinos and watched people gamble. I was soon trying my hand at the tables, picking up tips from dealers I knew, and before long I got to be a pretty good blackjack player. I learned when to double down and when to split, and I got good enough that years later I won a blackjack tournament on a cruise.

We included comedy in our shows. Casino audiences were very different from the club crowds I was used to playing. In Vegas, you have to put on a show. People aren't dancing or socializing; they sit at a table waiting to be entertained. So any band who wanted work had to do more than just play music. That knowledge would be useful for me in the coming years.

Band business was handled in a very professional manner. We all lived at the same pay-by-the-week apartment complex. We rehearsed every day. We had a manager, and we were signed with the William Morris Agency, who had gigs lined up for the whole next year. The problem was that for the first time in my short career, I had a boss. All the bands I had been with until then were group efforts. We all pitched in, and we all had a say. Not so with the Swingin' Dolls.

Our living arrangements when we left Vegas on the road weren't to my liking either. I was rooming with Dolores, the bass player. I felt like a Satanist every time I went out and partied, because Dolores was a devout Mormon, and I was still partying a lot during those days.

Sal, the Burbank policeman, was a casualty of the road. We continued seeing each other off and on after I left Los Angeles, but spending most of your life on the road is not conducive to stable relationships. People grow apart, and sooner or later somebody starts dating others.

The last time I saw Sal was on his birthday, when I flew, gift in hand, straight from my last show in Lake Tahoe to Burbank, where he picked me up at 3 A.M. What I wanted to hear from Sal was a marriage proposal. What I heard within an hour of my arrival was the news that he'd been seeing someone else.

"If that's the way it is, just drop me off right here," I said in anger.

He did. It was 4 A.M. and he just pulled over and I got out of the car. I didn't even know where I was! I really thought he'd turn around and come back, because I couldn't believe anyone, especially a police officer, would leave another person in that kind of peril. He didn't return, so I walked to a pay phone and called his parents, who came and got me for the night. They couldn't believe their son dumped me on the side of the road, either.

I left my gift with them and flew back to Tahoe the next morning. Sal's mother called me later in Vegas to tell me Sal was marrying the other girl and give me her theory as to why. The other girlfriend had given him an expensive engraved mug for his birthday, whereas I had given him a Pendleton shirt. "She bought him away with a nicer gift," Sal's mother said.

I was devastated. To drown my sorrows I went out the next night and drank until I was numb. I woke up in the morning, not knowing how I got back to my hotel. I had a horrible hangover. I mean horrible. My head hurt, my stomach hurt, my skin hurt, and so did my heart.

Drinking to numb myself from the pain of a relationship gone bad. Now where had I seen that before?

I didn't like working for Marlane, but the work was steady, the money was good, and we had an upcoming tour in the Orient. I was excited about going but very apprehensive about showing anyone my passport. Nobody knew I was a Canadian citizen, working in the States illegally. I finally had no choice but to turn my passport over to the manager of the group. It turned out later that I'd had good reason for concern.

The thought of going to work overseas was more exciting than actually going. First, it was too expensive to transport our own instruments, so we had to depend on whatever was provided. Neither the band instruments nor the facilities on Vietnam War–era American military bases were anything close to what we were used to.

There were no dressing rooms, so we dressed in offices or in whatever empty room they provided. One of those offices had so many cockroaches you had to look for a spot to stand in between them. There were no stage lights and little equipment, not that it mattered to our audiences. The soldiers didn't care that our speakers only worked half the time and that I sometimes had to use pots and large cans as my drums. They treated us like royalty. Once, when we had to leave the stage in a downpour, the soldiers took off their coats and made a canopy for us all the way to the bus. That touched me very much. It was my first taste of being a star; the ovations we received were overwhelming, and, they were understandable. We were four young women dressed in slinky dresses all wearing push-up bras. Some of our dresses were designed and made by an excellent dressmaker—my mother.

We played in Tokyo, Bangkok, and Seoul. We got to do some sightseeing, like the floating market tour and the Golden Buddha in Bangkok, which added to the excitement of being in the Far East. The food was another story. One day they gave me something that looked like cow noses on a stick! It was all too foreign for me, and I was thrilled when we had a chance to eat at the military bases.

Can we see your green card, please?

Like I said, I tended to defy authority and was not happy working for Marlane. I wanted my own band, so I decided I would quit when we returned. Our next gig was at a club in Riverside, California, and at the end of our first night I gave two weeks' notice.

The next night when I came in to work, two immigration officers were there with a warrant for my arrest. I looked at Marlane as the officers questioned me. She turned away, but I caught the smirk that told me all I needed to know.

"You can go ahead and play the rest of the night if you want," one of the officers said. "We can take you in later."

"No," I said. "Let them play without a drummer." Later I found out that the bass player tried to play drums and the band kind of fell apart that night. That gave me a small amount of satisfaction.

The officers took me in, fingerprinted me, filled out a bunch of papers, and told me I had twenty-four hours to leave the country. I couldn't believe I was being deported. "Please, I have a car I'd like to drive back to Canada, and all my things are in Las Vegas, and I have to get back there and get them," I said. They gave me seven days.

The next morning I made the five-hour drive to Las Vegas, trying to figure out what to do. I'd always heard that once a country deported you, you could never set foot in that country again. I kept remembering how the bandleader looked at me while I was being arrested, as if to say, Poor thing, it's terrible that someone would do this to her. I remembered that her husband and her father were both there as well, which was a rare occurrence at any venue. There was no reason for them to be there, unless she thought there might be trouble. I felt angry and betrayed.

I started packing my things and making some good-bye calls, preparing to leave for Canada the next day. Then my phone rang, and it was an agent asking if I was available. "Yes and no," was my answer. "I'm available, but I've just been deported and am leaving for Canada tomorrow."

"Let me see what I can do," the talent booker said. "I may be able to help you and help myself at the same time. Stay where you are, and I'll call you right back." I waited by the phone and suddenly remembered that I'd been asked to join a topless female band. Even if I had breasts, I'd have to say no.

It seemed too good to be true, but by the end of the day he got me a visa and I was back in business, playing with another fully clothed all-girl band at the Four Queens Casino in downtown Las Vegas. I was careful to keep my visa and green card updated through the years, and finally became a U.S. citizen nearly ten years after this incident.

An unexpected trip

The starstruck syndrome is a common affliction among young girls who move to Las Vegas. They come seeking fame and fortune and suddenly find themselves surrounded by an abundance of men who possess both. Being intimidated by their stardom is almost always risky. Sly Stone taught me that not long after I got to town.

Sly and the Family Stone was one of 1969's biggest musical groups and Sly Stone was known as one of the godfathers of psychedelic soul. He was the first real celebrity I ever met. When Sly brought his show to town, I went to the concert with another female musician, Bobbi, who was also a big fan.

I didn't know anything about stars picking up girls from the stage until that night. I had no idea that male performers often had roadies whose primary purpose was to find girls they thought the star might want to meet and take them to his dressing room. At the end of Sly's show, a young man came over and said I was invited backstage. I didn't want to go without my friend, but Bobbi insisted. "Go on, go on. It's Sly Stone!"

I was so in awe of him I could barely speak. But I finally got up the nerve to say hello. He invited me up to his room and then asked me if I wanted to smoke some pot. I'd been wanting to try it and told Sly so. But as a nonsmoker, I didn't think I could. Sly said he could take care of that. He left for a moment and came back with a pill in his hand.

"It's pot," he said.

I'd never heard of pot in a pill, but I was dying to get high, so I swallowed both the pill and the story.

Looking back, I realize how naive it was to be going alone to the hotel room of a psychedelic soul man famous for doing drugs. But I was young and starstruck and loved the idea of hanging out with a rock star. After I took the pill, we started talking about music, his career, drums. I started feeling funny and felt a burning sensation in my stomach. When I went to use the bathroom, I glanced in the mirror and my face looked sort of blotchy, almost as if I were seeing through the skin. By the time I came out, my stomach seemed to be on fire.

"Maybe I ought to leave," I said. "My stomach is really hurting."

"That's just the acid," Sly said with a shrug.

"Acid from what?" I thought maybe he thought I had indigestion.

"The acid I gave you."

Then I knew what he was talking about. The supposed marijuana pill had been LSD. I'd heard of people sneaking psychedelic drugs into punch bowls and people's drinks back then, but I never dreamed someone would do it to me. I wasn't any angel. I wanted to know what it was like to smoke pot. But LSD scared me. I don't remember if I got mad or what I said to Sly. I was so upset all I could think of was going home. I managed to get back to my apartment, where I sat with my arms crossed over my aching stomach and wondered if I was going to overdose. Luckily, I had no other side effects and no flashbacks later on.

13

The Cover Girls

Las Vegas guys are famous for wearing lots of jewelry and for being seen with flashy women, and my next big opportunity came through someone who fit the bill perfectly. Penny Mayo was almost a caricature of a Las Vegas agent. He was always making a deal. He loved flash and he surrounded himself with it, from the acts he represented to the woman he married. His wife was a striking, buxom young woman, a Jayne Mansfield–type blonde who, if you believed the rumors, he'd married when she was around fourteen years old. He was in terrible health by the time I met him, overweight and diabetic, yet he still wheeled and dealed all over town.

Penny decided to put together an all-girl band. His vision was of a glamorous, glitzy, flashy quartet who also happened to play great music. He signed the rhythm section first, a beautiful tall brunette bass player named Terri O'Brien from Los Angeles and then me. (It wasn't hard to figure out how he found me, since there wasn't a surplus of girl drummers in the musicians union in 1969.) Then Penny signed Vicki Manning, a pretty, raspy-voiced singer and keyboard player from Phoenix, and we were left to find a guitarist. We got word through the San Francisco Musicians Union of a good female guitar player named Stephanie Teel, and we flew her in to audition. She walked in carrying her guitar and wearing a tie-dyed shirt, torn blue-jean cutoffs, an Australian outback–style cowboy hat, sandals, no makeup, and a toe ring. But she could really sing and play the guitar, so we hired her on the spot.

Penny wanted to call us Jenny Jones and the Jones Girls, and for lack of a better name that's how we billed ourselves while we were still just rehearsing. Once we started working, we changed our name to the Cover Girls; even though I was the band leader, I viewed us as a team. We had our own logo designed, and the money was good enough that I made a down payment on a van and had the logo painted on the side. I let Stephanie drive the van, since she didn't have a car.

One of Penny's other acts was a comic named Al Bello, who had a successful comedy revue on the strip. He hosted a novelty variety-type show, featuring a band and a troupe of female dancers. Al approached Penny with the idea of replacing his all-male band with women. He decided an all-female revue would be an even bigger draw, and the newly formed Cover Girls got the gig.

Al was a good comic and front man, but what he really wanted to do was play golf. Penny, who always believed in me, suggested that I could front the show as well, using Al's material. So Al got to play more golf, and I ended up fronting the revue from the drums on a semi-regular basis. We worked an entire summer at the Mapes Hotel in Reno, and the Cover Girls became a family. We ate together, rehearsed together, worked together, hung out together, and partied together. The partying was on a pretty regular basis—like every night after work. We'd all go out to drink beer and shoot pool. The drinking didn't seem to be a problem at the time, but later it became a serious problem for one of the other band members and could have easily become serious for me.

Ba-da-bing, ba-da-boom!

After leaving the Al Bello Revue, the Cover Girls worked solidly through 1970. One thing I'd learned from working the Vegas circuit was that people want more than just music. They like to be entertained, and what better way than to make them laugh? One of our comedy routines was a takeoff on something we saw on *Laugh-In*, which was so popular in the seventies. We'd play four bars of music, stop and tell a quick joke, then more music, and another quick joke. We each got to bring in new jokes, and at the time they actually seemed funny. Like:

"I went to the doctor because I had water on the knee. He told me to start wearing pumps!"

Ba-da bing, ba-da boom!

We had fun on the job, but I was a strict leader. Years later the girls told me we needed strong leadership because we were all young and running a bit wild. We behaved more like college kids doing pranks on campus, except our campus was a string of motels and hotels across America. One of our favorite things to do was to put speakers outside our motel windows and play sound effects such as people screaming and people falling down stairs. But in spite of my involvement in the pranks, I was still the leader and made a list of rules for the girls. Some of the written rules that were strictly enforced included:

> Never be seen without makeup.
> Never date a club employee.
> Never drink on the job.
> Always behave in a respectable manner
>   to reflect well on the group.

Being in the band was rough on Stephanie, who was really a hippie, a naturalist. She had to wear glitzy costumes—some of which I made myself—style her hair every night, and put on makeup. Lots of makeup. We all gave her lessons in applying two or three pounds of eyeliner, frosted eye shadow, false eyelashes, and bright red lips. God never meant for Stephanie to wear makeup, but she did what was required and never complained. The minute we finished our sets, off came the clothes and makeup, and back on went the jeans and tie-dye.

The Cover Girls got into a lot of innocent trouble back then. When we finished the show, we were ready to party. And every night we tried to outdo each other with stunts designed to break the monotony. One night, during our stint with the Al Bello Revue, we decided it would be fun to break into a house in Reno that was deserted and rumored to be haunted. We finished our show and headed out. There were ten of us: the four band members, five of our dancers, and Penny Mayo, who'd decided to turn it into a seance and brought candles to burn. He wasn't a medium, nor was anyone in the crowd, so I have no idea how we thought we were going to conjure up any spirits.

We were circling the house, trying to figure out the best way to bust in, when Stephanie offered to break in through a window. As soon as she was in, the cops showed up. Within seconds, two cops jumped out of a squad car and told us to freeze. It was the K-9 unit, and they had a big attack dog with them. But instead of any serious criminal types, what they found was a bunch of drunken musicians and dancers and one chubby agent waving a candle. The cop read us our rights anyway.

I still had my delinquent tendencies, so I started spouting off to the police officer. "You can't arrest us." I laughed. "There are ten people here, and you've only got one squad car!"

Terri said she almost died.

"Fine, sister," the cop said. "We'll just bust you for breaking and entering and public drunkenness. Get in the car."

Penny finally interceded in my behalf. When he explained that we were playing the Mapes Casino and were just out for a little harmless fun, they agreed to let me go.

Another time on the road we broke into a water-slide tourist attraction called the Super Slide. We knew you had to have mats to slide on, so we borrowed some blankets from the motel. We got off work at 2 A.M. and headed for the slide. We had to climb a pretty high fence. Naturally, Stephanie offered to go first. We were having a ball going down the slide on our blankets until the police showed up with flashlights. We scattered and hid under some cars, busted only after we started calling out to one another from our hiding places. We had our story down, though, and told them that the tourists always talked about the Super Slide, but it was always closed by the time we got off work. They told us to pack up our blankets and go on back to the motel.

The Cover Girls, Penny-less

One day, when we were on the road in Fairfield, California, we got a phone call with some shocking news. Betty Sue, a sax player I'd worked with at the Four Queens, was found murdered in Las Vegas, strangled with an electrical cord. They said there was no sign of forced entry, so it appeared that she knew her murderer. Betty Sue was a total opposite to the partying Cover Girls. She didn't drink, hardly ever dated, and was considered a homebody. The news came as such a shock and scared us all so much we spent that night in the same room, afraid to be alone. The next thing we knew, Penny was reported missing. Rumors flew all over town. Some people said Penny had murdered Betty Sue and was on the run. Others speculated that he had gotten into a mess with some mobsters, and they had killed him and stuffed him in the trunk of a car.

One day, almost a year later, he showed up back in Vegas, simply saying he'd had a nervous breakdown. Penny was never the same after his unexplained absence, but he remained friendly with all of us until his death in 1985.

We were like a gypsy family out on the road. We ate all our meals together, including one Thanksgiving dinner at a Denny's. I can't even remember having Christmas with my family in London, so it's not surprising that holidays don't mean much to me. I'm never insulted if my friends and family forget my birthday or don't send me anything for Christmas. The lack of a sense of family other than the Cover Girls was compounded during those early days out on the road. I often worked on holidays and spent many Christmases on the road, and that was fine with me. About the only time the Cover Girls were apart was if one of us had a date, and even then we knew all the details by breakfast the next day.

We got a lot of work, too, because we were good, and word about us began to spread. One of the offers we got was for a Canadian tour that included a show at the Iroquois Hotel in London, Ontario. I had mixed feelings about going home. Sending back good press clippings seemed to have eased Father's critical attitude. But he'd never seen me work, and I wondered if he would still have disdain for my chosen profession. To my relief, Father and Roula sent me flowers on opening night, and when they came to see the show, Father said he liked it.

It was fun to come home in style. I don't think the Cover Girls ever played better than we did in London. Father and Roula even had a party in our honor. One night I was up very late talking to my father, when the conversation started to sound familiar. He told me he was having a cash-flow problem. He had some creditors to pay and was in a bind.

"How much do you owe?" I asked.

"About two thousand," he said grimly.

I took out my checkbook and wrote him a check for two thousand dollars. I explained that this was money I'd put aside for payroll taxes, so I'd need it back. If he was really only in a tight cash-flow position, he should be able to pay me the money by the next quarter.

Father was stunned. He could not believe I actually had that much extra cash or that I'd put it aside to pay my taxes. He couldn't believe I was that responsible. He accepted the check, and, as he did, our relationship was forever changed. It was a great moment for me. He saw me as an individual who could be trusted to hold a job and be responsible.

14

Going to the Chapel

I may have been fiscally responsible, but socially I was headed down the wrong road. Too naive and too impulsive, I was partying far too much—so much that in 1969 at the age of twenty-three I ran off and got married. I'm not sure why; it was a crazy stunt. Soon after, the marriage was quickly annulled.

I am very lucky. I didn't have to hit bottom before I quit drinking. There was no single moment when I suddenly thought, *You could end up an alcoholic just like your mother.* My change in lifestyle just evolved. The more responsibility I took on with the Cover Girls, the less comfortable I felt going out drinking. It wasn't that I was afraid for our image. I was concerned about not being in control of my actions. The idea of anyone finding me passed out naked in a bathtub, as I had once found my mother, was repugnant. I was also growing increasingly interested in nutrition, so I stopped partying for the most part. I didn't completely abstain, just drank moderately when I drank at all.

I seem to stay surrounded by alcoholics, though, the most obvious one being my mother. There have been many more problem drinkers in my life, and I think an expert would say it's because children of alcoholics want so badly to have some control, to change the tide, that they become magnets for people in need of help.

One of my best friends was a female musician in Vegas. She was also an alcoholic. In fact, when I was doing stand-up comedy, I was headed out on the road and my friend, who is a lesbian, was going to stay at my apartment while I was gone. She'd had a DUI, and her court date was the following morning. I thought she might need a peaceful sanctuary. But when she showed up at my place, I could tell she was intoxicated. I didn't think it was just alcohol, and phoned some of her friends to see if she'd taken some drugs too. Nobody seemed to know.

She started rambling, sometimes talking to herself and sometimes to me. Every so often she would seem to forget where she was and begin addressing me by the name of her old girlfriend. Finally she put her arms around me and tried to kiss me. I knew better than to act confrontational when she was so drunk, so I just took her arms and gently pushed her away.

"You don't mean this," I said. "This is Jenny."

She went crazy and started hitting me, screaming how much she hated me. Then she started telling me I was the only woman she'd ever loved, and the reason she loved me was because she couldn't have me. I still believed she thought I was her old girlfriend. I kept trying to stay unruffled. All of a sudden she was all over me. She punched me and even bit me before I got her calmed down. Her next actions frightened me even more. She got a brush and began brushing her hair in an obsessive manner, as if her very life depended on each brush stroke. She wandered around the apartment, looking for nonexistent items she thought she'd lost. I kept telling her nothing was there, but she couldn't seem to hear me.

Finally I thought she had passed out for the night, and I went to bed. She didn't stay down. She would stagger off the couch and fall onto the coffee table. She talked to people who weren't there. And she kept coming in and out of my room, so I was afraid to sleep. I kept wondering what I would do in the morning when I had to leave to go on the road. It was the first time I realized just how serious her illness was. I knew I was going to have to tell her she couldn't stay there alone while I was out of town. I wasn't mad at her, just sorry for her.

Over the years I encouraged her to seek professional help, but I tried not to preach or withhold my friendship if she did not. And

I am very proud to report that in 1997 my friend entered treatment and is doing fine one day at a time.

Did I mention he was Italian?

I was twenty-three years old when I first saw Al Gambino, my first "real" husband. (The first time I got married was more like a date gone wrong.) Al used to come sit at the bar at the Aladdin and catch the Cover Girls' show. He was a struggling Vegas singer and musician who often earned extra money by writing musical charts for big bands. In many ways he was ahead of his time. Al was the first person I knew to experiment with computerized music, and he was very good at what he did. Some journalists at the time went so far as to call him another Sinatra. Unfortunately, in show business, having talent doesn't guarantee success.

I was immediately attracted to him. Did I mention he was Italian? We started dating steadily, and things were great. We had a lot in common, and it looked like he had a good future in music. He had a manager and had just moved to Las Vegas from New Jersey. When I was approached by his manager with an offer of $1,000 to have sex, I told Al, but he didn't seem bothered by it. I wanted him to defend my honor and confront the man, but he didn't. It should have been a red flag.

Al was the only man to stir up my emotions like Sal had, and the timing was right because I was ready to get married. And he was a nice honest guy, too. So often the men I met were not what they seemed. I'd gone out with one of the pit bosses at the Mint Hotel a few times and really liked him. One day I called him at home. A woman answered and said, "He's not here. This is his wife. Can I help you?" I made up some excuse why I was calling and hung up. When I confronted him about it, he looked at me very casually. "Of course I'm married," he said. He didn't even seem to care that I'd called him at his house and spoken with his wife. There wasn't a trace of embarrassment.

Al Gambino was a welcome change.

I went to Al's parents' home in New Jersey to visit, and we both went to London to visit Father and Roula and Mother. Everyone seemed to hit it off. Father even liked him, although he did quiz me about why I wanted to get married. I told him I was crazy about Al and couldn't stand to be away from him. Father seemed to understand and offered to give me a wedding dress. After I was back in Vegas, we exchanged photos of dresses back and forth while we decided on the final design. I chose a dreamy full-length gown, sheer white over powder blue, and sent him my measurements from Las Vegas. When the dress arrived it was a perfect fit.

We got married on December 27, 1970, at the Little Church of the West next to the Frontier in Las Vegas. Mother and Father were both in the wedding party, and Roula was an honored guest. We were one big happy family. At the wedding reception at Cioppino's Restaurant, Father gave a toast. "Jenny is my million dollars; now, with my new son, I have two million dollars."

Unfortunately, I was prepared to *get* married, but I wasn't ready to *be* married. I envisioned life with Al to be a continuation of the dates we'd gone on, lots of laughing and talking about the Las Vegas music scene. I didn't anticipate the tensions that would necessarily follow when Al's career didn't take off and we struggled to pay bills at the very time the Cover Girls had decided to call it quits.

There was no comprehensive reason why the Cover Girls broke up, but I think being out on the road so much took its toll on all of us. We'd had our fun, but we were all suffering from burnout. And although everyone was sad about it, we all knew the band's time was over. Our last booking was at the Nevada Lodge in Lake Tahoe. It was a very emotional night because our family was splitting up, so we turned the whole last show into a party. My rules went out the window, and we wore things like pajama tops and Mickey Mouse shirts instead of our glossy stage clothes. (It was perfect for Stephanie!) We played the last song, hugged, and had one more drink to say good-bye. It actually turned out to be "see ya later," because we have stayed in touch over the years.

· *Where are they now?* ·

Terri is a barber in Palm Springs, Vicki is a hairdresser in Phoenix, and Stephanie still plays guitar with her own band in San Francisco.

Girl drummer for hire

I was ready for a change, especially to be off the road, and I'd noticed how many comedy shows, like Bottoms Up, played steadily in Las Vegas. Since I had experience in music and comedy, and Al was a musician/arranger, we decided to put a show together and audition for some buyers.

I really wanted our comedy show to work, because if we couldn't sell some agents on us, I was going to have to start free-lancing as a drummer, and there was no job security there. So we rehearsed our routines and booked a stage at the old Thunderbird Hotel to audition for talent buyers.

Now I realize how amateurish we must have been. I wore a big curly blond wig, and Al was the straight man. Our comedy was very silly, somehow employing props, including a big bowl of spaghetti. It was so lame I've blocked it from my memory. But we didn't realize how foolish we looked that night. We thought we were on our way to the big rooms. We anxiously awaited an offer for several days, but nobody called us back. Once again, I put my name up at the musicians union: GIRL DRUMMER FOR HIRE.

Finances were one big problem, and as time went by sex became another. I should say, *lack* of sex was a problem, because Al quit having sexual relations with me. Nine months went by, and Al never once approached me for sex. I know I should have approached him, but I didn't know how. I was sure he'd lost interest in me because of my flat chest. I became insanely jealous every time he was around attractive women, which was all the time.

Al put a group together and hired two dancers as well. They all wore skimpy little costumes, and the men in the audience just drooled over them. One of the girls had the biggest, most outlandish breasts I had ever seen. Every time Al looked at her, even spoke to her, I was convinced he was lusting after her.

I was naive enough, though, to think Al was being faithful to me when we weren't having sex. I still trusted him, even when he'd come home smelling of women's perfume and, yes, the ubiquitous lipstick on his collar. When I asked him about it, he'd explain, "Well, I have to dance with the women between shows to keep them coming back. So of course their perfume will be on me too."

He got angry that I was questioning him, so I backed off.

15

The King Of Las Vegas and I

Just as my marriage was hitting a low, my career got a big boost. One day in 1971, Wayne Newton's music conductor, Don Vincent, called me to audition for a job singing backup with Wayne's show. Wayne Newton was the King of Vegas, and I couldn't believe his conductor was calling me. I wasn't a singer, I was a drummer who sang. There's a big difference.

Don explained that one of the backup singers was suddenly called out of town, and they needed someone that night. Wayne's drummer had heard me singing harmonies with the Cover Girls and recommended me. I didn't know what to say. I was afraid to audition, since I had never sung solo and didn't want to embarrass myself. On the other hand, I did have a good ear for harmonizing. I said I'd have call him back.

I thought about it for a while and decided I didn't want to wonder for the rest of my career what would have happened if I had auditioned. Plus, I've never been one to back down from a challenge. I called back and said I'd be right there. By the time I arrived at the casino, rehearsal was over, the band was packing up, and Wayne Newton had left the building. They must have been desperate by then, because they handed me a tambourine and a dress and told me to come back at seven-thirty.

I went home and tried on the dress. It was too long, so I pulled out my sewing supplies and quickly took up the hem. When I got in the car to head to the Frontier, it finally hit me. I was going to perform with one of Las Vegas's biggest stars, and I didn't know anything about his show. I didn't know where I would be standing, what songs he was performing, or what harmony part he expected me to sing. I started to get extremely nervous.

When I got backstage, Wayne was standing there looking bigger, taller, and more imposing than I expected. I introduced myself, and he reached out to shake my hand.

"It's nice to meet you. Thank you very much for helping us out." Then he headed for the stage.

Time was running out, and very soon everyone would know me for the pretender I was. I would look like a fool in front of Wayne, his band, his friends, and his audience. Before I knew what was happening, the other backup singer took me by the arm, led me to the stage, and pointed to my spot. It was right up front, in front of the string section. I'd never been on one of the big stages before, nor had I performed with a string section. I'd never even *heard* a live string section. I was a lounge act and I knew it. Soon the world was going to know it too. The other singer must have noticed the sweat starting to pour down my back, because she came up behind me just before the curtain rose.

"Don't worry about it," she reassured me. "Just find a part nobody else is singing and jump in."

But that didn't stop my knees from trembling. All of a sudden the audience lights lowered and the curtain rose. I stood there with my mouth frozen in a smile and my eyes glassy with terror.

"Ladies and gentlemen, Wayne Newton."

Wayne was casual about having a novice backup singer in his show. Maybe he couldn't even hear us. He had a thirty-piece orchestra, and we were just two women singers. Luckily, Wayne sang a lot of standards, like "When the Saints Go Marching In," and I could wing it. Wayne does a long show, and it seemed to go on forever. I stood there sweating and shaking that tambourine and trying to join in when the other backup singer sang, until at long last the curtain came down.

It was over. I couldn't believe I'd made it through without anyone pointing at me and laughing. I also couldn't believe that I hadn't brought a tape recorder. At least I could have rehearsed between the first and second shows. But I don't think Wayne realized how bad I was, because the conductor came up to me after the second show and told me to report back to the casino the next night. That night I made sure I had a tape recorder. On the third night I sang with the show, I knew the songs.

I was with the Wayne Newton Show for almost two years. I don't know if I was more excited about working with a big star or about having steady work, but it was a great experience as well as an educational one. I learned a lot from Wayne Newton. Each night before going home the core group had a meeting. Included were the conductor, the rhythm section, the backup singers, and, of course, Wayne. The show was discussed from start to finish.

What could have been better?

What worked perfectly?

This is a guy who is considered the best in Vegas, and every night he asks, What could have been better?

Within a matter of weeks Wayne appointed me leader of the backup section and vocal arranger, and we hired a third singer. And there was one more contribution I made to Wayne's show. One of his signature performances was his version of "Dixie," but he thought it was missing something. It needed a harmonica solo. No one in the band played harmonica, so Wayne asked if anyone was willing to learn. When no one offered, I volunteered. How hard could it be? I knew I could do anything if I just committed to it, so I went to the music store and bought a blues harp and an instruction book.

I made my television debut while I was working with Wayne in May of 1972. One night Wayne announced that Merv Griffin was coming to Las Vegas to tape his show. The most exciting part was that Wayne decided to perform "Dixie" on the show, and I got to play harmonica on national TV.

I never really socialized with Wayne, but I was invited to his house once. He'd been in a movie, and he had a private screening party for his friends and the people in his show. I was very nervous about going. I'd never been to the home of a celebrity, and I didn't know what to wear or how to act. When I got there, I thought I was at a country club, except that this club was home to some beautiful Arabian horses. He lived just the way you'd expect a star to live, in a lovely house with grounds that were so painstakingly manicured they looked like a golf course. Another thing Wayne's yard had that a country club probably didn't have was a live wallaby hopping around.

Elaine, Wayne's wife at the time, was a surprise to me. I don't know what I expected, but she was a very warm, down-to-earth woman who'd been a flight attendant when she met Wayne. I was a bit in awe of her: First, she was gorgeous, and second, I thought of her as a celebrity too. But she chatted with me and the other backup singers just like we were old friends. I was shocked when she began confiding her marital troubles to us. She'd say things like "Wayne thinks *I* should leave, but I'm not going to do it. *He's* going to have to leave." I don't think she was being vindictive. I think she was just one of those open, unaffected people. In fact they eventually divorced.

Hearing someone like Elaine Newton speak so candidly about some very personal problems gave me the confidence to bring up my own issues.

The woman I entrusted with my troubles was a neighbor and fellow backup singer in Wayne's band. Lynn had never sung professionally when I met her, but when I heard her sing I was so impressed I recommended her to Wayne. After all, he'd hired me with no real experience, so I knew he was willing to take a chance. My belief in her proved to be justified, and she turned out to be a mainstay of the act. We sat at a bar one night after work, and I had to have a drink to get up the courage to talk to her. She was shocked when I told her Al and I hadn't had sex in almost a year and finally asked me a pointed question.

"Jenny, have you ever just looked at your husband and said, 'I want you so much'?"

"That's just not my style," I said.

"Have you ever had an orgasm?"

"Uh, I don't know. What does an orgasm feel like?"

"If you have to ask, you haven't had one," she said, shaking her head.

I knew I hadn't ever had one, too.

Having sex with a woman never crossed my mind

One afternoon I learned more about our sex problems than I really wanted to know. I was looking through some old papers in the file cabinet and found a big envelope I'd never before noticed. I opened it and found pornography magazines—women with women. I was stunned. I didn't know what it meant. Was my husband a pervert? Was he just bored with me? I had no experience with pornography or people who looked at it. It's easy to laugh about porn movies and that sort of thing, but when you find it hidden in your file cabinet it's unnerving. And it's threatening.

I finally worked up my courage and confronted Al. He stammered a little, obviously embarrassed at having been busted. I asked him if the pictures had anything to do with the fact he didn't want sex with me. He looked down at the floor. Then he said, "Would you be willing to have sex with a woman and let me watch?"

He caught me off guard with that question. Having sex with a woman had never crossed my mind, but if it meant saving the marriage. . . .

"Is it that important to you?" I asked.

"It would make me the happiest man in the world," he said.

I had never seen him so excited as when he realized I was considering it. I began to rationalize, thinking that if I closed my eyes and let her do things to me, I could make him happy. The more I entertained the idea, the more excited he became, making it difficult to say no and disappoint him.

"All right, I'll do it," I said.

It didn't happen, though. In the ensuing days, when the reality of having sex with another woman to save my marriage was taking form, I became less and less willing to participate. I finally realized that I'd be doing it for the wrong reasons and told him I had changed my mind.

We grew farther and farther apart after that, and finally I didn't see any reason for us to be together.

When I moved out I took three things: my clothes, my drums, and my car. Every time I've parted company with a man I've made sure I only left with what I came in with. In this case, it was clothes, drums, and a car. We didn't own any property and didn't have any furniture I cared about, and by then I didn't really care about Al. I moved into a pay-by-the-week motel.

Telling my parents was not something I looked forward to, but to my surprise Father took it quite well. Then again, I was just following in his footsteps. Mother didn't seem affected one way or the other.

I didn't stay single long. One night in 1973 I noticed a well-dressed man walking through the backstage area at the Frontier Hotel. He was slightly balding and appeared to be in his early forties: not exactly my type, but there was something about him I liked. Among all the musicians, he stood out as a mature, sophisticated businessman. He looked like someone with some substance.

Wayne introduced him to several of us between shows; he was a Los Angeles–based Capitol Records marketing executive, in Vegas to meet with Wayne regarding record releases. His name was Buz, and in addition to working with Wayne, his other Capitol Records artists included Anne Murray, Glen Campbell, and Merle Haggard. After that first encounter, Buz often came to Wayne's show to discuss record company business. And he always found time to talk to me between shows.

Buz was very different from the men with whom I'd been associating over the past few years. For one thing, he was older. He had a steady job and made a good living. Not only did he represent security to me, he treated me like I was special. Even when he was hitting on me, he did it in a thoughtful way. There were no come-on lines. Instead, he would sit backstage and rub my recently sprained ankle between shows. Considering that my former husband would go months without wanting to touch me, feeling desired and pampered was a welcome change. Buz had been married twice and had six children ranging in age from eight to twenty-four. I was twenty-seven.

I didn't think Wayne would approve of an employee having a relationship with one of his business associates, so Buz and I started dating secretly. I didn't know how long we could carry on our clandestine long-distance love affair, with him flying to Vegas to see me or me flying to Los Angeles to see him.

Then one day, I was on a flight to LA, where Buz would be waiting to meet me at the airport. When I heard that Wayne Newton was also on the flight, I decided this would be a good time to come clean. I asked for permission from the flight attendant to visit in the first-class cabin and I approached Wayne's seat, so nervous I thought my throat would close up.

"Wayne," I stammered, "I have something to tell you and I hope you won't be upset. I've been dating Buz."

"Oh, I know," he said casually. "He's a great guy."

So much for dating a co-worker.

The longer I worked with Wayne, the easier it became to talk to him. So when I began to consider getting my large nose fixed, I decided to ask Wayne for advice. I had been self-conscious about the size of my nose since my teens. (In fact, I tried to find a profile photo for this book, but I'd been so embarrassed about it I never took a picture from the side.)

I hadn't told anyone that I wanted a nose job, and I was embarrassed to tell Wayne, thinking he would just say, "Oh, you look fine the way you are." But instead he said, "I believe in doing whatever makes you feel good about your appearance." That was all the permission I needed. But he gave me more than permission, he

gave me the name of the best nose doctor in Beverly Hills and offered to let me recuperate at his Los Angeles residence.

I couldn't get to the doctor fast enough to schedule the surgery.
I was already seeing Buz at the time, so I recouped at his home, a
beautiful Spanish-style house in the Hollywood Hills that he called
Casa Loma. I wanted to move to California to be closer to Buz and
decided to quit my job with Wayne. I gave my two weeks' notice
and was told that, while I'd be paid for the two weeks, I didn't need
to come back. It was all very friendly. That's just the way they operated—if someone wanted to leave, Wayne didn't want to hold
them up. It was fine with me. I didn't mind getting two weeks' pay
for doing nothing.

Not long after we started dating, it was time to meet Buz's children—
and, as he and his ex-wife had shared custody, that also meant
meeting her.

Buz's second wife was a beautiful woman. She completely intimidated me. She had a great body, which was even more impressive considering that she had borne four of Buz's children.

The worst part was Buz's feelings about her. According to him,
the two had stayed married several years longer than they should
have, since they no longer really cared for each other. But, he said,
he couldn't stand to leave her because of her beauty. That's not exactly what an insecure, flat-chested new girlfriend wants to hear,
especially one recouping in his home with a bandage across her
swollen nose.

I couldn't have felt more unattractive, and she couldn't have
been more together. My face was still swollen from my recent
rhinoplasty, and I thought I looked like a blowfish. My insecurity
was intensified when I found out Buz had been dating a former
Miss Ohio just before he met me. Clearly, this was a man who
wanted a beauty on his arm.

I didn't think I qualified on any level.

My insecurities faded somewhat after Buz took me to New Or-

leans and asked me to marry him. I accepted, and we decided to
return to New Orleans for our wedding, an extravagant affair, which
he organized. I wore a romantic *Gone With the Wind*–type gown
and carried a parasol. After a ceremony at Beauregarde House, we
rode in horse-drawn carriages through the French Quarter, escorted
by the Olympia Brass Band.

When we got back to the hotel, Buz had catered a magnificent
reception, with piles of shrimp and crawfish and magnums of champagne. Mother didn't come to the wedding; Father and Roula came,
and Dad was so impressed by the blowout that he toasted Buz and
said, "This is a real man. This is what my million dollars has
needed."

Translation: This is a *rich* man.

16

Readymade Family

Buz wasn't a rich man, but he did earn a good salary and liked to live well, so my life changed drastically. He moved me from a little apartment in Las Vegas to his elegant home in the Hollywood Hills. It was a wonderful house, white stucco with a red tile roof, Mediterranean archways, and a tiled swimming pool off the den. You could see the Hollywood sign from the backyard.

I couldn't wait to become the mistress of my new domain. I thought it was my chance to be part of a real family, a *Father Knows Best* kind of family. I anticipated a new marriage where my husband would go off to work with his briefcase and I would stay home and be the lady of the house, never worrying about bills or stability. My only concern would be that dinner be ready when he came home. It was an unrealistic, dated dream fostered by 1950s television and the movies, but even with my independent streak it's a dream I'd bought.

Unfortunately, a houseman was already in charge of Buz's household. Buz was impressed by the fact that this man had once worked in the same capacity for Hugh Hefner. This houseman did everything: cooking, cleaning, shopping, even planning dinner parties. I didn't need someone cooking, cleaning, or party-planning. I was very proud of my culinary talents and wanted to show them off for my new husband. I soon learned that the houseman didn't want me involved in the household management because he was stealing liquor. Buz entertained both frequently and lavishly, so it was a simple and lucrative heist. Once Buz learned what was going on, he fired the man, and I got down to the business of being a wife and a stepmother. I was about to find out what it was like to be Roula when she married my father.

When his children came to visit, we got along well, but they didn't think much of my cooking. The only food they liked was fast food, and I was getting very serious about eating healthy. I'd fix soups and whole grain breads, and they'd beg for French fries. I suppose they weren't any fussier than most teenagers, but I took their criticisms personally, since I wanted them to like me and be glad I was a part of the family.

My role in the family was never well defined. I wanted to be a friend to Buz's children. I wanted them to feel they could come to me with any problems, but I didn't want to be a mother figure. Occasionally Buz tried to put me in that position, and I didn't like it. Once when we were driving somewhere, the children were misbehaving in the backseat. Buz was driving and suddenly said, "Jenny, would you please be the disciplinarian?" It was an uncomfortable moment. I wasn't sure what to do. He finally had to pull over to handle the situation himself, and I felt like a failure. I had disappointed my husband. But I would much rather have been the children's friend than an authority figure. It was the only thing I knew how to do.

Buz spoiled his children, buying them anything they wanted the moment they wanted it. There was no anticipation in that family. At Christmas he could never think of anything to get them, because they already had everything they wanted. I disagreed with all the coddling. A little hardship builds character. And you don't develop a sense of appreciation when everything comes so easily. It seemed to me they should have had some responsibility at some point.

But Buz didn't care to hear my opinions about his children. Looking back, I think he was a typical divorcé, who feels guilty for not being there in person and tries to make up for it with material goods. My strong feelings about the pampering of his children were the cause of many disagreements and contributed greatly to the downfall of my dream marriage. My advice to any woman marrying a man with children is to know that his children will always come first.

Too good to be true

Buz had already left Capitol Records to start his own music marketing company in 1973. He opened an office in Hollywood and barely got things off the ground when he was approached by a man from Atlanta with a business proposition. His name was Mike Thevis. He told Buz he wanted to go into the record business and was looking for someone with experience in the music industry to help launch a new record label. Mike claimed to have deep pockets, and when his finances checked out, Buz went to Georgia to meet with him. They struck a deal, and for two years Buz and I commuted between Los Angeles and Atlanta.

I thought I had seen lavish homes in LA and Vegas, but they were nothing compared to Mike's mansion in the South. The two-story brick home was so long you could justifiably mistake it for a motel. When you first walked inside, you stepped into a huge entryway with a gigantic curved staircase on either side. The swimming pool even had a bridge across it. I'd never been in a home where every item was original and expensive and hand-picked. He'd purchased the floor of a room in an English castle and had it moved piece by piece to his den. There was a handmade custom pool table. There was a story behind every single statuette and candlestick. Nothing got in its place by accident. It was the most dramatic residence I'd ever seen, and that included Wayne Newton's house.

His wife had a thirteen-carat diamond ring, and the stone was so heavy it had to be weighted to keep it from slipping from one side of her finger to the other. With this conspicuous show of wealth, you'd think these people would have been snobbish and condescending, but they seemed to be a really nice couple. They had lovely, well-brought-up children. They were multimillionaires, and they wanted to set Buz up as a business partner. The whole setup appeared too good to be true.

Mike put us in an upscale apartment in Buckhead and gave Buz almost unlimited funds to hire a staff and open an office in Atlanta. I was thrilled that they also formed a song publishing company. I'd been trying to write songs since my early band days and never had a publisher. Now I had a place to publish, and hopefully record, my songs. I began to write in earnest.

One night Mike phoned and in hushed tones told me an associate of his had been murdered. He wouldn't give me any details, just told me to have Buz call him. I thought a burglar must have broken into the Atlanta office and killed one of the staff. Buz was mystified too, because as far as he could find out there had been no robbery.

Once the investigation got under way, we learned how close to trouble we had been living. Mike's money came from pornography, and the authorities had been trying to bust him for interstate transportation of pornographic materials. We started hearing rumors of underworld ties. No wonder Mike's Atlanta home had such tight security that Buz and I couldn't leave our bedrooms once we settled in for the night!

Not long after that, a fire set under mysterious circumstances destroyed one of Mike's offices. They finally arrested Mike on the porn charges. But he somehow escaped and wound up on the FBI's Ten Most Wanted list. He was recaptured and convicted of racketeering and conspiracy to commit murder. (He is now in a state prison.)

When Mike got arrested, the bottom fell out for Buz. He'd invested a lot of time and effort in Mike's so-called record company and had closed his own business. I learned that Buz didn't really own the Spanish-style mansion. It was a lease-purchase arrangement and we couldn't afford to buy it, so we had to let the house go.

Changing roles

We moved into the Mariners Village Apartments in Marina Del Rey, and I went back to work. I started out in a duo, keyboards and drums, went to a trio, and then finally a four-piece band. I was singing a lot more from the drums and wondering if I was good enough to stop playing drums and be out front. I decided I would never know if I didn't try. Determination had already seen me through several career changes. So I hired a drummer and on that day became the vocalist for Jenny Jones and Company.

Singing lead for the first time wasn't as difficult as I expected. I had the experience of singing with Wayne for two years, and if I was good enough for a man with perfect pitch, I could surely front a four-piece band. Stage presence was another matter. I didn't know what to do with my hands, which were no longer holding drumsticks. I solved the problem by playing percussion instruments—a tambourine, a cabasa (a round wooden instrument with beads or metal chains around it), a cowbell, maracas—and the added sound contributed a lot to our music. I even got to play the harmonica again, and even occasional keyboards.

Our repertoire included songs by the Bee Gees, Linda Ronstadt, Stevie Wonder—whatever was popular at the time. We were there to please, so we took requests from the audience. Unfortunately, the most requested songs weren't always ones we'd have picked. At one point I thought if had to sing "Feelings" one more time I'd break out in a rash.

We landed the house band gig at the Lobster House in Marina Del Rey, a dream job for me since it was five minutes from home and it was steady money, something Buz was having a problem generating. My dream marriage wasn't turning out the way I had expected. In *Father Knows Best*, the wife doesn't bear the brunt of the financial responsibility. Buz and I grew farther apart as I was either rehearsing, managing the band business affairs, or working at night. We had little family life.

I didn't have much contact with my other family, either: Father, Mother, Roula, and Liz. Divisions seemed to be forming, lines drawn within our family. I was closer to Father and Roula; Liz was closer to Mother, who by now had very little contact with the rest of us.

Like many small businesses, Father's bridal shop had fallen victim to overexpansion. In the early 1980s, with the business flourishing, Father opened additional shops in Windsor and Toronto. He had no plans to be a hands-on manager at his two new stores but to function strictly in a supervisory position. He regretted the expansion almost immediately, facing problems with poor store managers, increased shoplifting, and an inability to keep control over the inventory in his unmanageable business empire.

When his accountant sent him a report that said his volume was up and his profits were down, Father decided it was time to retire. He liquidated everything—the stores, his home, and his rental property—and he and Roula moved to Clearwater, Florida. True to form, Father decided to make a splash in the local community. He recalled it in his memoirs.

> *We wanted to establish relationships with our fellow Floridians. In order to introduce ourselves and our lifestyle, and also to make new friends, we decided to give large, elegant parties and invite at least seventy people to each one. We often had company for formal dinners. We accomplished what we wanted, because we have a large circle of friends.*

His parties were quite impressive. Once he hired a belly dancer who draped a python over her shoulders while she entertained. He reinforced this inflated image by finding a homeless man and allowing him to live in the garage and eat three meals a day in exchange for doing chores around the place. So it looked like he had a hired man.

I understand his wanting to impress his neighbors but he'd received far less for his businesses and properties in Canada than they were worth, and he lost even more money on a bad investment in Florida. He was not the rich man he liked people to think he was.

Liz and I talked on the phone occasionally, but once we finished making small talk about her two daughters, Lisa and Andrea, we had little to say. We'd headed in different directions, and neither of us understood the other's lifestyle. She said I "went Hollywood," and I said she never came out of the sixties.

Mother's health was deteriorating—smoking and drinking will take its toll—but she also paid me an occasional visit. She always loved to watch me play in bands, and I'd send her an airline ticket whenever she got the urge to listen to Jenny Jones and Company. As long as I never questioned her drinking, we remained on fairly good terms.

Jones and Company

Jenny Jones and Company was one of the best bands I'd had. We worked the LA area and had a good loyal fan following that enjoyed our music and especially my comedy, such as it was. I told jokes and picked on some of the regulars, and they, in return, picked on me. It was all in good fun. Often the jokes on me focused on my figure, but it didn't bother me since I was pretty used to such teasing. One night the bartender told me a letter addressed to me had arrived in the mail. I didn't notice that people seated at nearby tables were snickering while I opened the letter. It read:

Playboy Magazine
New York, New York

Ms. Jenny Jones
c/o Holiday Inn
Pasadena, California

Dear Ms. Jones,

> *We wish to thank you for your letter and picture which we recently received. However, we will not be able to use your body in our centerfold.*

On a scale of 0 to 10, your body was rated minus two (-2). The ratings were done by a panel of men ranging in age from 65 to 75 years old. We tried to have our panel of men in the 25-to-35-year-old bracket rate you, but we could not get them to stop laughing long enough.

Should the taste of American men ever change so drastically that they would want you in the centerfold, you will be notified by this office. In the meantime, however, don't call us, we'll call you.

Sympathetically,

Hugh Hefner

I laughed as hard as anyone, but underneath I hated having a laugh-worthy body.

For the next two years we worked solidly, both on the road in clubs like Fitzgerald's in Reno and in the LA area at venues like the Holiday Inn in Pasadena. We played one particularly memorable date at the Lompoc Federal Prison, where they not only searched us on arrival, they searched our instruments. The show was in a huge auditorium, and it was standing room only. We all put on our stage clothes, mine being a skin-tight hot pink jumpsuit, and made our entrance onto the stage. I'd never heard an ovation like that before, nor have I since.

Their applause was so deafening we truly could not hear our instruments or vocals, but we just kept singing "Stayin' Alive" by the Bee Gees, not realizing then what an appropriate opening number it was. Halfway through the song I noticed some of the men in the audience motioning for me to turn. I kept looking behind me, thinking an escaped prisoner was coming up in back and they were trying to warn me. Finally I realized they wanted *me* to turn around, so they could see my behind.

My father as a twenty-one-year-old Polish Army recruit in 1936. The braid was awarded for expert marksmanship.

My mother and father in their wedding clothes in the Soviet Union in 1942.

*M*other visits my brother's grave in a Teheran cemetery.

My parents, Sophie and John, in happier times. (Palestine, 1944)

*Y*ours truly, playing ball in Rome, Italy, in 1947.

*M*y mother with her two daughters arriving in Italy from Egypt in 1947.

*T*his picture of me was taken by a door-to-door photographer on Sackville Street in London, 1949.

That's my sister, Liz, on the left as we strolled in Italy in 1948.

Liz and me, shortly after arriving in Canada, 1949.

The family that could have been, circa 1950.

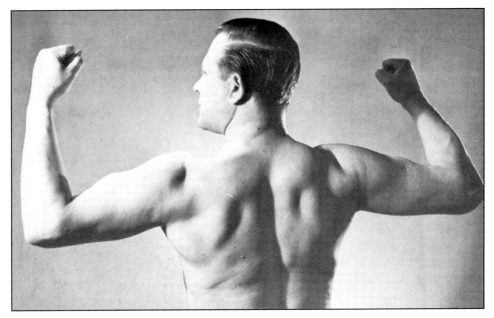

*H*is dream was to be a professional wrestler, so my father trained at the Y.M.C.A. in 1950.

*M*y first Communion, 1952.

*S*ummer of 1955 was spent at a Canadian tobacco farm.

We always wore uniforms at St. Monica's Catholic School in Montreal. This was 1957.

The newly opened bridal shop named after my mother on Richmond Street in London, 1952.

Mother played guitar and sang me to sleep when I was a child. She was at her most beautiful in 1957.

Liz had the figure—I was the cute one, 1962.

𝒢oing to the prom at London Central and yes, that is sparkle in my hair, 1962.

𝓜aking it as a model. At seventeen, I landed the Catalina swimsuit catalog.

Pure glycerine soap

Select

Specially made to
LEAVE SKIN MOIST
AND SMOOTH

Mild non-drying glycerine soap

MADE IN CANADA

𝒜nother huge modeling assignment—this box of soap was marketed all across Canada.

This photo was taken just after I arrived in California, in the courtyard of my North Hollywood apartment, 1967.

December 28, 1970—headed for the Little Church of the West to marry Al Gambino.

My first professional photo was taken in 1964. No, that's not a spot on the paper, it's a beauty mark. I changed the spelling of my name in 1980 to "Jenny."

*T*his has always been my favorite photo. I was only eighteen, but these massive drums brought me independence.

"*J*ennie and the Up-Set" in 1965. Jeff Pelsone (left), Joe Campese (right), and Johnny Vossos (below). I was in love with Johnny.

*T*he Al Bello Revue featuring the Cover Girls. We were some wild and crazy girls!

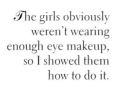
*The girls obviously weren't wearing enough eye makeup, so I showed them how to do it.

*The Cover Girls in 1969. That's me, the drummer, sitting down wearing a fall. Left to right: Terri O'Brien (bass), Stephanie Teel (guitar), Vicki Manning (keyboards).

We went everywhere together, sharing good times and bad.

The Cover Girls disbanded in October of 1970. This was our last night playing together in Lake Tahoe.

At thirty years old, I was no longer a drummer, but the lead singer of "Jennie Jones & Company."

By 1977 I was writing music and occasionally I accompanied myself on piano to sing my own songs.

Yet another Jennie Jones & Company. The black jumpsuit is the one I was wearing the night of my assault in 1979.

You go, girl! I miss singing.

Playing drums at the Lobster House in Marina Del Ray.

JANINA'S KITCHEN

Healthful Treats
Fresh from my kitchen
Delivered to your home

Hi Neighbors. I've had a love affair with cooking for years and have developed a lot of delicious recipes. So many friends have suggested that I offer my foods for sale, that I have finally decided to "go public." Being nutrition-conscious, I make everything with the highest quality natural products, a minimum of sweetening and cholesterol, and maximum protein, vitamins and fiber. Every dish is made at home, and only to order. The taste will speak for itself. Since I live in the Marina, I can deliver my "creations" fresh from my kitchen to you. If you don't have time to cook, or if you're tired of commercially prepared food... Call me.

Janina

ilburn
cane St.
el Rey, CA

Janina's Kitchen was more successful that I ever expected. I prepared the food, then delivered it on my bike, 1979.

Mr. and Mrs. Buz Wilburn in 1974.

I took that as a sign that my bosoms were so uninteresting they preferred my backside. My father had been right. My chest wasn't even interesting to a thousand men who had no access to women. I was too insecure to realize they just wanted to check out the whole package. Then a huge, hulking, monolithic inmate stood up from the front row and started making his way to the stage. And no one tried to stop him! I figured I was dead: LOUNGE SINGER SLAIN IN PRISON RIOT.

He walked on stage, past the guards posted at either end, and came toward me. I tried not to show my fear, but I was in a federal prison and the inmates definitely outnumbered the guards. He walked right up to me, as we nervously continued to play "Brick House," and started to dance with me. So I joined him in the bump while the inmates roared so loud I thought the walls would come down. When the show was over, I asked the warden why no one stopped the dancing inmate.

"We knew he was from minimum security and wouldn't harm you," he explained. "If we'd tried to stop him on principle, then we could have had a riot." As it turned out, I was far safer at Lompoc Prison than in my own apartment complex in LA.

Leaving the prison was sad. As I walked away from the barbed-wire fencing I could hear voices saying "Thank you, Jenny" and "Bye, Jenny." I looked back and saw that the men were all back in their cells, with windows barely big enough to look out of and nothing to see if they did. I wondered what crimes they had committed, and if any were actually innocent of the actions for which they were convicted. The few inmates we did speak to seemed like decent human beings. A lot of them were just boys. Maybe they took a wrong turn. Now that I've done the talk show and have a little insight into troubled teens, I'll bet if I had said, "All the men without fathers, raise your hands," most of the hands would have gone up. One of the great tragedies of our time is the number of unwanted children, particularly fatherless boys.

I feel selfish that I see my childhood as imperfect, simply because my mother and father divorced. At least I had both parents.

17

If You Scream Again,
I'll Cut You!

By this time Buz and I were not on good terms. He was trying to get his career back on track, and I was playing six nights a week. Working nights was a familiar way of life for me: I'd play from 9 P.M. to 1:45 A.M., wrap up with the band, and head home by 2 A.M.

We were playing the Plush Horse in Redondo Beach in August of 1979. Since these clubs had no dressing rooms, I always went to work in my stage clothes and full makeup. I seldom even took a purse, just a small makeup bag. One night I arrived home at Mariners Village apartments about 2:15 A.M. and drove into the underground garage, parked, and started for the stairs, still wearing my slinky stage costume, a black jumpsuit cut down to the navel, with lacing up the front. Buz and I had been arguing when I left for the show, and I was still angry and distracted. I never saw my attacker coming. He was just there.

Since then, I've often heard other crime victims describe it that way too: "He was just there." You never really know what you'll do in a crisis until it happens. You don't know if you'll scream, fight, or run. In this case, I screamed. In one swift movement he stepped behind me and slapped his hand over my mouth. "If you scream again, I'll cut you!" he whispered. I couldn't see what he had in his hand. Maybe it was nothing, but I believed it was a knife. So I didn't scream again.

He dragged me back over to the car, but I was shaking too hard to unlock the door, so he grabbed the keys from me and unlocked it himself. Then he pushed me down in the passenger seat, locked and slammed the door, and walked around to the driver's seat. I reached back up and unlocked the door, hoping he wouldn't see me do it and kill me right then. I thought I might stand a chance if I could jump out of the car while he was driving. I was prepared to risk breaking my shoulder or worse if I jumped.

When he got inside and started the motor, all I could think to say was "What do you want?" He didn't answer. He just looked ahead and drove from the garage as though he had a purpose. I stared at his face from the side, trying to memorize his features, hoping I could identify him in a police lineup if I wasn't killed. All of a sudden it dawned on me. He made no attempt to hide his face. He wore no mask. He didn't tell me to turn my head away. He didn't plan to leave a witness around to identify him.

I decided the best time to jump would be when he left the parking lot and turned onto the street. But instead of heading away from the apartment complex, he drove toward another underground parking garage. I felt if I got inside that garage I'd soon be dead. Inside might be a group of men or a van to transport me somewhere in complete secrecy. So I jerked the car door open and jumped.

Parts of what happened next are a jumble inside my mind and will probably never come back to me. But I do remember being half inside the car and half outside it. He stood over me, pounding me again and again on the head. I could see his fists coming and I could hear them hitting my head, but I felt absolutely nothing. I actually wondered if this was what being dead was like. I wondered who would find my body and in what location it would be. I heard myself pleading with him. "Take my money," I begged. It was a desperate bluff, because I had no money in my bag, just makeup.

He stopped hitting me and grabbed the makeup bag from the floor of the car. Then he turned sharply, as if he'd heard something. I screamed out again, in case someone had driven up. I don't know what happened to startle him, but he began to run. I lay there for a moment, unable to believe that I was alive and he was gone. Then

I got to my feet, discovered nothing was broken, and got back into my car. The keys were still in the ignition. I was shaking uncontrollably as I raced out to the street.

Boys Market was a twenty-four-hour grocery store in Marina Del Rey. I drove by it all the time, and I knew that in the bakery department they made fresh doughnuts very early in the morning. Cops hanging out at a doughnut shop sounds like an old joke, but the truth is, I always saw police cars there in the early morning hours for the fresh buttermilk doughnuts. So that's where I went. In less than three minutes I was babbling to a couple of policemen. "You've got to get back there," I said over and over. "This just happened. Maybe he's still around." I got completely hysterical when they didn't make a move toward their cars.

"Just calm down," one officer said. "We already got the call."

But nobody made any fast moves to do much. Maybe they knew. Maybe in their years of experience they understood that the guy was already long gone. Then again, maybe my revealing stage clothes and heavy makeup made them think I was a prostitute involved in a dispute with her pimp.

Finally, they told me to get into the police car so they could drive me home. When I sat down in the backseat, I realized I'd wet my pants. I knew exactly when it had happened, too. It was when the man had grabbed me from behind and threatened to cut me. You feel adrenaline shoot through your body when you're scared, and in my case it had shot through so powerfully I wet myself.

Having been a bed wetter until I was almost fourteen years old somehow made the embarrassment worse.

Even though my clothes were half torn off of me and welts were starting to form on my face, my husband said very little to me when I got home. It shouldn't have come as a surprise, because we hadn't been speaking except to argue for several days. He just listened and shook his head. He wouldn't even hold me. He didn't wrap his arms around me or try in any way to comfort me. I had to take myself to the hospital to have my head checked. Later, I wondered if he felt guilty for not taking me to and from work each night or meeting me at the parking garage. Whatever his reasons, I could never forgive his lack of response.

That was a pivotal moment in our relationship. I had grown up starved for unconditional love and unconditional support. My mother's acceptance ran hot and cold, and my father turned his back on me as soon as I left home. I couldn't choose my parents, but I could choose my husband.

I went down to the police station and looked at mug book after mug book. I tried to describe my attacker to the police sketch artist. I gave countless police interviews. But they never found him.

I started having nightmares so horrifying that I dreaded sleep. Some of my bad dreams revolved around the actual incident, while others involved me running from some unknown horror. I was always somehow cornered, and at just the moment I was about to be killed, I woke up. These nightmares have never really gone away, after all this time. I never have good dreams. At least none that I remember.

I was fearful of other people for the first time in my life. The only thing I'd ever feared was the dark, and that was because of my sister's childhood pranks. When I was very small, Liz would tell me there was a monster in the closet and then shove me in and lock the door. Sometimes she kept me in there for an hour as I screamed in terror, or at least it seemed that long. She thought it was funny and still does. I don't see the humor. I never walk into a darkened room.

But I wasn't afraid of people until the attack.

I went into therapy to try and deal with the fears, but it didn't help. My counselor just talked a lot about the fact that it was probably a random act and I'd never see this man again. After all, the police thought it was a random act. But I wasn't convinced.

The band couldn't work without a lead singer, so I went back to work right away. My injuries presented a problem at first, because in addition to severe headaches I had a painful and bleeding throat from screaming. The band was very supportive, much more so than my husband, and covered a lot of my vocals. They gave me the emotional hugs I so badly needed. I didn't tell anyone in my family about the assault for years.

One night I was onstage with the lights shining on me when I saw a man standing in the audience. The glare of the light was so bright I couldn't really tell, but I thought he resembled the man who'd beaten me, and I panicked and froze, forgetting the lyrics to what I was singing. There were other incidents. One evening when I was leaving the grocery store, I saw a man who looked vaguely familiar, and I thought, What if it's him? What if he's come back to finish what he started?

I never got on an elevator if the only other occupant was a man. (I still don't, by the way. I think that's just being cautious.) But in other ways I was not being cautious, I was being paranoid. If a man even spoke to me on the street while dozens of people were around, I would come apart.

The nightmares got worse. They were always similar, with me being cornered by a strange man, unable to get away, then waking up with my heart pounding, my nightgown soaking wet. One particular night, just a few days after the assault, I bolted up in bed and in my mind I saw a man standing in the bedroom doorway. I screamed hysterically. No one was there, but it was real to me. The nightmares have become less frequent over the years, but they still haven't stopped. I don't know if they'll ever go away .

I replayed the events of that night in my mind hundreds of times, always wondering *what if?* What if it had been three men and not one? What if I had kicked him in the groin? What if he'd had a gun? What if I'd had a gun? I thought to myself, If I had been carrying a pistol, when that man went around to the other side of the car I could have taken it from my makeup bag and shot him when he opened the door. I would have done it, too. I believe if you are that terrorized by another person, you can shoot.

Still, I was hesitant to buy a gun for several months. Instead, I got a Doberman pinscher. It didn't take long before the apartment managers learned about my Doberman, whom I'd named Sir Duke, after a song I often performed, Stevie Wonder's tribute to Duke

Ellington. One of the managers came around and told me I'd have to get rid of Sir Duke or get out.

"The dog stays until I'm ready to leave, which can't be soon enough for me," I said.

I hadn't been a happy tenant there anyway, complaining several times about inadequate lighting around the property. There were so many places a rapist could hide. And, as with so many of the places I've lived, I got no consideration for being a morning sleeper. Only another person who works at night and has to sleep into the day can really understand the frustration I've experienced. It's a nine-to-five world out there, and if you sleep until noon you're flat-out lazy. I've had screaming confrontations with hotel housekeepers, apartment managers, neighbors, gardeners, repairmen, and deliverymen. At Mariners Village one morning they started replacing the floor above my bedroom at 8 A.M. I was into my fourth hour of sleep. I put on a bathrobe and sunglasses and walked out to the management office.

"I work at night and need to get some sleep. Is it possible you could reschedule the floor work until later in the day?" I tried to be very polite, hiding the anger that burned inside me.

I'll never forget the woman's answer, because it's one of my all-time favorites. (I'm getting angry again just writing this.) "If we do it for you then we have to do it for everyone else."

I think anyone who says that shows an insensitive lack of understanding. If it's the right thing to do, then *do* it for everyone else.

18

Janina's Kitchen

Buz and I moved out of the complex just down the street into a beach house on Hurricane Street on the Marina Peninsula. We could not have afforded to live on that upscale strip along the beach except that the house was supposed to be torn down and they needed interim tenants to keep the insurance rates down. One of my neighbors was Suzanne Somers. I used to see the limo pick her up every day to take her to *Three's Company,* and in my wildest dreams I couldn't have imagined that she would one day appear on *The Jenny Jones Show.*

I was thrilled because I now had a big yard for my new Doberman. Buz liked Sir Duke well enough, but he despised the one bad habit the dog had: passing great amounts of deadly smelling wind. I didn't care much for Sir Duke's flatulence either, but I wanted protection.

I loved living at the beach. I took Sir Duke out every day for an early morning run on the beach, and sometimes I'd roller-skate down the sidewalk with Sir Duke in tow. Once, when I was on skates, Sir Duke took the lead and I landed on my butt, cracking my tailbone.

I loved the little kitchen at the beach house and spent a lot of time cooking. Since I was health conscious, I decided to develop healthier recipes than the ones I saw in cookbooks and women's magazines. (This was a long time before people were notably nervous about fat grams.) Once in a while a neighbor would drop by and sample my olive bread or peanut butter muffins or the Greek spinach squares Roula taught me to bake. On the surface, Buz and I had a solid marriage and a pretty good life.

But we were in marital limbo the entire time we lived on Hurricane Street. We just went along, not communicating, seldom talking. Our roles had reversed and I was paying the bills with my band income, while he tried to get something going. He was a personal manager to several performers, including singers Chris David and Vic Genre, and a poet named Bruce Sievers. We tried having him manage my career for a while, but working together was a mistake.

I don't know why I didn't leave. Maybe it was because Buz's business problems were so severe. He couldn't even afford an office and was working from home. We were having serious financial problems, even though I played as many club dates as I could book for Jenny Jones and Company.

But after the assault, going out at night to work was traumatic for me. One night I was so afraid to walk out the front door to the driveway I actually called the police to escort me. I was a bit embarrassed, but not too embarrassed to ask. Between my fear of being out at night, my discomfort in smoke-filled rooms, and simple burnout after all the hard work, I was ready to quit the band. Finally, I came up with an idea. I would go into the catering business. After all, I had (and still have) a true love of cooking and people always told me I should open a restaurant, so why not market the skill?

I took three weeks planning what items to offer and what ingredients I could use to make each item less fattening and more nutritious. I thought the catering business through carefully before I did it. I decided to use my full name, the more homespun Janina. Then I designed a flyer and menu for Janina's Kitchen, made copies, and walked through the neighborhood dropping them in people's mailboxes. Two days later I got my first call. It was the post office.

"We found one of your flyers in a mailbox. Did you know it is illegal to put anything in people's mailboxes?" The woman's voice was stern.

"I'm very sorry, I didn't know," I said. "It'll never happen again." After that, I put them under my neighbors' doors.

In addition to the menu, my flyer listed the ingredients I used: stone ground flours, unhydrogenated oils, unsulfured molasses, raw honey, wheat germ, natural bran, sea salt. Along with olive bread, peanut butter muffins, and Greek spinach squares, I offered such foods as buttermilk spice cake, zucchini chocolate cake, Earthday carrot cake, and Boston brown bread.

I included a fresh orange cake made with oranges, nuts, and raisins; my Father's favorite Polish cabbage rolls; and my tour de force, Sicilian cake, a pound cake layered with ricotta cheese and fruit under chocolate-coffee frosting. Every item was made from scratch, using no shortening, bleached flour, butter, food coloring, saccharine, or mixes. I took a lot of pride in my cooking, and I still do. (In fact, I'd like to share one of my favorite recipes with you, so below you'll find a Pumpkin Chocolate Chip Muffin recipe.)

Within a week of delivering the flyers I had $100 worth of orders. Within a month I had catered two parties. I'd start baking at 9 A.M., and at 4 P.M. I'd get on my bicycle with the basket full of packages and delivered the orders. Within a couple of months I was filling between sixty and eighty orders a week. Once in a while I'd get so many orders that my small Gaffers & Sattler oven wasn't enough, and I had to use my neighbor's oven to get everything done by 4 P.M.

The business got so successful that I had to hire some help. I asked my friend Bonnie if she'd like to earn some extra money, and she agreed to come and help. She did everything from taking food orders to decorating cakes and washing dishes.

Pumpkin Chocolate Chip Muffins from Janina's Kitchen

2 eggs
1 cup skim milk
⅓ cup canola oil

1 cup canned pumpkin (½ can)

2½ cups unbleached white flour
½ cup sugar
1 tablespoon baking powder
1 teaspoon each cinnamon and nutmeg

1 cup semisweet chocolate chips

Have all ingredients at room temperature. Preheat oven to 400 degrees. Combine eggs, milk, oil, and pumpkin and set aside. Sift dry ingredients into large bowl. Make a well and add liquids. Stir gently until barely combined. Fold in chocolate chips. Gently divide batter between 12 muffin cups. Bake at 400 degrees for 20 to 25 minutes. Let stand in pan 5 minutes, then remove to cooling rack. Makes 1 dozen.

Muffins don't keep well, so I freeze them as soon as they've cooled. They're quick to microwave, and they provide valuable beta-carotene. You can use walnuts instead of chocolate chips.

Make me laugh

What I really wanted to do was stand-up comedy, and my catering business played an indirect role in my making the transition. During the time I played clubs, I seldom watched television. We performed at night and rehearsed during the day. But once I was working from my home I could tune in the TV and listen to what I'd been missing all those years. One of the first shows I saw was a comedy show called *Make Me Laugh*, and it proved to me that things hadn't changed much since my Las Vegas days: There still were very few female comics. Despite that showcase fiasco Al Gambino and I had staged at the Thunderbird Hotel, I still believed I could do comedy, and I saw an opportunity in a field with few women.

The immediate obstacle was that I didn't have any material.

But I kept thinking about Bob Hope. I knew he employed writers to supply him with jokes. All I had to do was find some good comedy writers and let them put together a show for me. I knew if I had some funny material, I could get work. Once again, I'd be a novelty, a woman in a field dominated by men.

I started asking some of my old club contacts about comedy writers, but nobody seemed to have any idea about that end of the business. So I found a TV sitcom that I thought was funny, watched the end credits, and contacted the writers. They were a two-man writing team who said they wanted $500 for a five-minute routine. We met at a little restaurant at the marina, and I gave them a check for half the fee as a deposit.

"What do you want to talk about?" one of them asked.

"I don't know. That's why I'm hiring you," I said.

"Well, what strong opinions do you have? What are your likes and dislikes?"

I thought about it a minute and had to admit that I didn't have any strong opinions about much of anything. I realized that no one had ever asked my opinion about anything growing up, and I was rarely asked as an adult.

"I don't care what kind of comedy you come up with," I said. "I just want to be a comedian."

We spent about two hours talking about me: my life and my hopes for a comedy career. When they left, they said they'd have something for me in two weeks. I went home and waited with high hopes, but in two weeks the writers sent my $250 check back with this note:

Dear Jenny,

We're sorry, but there's nothing about you that we can write about. You don't have any persona.

So I stayed in the kitchen awhile longer. I had to rethink this comedy thing.

You wouldn't think a home-based catering business would get

drop-in trade, but people started coming by the house to see what I was cooking. One afternoon I had just finished my deliveries and was stirring a pot of soup I'd made for our dinner. A guy knocked on the door, and when I answered it he said, "Janina, I hate to bother you, but do you have any food I could buy?"

"Just this vegetable soup we were going to have for dinner," I told him.

"I'll take it," he said. So I sold him the soup, and Buz and I ate sandwiches.

I was proud of Janina's Kitchen. Taking an idea and making it happen was very satisfying. I think things work out when you make them work out. If you have a talent, jump in with both feet.

I also believe that if you are a good cook, catering from your home is a great way to earn money. Here in Chicago, there are cooks who go to people's homes, cook a week's worth of meals for them, and pop the food in the freezer. That way shut-ins, or professional people with no time to cook, can be assured they are getting healthy food.

Our beach house was a victim of progress. In 1980, a little less than a year after we moved to the beach, the house was scheduled to be demolished. It was really a shame, it was such a cute house: bright and charming, with a white picket fence. A big condominium complex now stands in its place.

I did find another way to generate some income, however. A friend of mine had appeared on *The Price is Right* television game show. Having been there herself, she told me I'd be perfect for the show. Her advice was that I not wear a bra, as she was convinced that's why she was chosen out of an audience of over two hundred people.

"I can't go braless on TV," I said, not because I thought it too racy, but because I was ashamed of my body.

"You can take a bra with you in your purse and then put it on in the restroom before you enter the studio," she countered. "They pick people while they're standing in line."

I took her advice, feeling a little guilty about the switch, but it worked. They told me to "come on down!" and I won $13,000 worth of prizes, including an MG Midget sportscar, a recliner, a barbecue, waterskis, a bikini, and $6,000 cash.

Buz also started getting his career together, so we were in a little better financial condition and rented a nice house in Northridge. It was close to his ex-wife's home, which meant he could see his children more often, and he asked me if I would be agreeable to his oldest son, Mark, coming to live with us on a permanent basis. I couldn't say no. I liked Mark, but I didn't like it that he was the most pampered and spoiled of all Buz's children. Mark could do no wrong in his father's eyes and was never disciplined that I was aware. I knew Mark would live with us anyway, so I said yes.

A few days before our scheduled move, I drove to the new house to look around, excited about where I would put things when we moved in. When I arrived, Mark's car was in the driveway. He was already living there. Buz surely must have known, but I was never told. Mark was very casual about it, showing me where he had put things in the kitchen. It's hard to describe how I felt: misled, betrayed, and disappointed. But more than that, I knew there were worse times to come.

The move put an end to Janina's Kitchen. It would have been impossible to try and keep my Peninsula customers working from Northridge on the other side of town. So I closed up shop. A couple of my wealthy clients approached me about opening a restaurant, but I had already decided to put another band together and go back to playing clubs. Maybe I was just anxious to get away from Buz, because I also planned to go back out on the road.

If I could talk to the animals

To make matters worse, Buz had issued a new edict: Sir Duke could no longer be in the house, only outside. Sir Duke was my best friend, and he always sat at my feet. When he was suddenly barred from the house he would sit outside the door and cry. I don't think he disliked being outside, he just missed his best friend. It broke my heart to hear him cry for hours. I cried for hours too. Sometimes I'd go outside and sit with him; then I would come in and we'd both cry again.

I know how much Sir Duke cared about me, because I took him to an animal psychic once. (I can't believe I'm putting this in the book!) I had seen a woman on *The Tonight Show* named Beatrice Lydecker who said she could read what animals were thinking. She even read Ed McMahon's cat's mind, and Ed said she was right on the money. So I tracked her down and made an appointment. We sat in her front yard, and she proceeded to describe the yard Sir Duke used to have, right down to the slope in the front and the broken piece of fence where he would watch for me to come home. She said he loved me very much and only lived for the times when we were together.

Wait a minute. That was supposed to be my husband!

It broke my heart to see Sir Duke sitting alone out in that yard in need of companionship. After much soul-searching, I found him another home. After he was gone I couldn't stop crying for three days.

I knew then that our marriage was over

I was seeing more of Buz's children than ever, especially Mark and his friends. One day, when some of Mark's friends were at the house waiting for him to get home, we started talking and the subject of marijuana came up. Being a musician for most of my life, I was no stranger to people getting high. I observed that some people seemed to be able to smoke pot and function perfectly, while others couldn't function at all. One of the boys laughed and said, "That's Mark! He's been smoking pot for years and nobody can tell!" I was stunned, because I hadn't been able to tell he was high.

I thought it was my responsibility to tell Buz, since he never used drugs and in fact was very much against them. It was a mistake. "Did you know Mark has been smoking pot?" I asked.

He immediately became angry. "No, he hasn't," was all he said.

"According to his friends, he's been getting high for years," I said. "I think you should talk to him about it."

Buz just went crazy. He got a wild look in his eyes and started yelling at me. I had never seen him act this way, and it scared me so much I ran into the bathroom and locked the door, fearing for my safety. He followed me and started pounding on the door. "Either you open this door," he screamed, "or I'll break it down!" I was scared. I felt the adrenaline rush through my body, just like that night in the underground parking garage.

I opened the door, hoping my compliance would calm him down. Instead, he barged in, grabbed me by the throat, and shoved me up against the wall. He put his other fist up to my face and said, "Is this what you want? Is this what you want?!" He shoved his fist into my face. I begged him to let me go. "Please," I sobbed, "you're scaring me." He was still out of control and looked capable of really hurting me. "I'm sorry," I said. "It was a mistake. I was wrong." I was lying, but he finally let me go. I knew then that our marriage was over.

That night I didn't sleep at all. I knew I'd be leaving the next morning, and I lay there all night, wondering what was ahead for me. In the morning, as soon as Buz left the house, I packed everything I came into the relationship with — my clothes and my drums — into my pickup truck. I was afraid to tell Buz face-to-face that I was leaving, so I left him a note. Ironically, Mark showed up as I was leaving to get into my truck. He seemed surprised that my truck was loaded up. I just hugged him good-bye and drove away.

I stopped at a pay telephone and called to see if I could stay that night at the home of my friend Bonnie. She and her husband said they didn't want to get involved in a family dispute and would rather I got a motel room. So that's what I did. Then I rented an apartment on Hazeltine Avenue in Sherman Oaks for $335 a month. I had no furniture, so I slept on the floor.

Within a couple of months I'd furnished my tiny one-bedroom apartment by going to garage sales. My bedroom lamps cost five dollars each, my silverware a dollar. When I spotted a beautiful three-hundred-dollar satin bedspread in the window of a fancy store, I went back with a pencil and paper and sketched it out, then bought similar fabric and made it myself for sixty dollars.

I'll take the .38 Special
. . . and some hollow-point bullets

That first night by myself was a rough one. I was alone, physically and emotionally, and I was afraid, the thought of a break-in only slightly more frightening than the nightmares that were sure to come when I slept. Even though I was apprehensive about guns, I felt I needed one for protection now that I was alone, working nights, and had no dog. I called the police department to ask what would be a good weapon to get. They suggested a revolver for personal protection and reminded me that it was illegal to carry a loaded weapon.

"Oh, I would never do that," I said, knowing full well that I had every intention of carrying it fully loaded. I would rather be arrested on a gun charge than be fished out of a lake somewhere. I asked the officer if he had any more advice.

"Yes. If you really want to stop someone, use hollow-point bullets," he said. "And if someone tries to break in and you shoot him, make sure he's dead and make sure the body is all the way in the house, even if you have to drag it in."

Hello.

I went to the B & B Gun Store in North Hollywood and asked about a revolver, pointing to a .22.

"Those won't necessarily stop someone," the clerk said. "Especially a big guy on drugs. It might hurt him, but he could keep right on coming." He handed me a slightly bigger gun.

"What you want is this Thirty-eight Special," he said.

I liked the two-inch barrel because it would fit more easily in my purse.

I said I'd take the Charter Arms .38 Special and some hollow-point bullets. He looked at me strangely when I asked for the bullets and asked why hollow points. That was some serious ammunition. I explained that I had recently been assaulted and that's what the police had recommended.

After my waiting period I picked up the gun and got the name of a shooting range. I wasn't surprised to find a lot of women at the range, but it had never occurred to me that a pistol shot is so loud that you have to wear earplugs, or that the kick is so strong. I signed up to practice, and they asked me what kind of target I wanted, a bull's-eye or the silhouette of a man. That was easy.

"I'll take the guy."

I was afraid to take my first shot, in case the thing blew up in my hand. The instructor laughed at me, so I asked him to go first. He shook his head, squeezed off a shot, and handed me the gun. I held the gun in both hands the way he did and pulled the trigger. The kick is so hard it can knock you back. It's not like in the movies, where people run around shooting revolvers with ease. The gun is heavy, and you have to pull hard on that trigger. When the gun goes off, it automatically kicks up in the air, and you must immediately pull it back down if you want to take aim again.

I practiced until I learned how to hold the gun somewhat steady and actually hit the target. I was determined, though, and got better with each shot. At one practice session, I took aim at the crotch area of the silhouette and hit it about ten times. There wasn't much left of the paper. I took that target home and taped it to my back window, hoping to discourage any potential attackers.

19

Starting Stand-Up

I'd had enough of playing smoke-filled bars late into the night, and now I was even more afraid to drive home alone. I was burned out on music. I couldn't even listen to it on the radio. It was time for a career change.

So in 1967, I took a day job. I wondered what a personnel director was going to think about listing the Swingin' Dolls and the Cover Girls as past employers. But on the other hand, fourteen years of handling bookings, publicity, travel arrangements, living accommodations, and day-to-day band operations had convinced me I could be good in an administrative capacity.

The first job I got was as an office manager for a fiduciary company located in the twin towers at Century City. It was a two-person office, the headquarters for a company that somehow transferred money and investments from another country. It was all a little vague, and I was never told what business really went on or if it was legal. My job was basically secretarial, and I did everything from planning my boss's vacations to handling all the filing, light bookkeeping, and correspondence. That was before fax machines, so I had to learn to send telexes.

My initial enthusiasm cooled rapidly, in just about the amount of time it took the boss to start chasing me. He pursued me quite aggressively, and I finally decided to go job hunting. Luckily, I didn't have to look far. I applied for and got a $350-a-week administrative position with the design firm of Tosh Yamashita, Inc., which was located in Century City's other twin tower. The company had a lot of high-end clients like Gump's and Neiman Marcus, and I enjoyed the responsibility of a busy office.

Because of a chance conversation with a co-worker at Tosh Yamashita, I made a decision for which I would pay dearly. One day a woman I worked with started talking about her breast implants. I couldn't believe it. I thought only celebrities got breast implants. I didn't know regular women had them. The woman just laughed and told me she knew lots of "regular" women who'd had implant surgery. She even took me into the women's rest room and showed them to me. They looked real, and for the first time in my life I thought there was a possibility that I could have a woman's figure. I started wondering how I could come up with the money for implants.

I also wanted to break into comedy, despite the discouraging incident with the writers who had returned my check. I met with several more writers over the next few months and started buying jokes from them. The going price was about $25 per joke, and I would negotiate the best deal I could. Some writers wouldn't write on spec—I had to pay up front, and then I owned the jokes, whether they were funny or not. One writer who let me "test drive" the jokes first was Larry Jacobson, who has since become an Emmy-award-winning writer for David Letterman. I started hanging out at comedy clubs at night, and as I sat in the back and listened to the comedians, I wondered if I'd have the guts to try it myself.

I eventually learned that the best comedy isn't about telling jokes. It's not about a setup and a punch line. It's about finding humor in everyday situations and delivering it in your own unique way. If you ask a comic to tell you a good joke, he'll probably go blank. They usually rely on their own experiences. Like musicians, most comics live on the road, which is one of the reasons you hear so many comics do airline and hotel material. But for my initiation into comedy I wasn't as concerned about the quality of my act as I was about not throwing up from anxiety.

I started going to "open mike nights," which means the microphone is open to anyone with nerves of steel. On open mike nights, when comics get there they put their names in a hat, and the emcee draws names throughout the evening. You might follow a terrible amateur or a guy who's just taped *The Tonight Show*.

Open mike

After several months of studying the other comics, I finally got up the nerve to put my name in the hat. I prepared five minutes of material and signed up at the Improv and sat down to wait to hear my name. I waited and waited. As time went by, I lost confidence. I just knew I'd be terrible and the audience would boo me off the stage. My heart was pounding so badly I thought the guy sitting next to me could hear it. The emcee called out the names, and new comics took the stage one by one. Some were good. Some bombed big time.

Every time the emcee pulled a name out of the hat, I prayed it wouldn't be me. At 10:00 P.M., I grabbed my purse and made my escape. "Sorry, I can't stay any longer. I have to work tomorrow morning," I told the emcee on the way out. I was so relieved. It was like God was with me that my name didn't get called.

I wasn't so lucky the next time. The emcee called my name early in the evening, and I made my comedy debut. Doing stand-up comedy for the first time is a terrifying experience. You are alone on a stage, talking to a room full of people who are waiting to see if you're funny. I was sweating profusely, my hands were shaking, my throat was dry, and my voice quivered.

"What did Adam say to Eve the first time they had sex? 'Stand back, Eve! I don't know how big this thing is gonna get!'"

And that was my closer. I think I was in denial about how awful I was the first time. But I did manage to get a few laughs. For some first-time comics, the experience is so traumatic, they never go back again.

I did go back, and each time it got easier. The first few times it was all I could do to simply remember my monologue.

Check out these babies

A lot of comics do self-deprecating humor, and I quickly became one of them. After all, I'd been making fun of my flat chest from the stage ever since I started telling jokes between songs. Fans were always bringing me things like a T-shirt with two fried eggs on the front. Since I joked about it so much, I'm sure they didn't know it hurt. One of my routines went like this:

"I walked into a lingerie department the other day and a tall, busty saleswoman asked if she could help me. 'I'd like to see something in a bra,' I said. She looked at my chest and said, 'I'll bet you would, honey.'"

Yes. I did want to fill out my bra. I'd grown up admiring movie stars like Jayne Mansfield and Marilyn Monroe, and I believed that big breasts were what separated the girls from the women. Now I know that women have been holding themselves up to an image of beauty that isn't real. Women with huge breasts, flat stomachs, and silky thighs are either implanted or liposuctioned, and their photos are probably airbrushed. Either that or they're unexplainable freaks of nature!

I grew up in a household where it was OK to make fun of people who had a different color skin, or attended a different church, or didn't have perfect bodies. My father thought nothing of advising me to rub ice on my breasts to make them grow. He proudly announced at the dinner table one evening that the best thing about Roula was that she had big boobs.

Maybe derogatory comments were more acceptable then, as opposed to today's political correctness, because I can remember many times in public when I'd hear comments like "Look at that big fat woman!" or "Look at the nose on *him!*" Those statements made me uncomfortable even as a child. I assumed that when I was out in public, other people were analyzing me the same way. Maybe even my own family!

"Look at that chest, she's flat as a board."

"Look at the size of her nose!"

Mother not only poked fun by tweaking my nipples and making silly sounds, I saw her do the same thing with Liz's daughter Lisa, continuing from one generation to the next. I consider Mother's touching her daughter and granddaughter in this manner totally inappropriate. It's no wonder I was embarrassed about my chest. It was a constant topic of conversation, and the comments were never good. Now, after all those years, I was excited at the possibility of never again apologizing for my body.

My co-worker sent me to her plastic surgeon in Beverly Hills, giving him her highest recommendation, even though he was not board certified. Since plastic surgeons aren't required to be certified, I just assumed it was a bureaucratic thing and nothing for me to worry about. He seemed to have done a good job on my friend.

I tried to go into surgery armed with some information, though. I didn't just wade in blindly. I asked the doctor a lot of questions, including the big one: Is this procedure safe? He explained that about 10 percent of women who have implant surgery develop hardness in the breasts, but that was the only risk. Besides, if my new breasts did harden, he'd replace them at no additional charge, which was a better guarantee than I got on my last muffler. The most important thing to me was the cost, so when he told me I could have breasts for $1,500, I was sold. I just had to come up with the money.

I had a garage sale and sold everything I didn't absolutely have to have. Once you start looking through what you own, you'll find that many of your possessions aren't vital to your life, especially if getting rid of them means you can fulfill a dream. Or in my case, fill up a bra. I sold books, pots and pans, clothing—I even sold chocolate chip cookies. In fact a woman drove up to my curb and yelled, "Are those homemade?"

"Yes," I yelled back from the driveway, "I made them from scratch!"

She held up some cash. "I'll take them all!"

I had outpatient surgery on May 15, 1981. I'd stayed up the whole night before, tingling with anticipation. What would it be like? I phoned Father, Roula, and Mother, and they all agreed I would feel much better about myself if I got breast implants. Like me, they'd heard no horror stories about complications.

At the doctor's suggestion I brought in a picture of what I wanted my breasts to look like. I bought a *Playboy* magazine at the newsstand. As I handed the clerk my money, I told him, "Let me be the first person to say I'm not buying this for the articles, I'm buying it for the naked pictures."

He didn't get it.

I found my dream breasts in one of the photos, tore the picture out, and took it to the doctor. My new breasts turned out to be at least a size larger than I'd ordered. Of course, the doctor was a man: Bigger was better.

There was a lot more pain than I expected. After all, this was a trauma to the body, but I didn't mind, knowing how these new breasts were about to change my life. I didn't even wait until the stitches were out before I bought a new bra, size 36 C. No more double-A cups for me. But I was curiously detached from these two objects protruding from my chest and felt as though I was carrying them around for somebody else.

I've since noticed that women who would shudder at the thought of baring their natural breasts will pull their blouses open and show implants to practically anyone who wants to look. It's not a personal thing anymore. Years later, when John Wayne Bobbitt appeared on my television show, he was very forthcoming when he talked about how his wife cut off his penis, but he spoke with complete detachment. (Yes, that's my choice of words and I'm sticking to it.) He said the words "my penis" as though it had nothing to do with him. He could just as easily have been saying, "I lost my wallet." The audience seemed shocked at how casually he told his story, without embarrassment, but I completely understood. His penis was well known, as were my breasts by then.

You become a spectator to your own drama.

From the first time I walked down the street with my new breasts, I noticed the difference. Men on the street whistled. Men blatantly stared at my chest. It was as if my whole sexuality was tied to these two silicone implants neatly stitched into my chest. It was nice, but it was disconcerting.

It was one thing when men on the street stared, but quite another when other comics at the clubs did double-takes. Even when I wore loose blouses, they could tell I had a chest where none had been. When they started greeting me with big hugs, I knew they were just checking to see what was in there. Word got back to me that Buz learned about my implants and said, "Just my luck. She gets them now."

No man will ever want to touch you again

Within a few months, one of my breasts began to harden. I wasn't taken completely by surprise, since I was told there was a slight possibility of hardening. It was especially embarrassing when people gave me hugs. One guy even pulled away from me and said, "What do you have in there, rocks?" I started holding my purse up in front of my hard breast when anyone approached me.

I don't think the purse trick fooled many people. There was one guy, a particularly vulgar and nasty comedian named Robert, who kept saying, "I want to ask you something personal." I knew it was about the implants and kept brushing him off. Finally he came right out with it.

"Word is that you've had your whole body done," he said with a little smirk.

I guessed he meant I'd had a face lift, a tummy tuck, implants, liposuction, and everything else in the plastic surgeon's book. I didn't know how to respond, so I just made light of it.

"Well, I'll take that as a compliment,' I said. "I must look good if you think I've had all that stuff."

He leaned back and looked me up and down like a piece of meat he was going to buy. "You must have done something," he said.

"What makes you think I'd tell you if I had?" I asked, sorry I'd let the conversation go so far.

He laughed. "I know a guy who says he hugged you, and your boobs were as hard as rocks."

I stammered out some explanation about how he'd probably mistaken my purse for my chest.

"Because if that's the case and your boobs are fake, no guy will ever want to touch you again," he said, not without some malice.

I just shook my head and walked off, hoping he couldn't see my face turning bright red. Had I spent money I could ill afford buying a body that nobody would want to touch?

On May 10, 1982, after six months of walking around with a purse clutched to my breast, I went back to my surgeon for a second operation. He used the same type of silicone implants, but this time he installed a size smaller.

20

Flop Sweat

On March 24, 1981, I got my first paying comedy job, at the Laff Stop in Encino for $15. I still have a copy of the check. It was a small amount of money, but it held a large promise for me; it meant I was good enough to be paid for telling jokes, and made me believe I was on my way to the big time. After that I had professional head shots done and started picking up paid dates for anything from $25 to $50. My confidence was growing, until a disastrous date at the Horn in Santa Monica. The club is closed now, but back then it was primarily a singers' showcase. A few comics showcased there, but it was rare.

I was scheduled to go on for twenty minutes after a Broadway-type singer, and I only had fifteen minutes of material. But comics usually throw in new material they want to test between blocks of proven material, and since I'd been working on some new ideas, I thought, Well, I can stretch it to twenty if I pad here and there.

As it turned out, the singer I was booked to follow was showcasing for a group of industry people. He had invited agents, managers, and record people. Most of the audience was there to see him. He had a high-energy three-piece band that just kicked it from the first note to the last song, a big up-tempo thing that brought the house down. People stood and cheered until he performed an encore and finally got off the stage. Then most of the audience left.

The emcee probably hoped that introducing the next act would stop some of his customers from leaving, because he didn't even allow time for the pandemonium to die down before he introduced me. He ran out on stage and said, "Now, ladies and gentlemen, here is a very funny lady, Jenny Jones!"

There is nothing harder for a comic to follow than high energy. Whether it is a comedian or a musician, it is tough to follow unless your act has the same intensity. I was doing a straight monologue. There was nothing I could do to get a laugh, nothing. There were about twenty people left in a big wide open room. Since part of my fifteen minutes included time for laughter, I went through my material in about nine minutes, less than half of the twenty I was booked for.

That's when I learned what "flop sweat" is. I was having it. I'm sure the audience could tell how nervous I was, and that made it worse. When I ran out of material, I had to start ad-libbing. I'd ask people where they were from and try to say something funny about the place.

No laughs. Zippo. Nada. Zero. *Niente.*

People started walking out. I felt I was up there for two weeks. It was a very humbling experience.

I quickly learned not to book myself right after a high-energy act. I also learned not to evaluate any new material on a late show on a Friday night. Friday night is party night. People leave work, go to happy hour, and by midnight everybody's drunk and loud. That's when you get disruptive crowds and obnoxious hecklers. The only night worse than a Friday night is New Year's Eve, which is every Friday night in the year all rolled into one. My advice to a new comic is this: Don't ever question yourself because of a bad Friday night or New Year's Eve.

Nobody was on the sidelines yelling, "You go girl!"

I quit four times that first year. But each time I refused to remain a quitter and went back. I knew I could do anything if I just worked hard and stayed focused. Part of the problem was that working a nine-to-five job and doing stand-up comedy at night is exhausting. I'd get back to my apartment around six, cook dinner, and maybe watch a little television while I ate, so tired that all I wanted to do was crawl in bed. Instead, I'd shower, get dressed up, and be back out at a comedy club by nine.

The worst times were when it was impossible to get a laugh no matter what I said or did. Sometimes the audience was drunk, and sometimes they just talked right through my act, not even respecting me enough to pay attention. Some nights I'd have to deal with hecklers. But on other nights I would kill, and I'd go home so elated I could hardly sleep.

Some of the clubs I frequented while starting out were the Ice House in Pasadena, Igby's in Santa Monica, and the LA Cabaret in Encino. I'd go any place there was a stage. I played restaurants, gay bars, and private parties; I did a motion picture mothers' luncheon; I even drove to Las Vegas when I heard there was an open mike night at the Continental Hotel, just to do twenty minutes for a new audience. Then I had to make the five-hour drive back home. There was also a tiny deli in Sherman Oaks, the Deli Smoker, where a lot of us started out performing in front of people whose only reason for coming was the knishes.

The first two years are an emotional roller coaster. You kill one night and are so excited you can almost see your star on Hollywood Boulevard. The next night you bomb and wonder why anyone would want to deal with this kind of rejection. I took every reaction personally. If they hated the joke, it meant they hated me. I drove home in tears many nights, swearing I was going to give it up.

I think the early rejection from some of the clubs made me stronger. Every time someone said I wasn't good enough, I tried to prove him wrong. I had never had overwhelming support from my family when I started anything. Nobody was on the sidelines yelling, "You go girl!" So I learned to take negative input and make it work for me. Every time I wanted to quit, I'd get mad and say, "Damn it! I'm not going to let them run me off!"

One night after a tearful drive home from the Laff Stop, I sat on my couch and analyzed what I was doing. I'd learned the value of closely examining every show from Wayne Newton. If a superstar could take a critical look at himself, I could too. I went over my material and my delivery. I replayed my cassette tape over and over. All of a sudden I saw the problem. There was nothing inherently wrong with my material. My delivery could use a little work, but it wasn't bad. I wasn't selling myself to the audience; I was just doing material. It was simple: I had to sell myself.

So I started thinking about comics I considered great, like George Carlin and Richard Pryor. The more successful comics I watched, the clearer it became that each one had a strong identity. As soon as they hit the stage you knew what to expect. I decided that I too needed an identity, and since I didn't have one I would have to create it.

By summer of 1981 I was on unemployment, doing comedy every night, usually for no pay. I had hoped to focus entirely on my new career, but even after selling my drums, sound system, and other band equipment, my bank account was quickly dwindling, so I signed up with a temp agency. I wasn't qualified for much more than receptionist duty, so they placed me at several companies doing just that, including at Famous Amos Cookies, where I worked for several weeks. They actually baked the cookies on the premises, and the constant smell of chocolate there was incredible.

Still eager to concentrate full-time on my comedy, I decided to try another game show.

I knew *The Match Game* liked bubbly contestants, so I went to an audition and bubbled my way to a spot. *The Match Game* was hosted by Gene Rayburn and featured six celebrities: Betty White, Charles Nelson Reilly, Brett Summers, George Kennedy, Barbara Rhodes, and Bill Daly. Gene would read a partial phrase, and both the celebrities and the contestants would fill in the blank. The match that won for me seems amazingly simple. Gene said; "Day-old *blank*." When both Betty White and I wrote down "Day-old bread," I was $5,500 richer and able to quit temping and finally get serious about comedy.

• Where are they now? •

Bill Daly, who played in I Dream of Jeannie *and* Newhart, *was recently a guest on* The Jenny Jones Show.

If they only knew

By the fall of 1983 my new breasts were hard again. This time my doctor decided to correct the problem with a nonsurgical procedure called a capsulotomy. He explained that a capsule had formed around the implants and it had to be broken up for the breasts to feel soft again. The procedure was probably the cause of many ruptured implants, including mine. Manufacturers warn today that excessive manipulation can lead to ruptures, but this was a standard practice in 1983. So he gave me an anesthetic and squeezed my breasts so hard they were sore for weeks afterward. When I went for my next checkup, the doctor told me he'd stopped doing the manipulation therapy, because it was too hard on his hands. He was getting arthritis.

With that, I started educating myself. I began to search for magazine articles—anything that would expand my knowledge. One of the articles I found spoke of a silicone implant called a Meme, which had a polyurethane coating to ensure that the breast remained soft. The same coating, I later discovered, stays in your system and breaks down into a chemical called TDA, which has been found to cause cancer in laboratory animals. When I phoned my surgeon and asked him about the Meme, he sounded encouraged. It might be the implant that could solve my problem. So on December 19, 1983, I had my third implant operation.

Once the pain of the surgery was gone, I realized I had no feeling at all in my breasts. It was a deep shock when I fully understood that in an effort to become more sexually attractive, I had disfigured myself to the point that I didn't care if I ever had sex again. I felt more self-conscious and unattractive than ever before, and the fact that men who didn't know I'd had implants still drooled over my figure only made things worse. All I could think was, If they only knew!

The lack of feeling in my breasts was the cause of much embarrassment. I should have been on my guard at one particular club booking, because I shared the bill with a comic who had a reputation among the waitresses at comedy clubs for being sexually abusive to women, even total strangers. I was leaning on a rail watching the opening act when he came up beside me. I felt something, as though he was bumping into me. A moment later he looked puzzled and said, "I can't believe you let me grab your breast and never said anything."

It was one of my worst moments. I mumbled something about adjusting my bra strap and walked away. I was intimidated by him because he was very popular at the time. I guess I thought when you're that successful, you're entitled to take sexual liberties. It was not to be my only encounter with this headliner.

When I called my doctor and told him the surgery hadn't worked and my breasts were getting hard again, he assured me that Vogue implants weren't supposed to harden.

"Vogues? These are supposed to be Meme implants," I stammered.

"Vogues have the polyurethane coating too, and I thought they'd be better for you," was his only explanation for the last-minute switch.

21

A Little Creative Booking

By 1983 I had worked most every comedy club in the Los Angeles area, where I crossed paths with most of the LA comics, in many cases not even remembering with whom I'd worked. For example, I had not realized until going through old records in preparation for this book that I opened for Robert Wuhl in Pasadena, Billy Crystal in Palm Springs, and Damon Wayans and Robert Townsend in West Covina. I played dates with Brad Garrett, Mark Schiff, Wil Shriner, Dennis Wolfberg, Yakoff Smirnoff, Pat Paulsen, Larry Miller, and Dave Coulier. I once did a radio show with another comic, and made a note on my calendar: "Did a radio interview with a fellow Canadian named Jim Carrey."

In June of '83, I worked with Gary Shandling and Ray Combs at the Ice House in Pasadena. Gary was the headliner, and made $650 a week, compared to my $175 a week as the middle act. Ray was the emcee. His tragic suicide in 1996 was heartbreaking. He was a very nice guy.

I was anxious to go on the road, knowing that to make it in television I had to appeal to all types of audiences. There were more and more clubs opening all across the country. But there were more and more comics, too, and I had unsuccessfully attempted to get an agent to represent me. No one seemed interested.

Most clubs were using three comics per week: an opening act, a middle act, and a headliner. Opening acts generally did about twenty minutes. The middle act had to be able to do thirty, and the headliner about forty-five minutes. After two years I only had a solid twenty minutes, which was all right; I wasn't a headliner anyway. I was fine with opening; I just wanted to work.

Since nobody would represent me for road bookings, I decided to represent myself. I got a list of the comedy clubs across the country and started phoning. I didn't have any luck at first. I had no track record, and most clubs used local comics as opening acts to save on travel expenses. I even offered to pay my own way if they would just put me up in a room.

After weeks of trying to convince someone to give me a chance, I solved the problem by creating a tour that didn't exist. You might call it dishonest, but I called it "creative booking." For example, I'd call a club in Columbus, South Carolina, and say I had an open week on my way to a job in Nashville. Did they need an opening act that week?

"I'll be coming through anyway so I won't cost you any travel money. Just a room and minimum pay."

Once I booked that date, I'd call the club in Nashville and say I had a week open between dates in Columbus and Atlanta. Then I'd call Atlanta, and so on, city after city. Same deal: no travel expense, little pay. But it did work. Within a few weeks of becoming my own booking agent, I had a solid ten-week tour.

It was like a wind chime made of cutlery

I wanted to do something special for Father and Roula for their twenty-fifth wedding anniversary, so I started making phone calls to solicit family members for the money so we could all send them to Hawaii. "Come on, let's do it together," I said. Nobody would contribute. So I put the tickets and hotel room on my credit card.

I brought them to Los Angeles first and gave them a little going-away party at my apartment on Hazeltine. I figured I'd be paying off that credit card for two or three years anyway, so I sent them to LAX in a limousine and had room service deliver flowers with their first breakfast in their oceanside hotel room in Hawaii. They were ecstatic.

After their vacation, they flew back to Los Angeles and stayed a few more days. On the last night we met some friends for dinner, and when we got back to my apartment my front door was wide open. I knew something was wrong and was afraid to go in, so I went to my neighbors, who, wielding baseball bats, led the way inside.

Someone had broken in and ransacked my apartment, stealing some videotapes, all the jewelry Buz had given me, and some cash. Luckily, I had been carrying my gun in my purse, or it too would have been gone. The burglar broke a back window, and I was afraid to sleep that night until it could be fixed. Father had the idea to hang some pieces of silverware in front of it so we could hear any intruder. It was like a wind chime made of cutlery. I don't know if the silverware would have alerted us or not, because I didn't sleep anyway. Once again, I felt frightened and vulnerable.

Nobody wins

Whenever I could book myself near London, I would visit Mother and she would always insist that I stay in her small apartment. I knew it would be better if I stayed at a motel, because of the hours I normally kept. I didn't want my schedule to become intrusive to her daily life, but on one trip it became a very big problem.

"I don't want you to feel like you have to tiptoe around me all day," I said, when she asked me to stay with her instead of in a hotel room.

"It's no problem at all. I'd much rather you stay here," she said.

Mother sounded great on the telephone. When I agreed to stay at her apartment, she even said she might consider coming back to Los Angeles with me for a while. I thought we were in for a nice visit.

When I arrived in London, it didn't take long to see that Mother had been on a nonstop drinking binge. She seldom ate anything, her face was puffy, and she seemed to have a perpetual hangover. I don't know where I got the nerve, but I told her I thought she had a problem and begged her to do something about it. I was surprised at her response. Instead of telling me to mind my own business, she promised not to drink for six months just to prove she could.

Most of the time when I brought up her drinking, it angered her and put her at odds with me. But there was an additional factor in our deteriorating relationship. Mother was programmed for failure. Since the day my father learned of her affair, she was told she was a tramp who would never be anything but worthless. I refused to see failure as inevitable, and she couldn't relate to that. I believe she saw my trying to succeed as abandonment.

Mother had never seen my comedy act, so I was excited when she and Liz's daughter Lisa drove to the show I had booked in Windsor.

I worked hard and was proud of my act. I'd even started incorporating props, including a series of dolls. I'd spent a lot of time and energy altering them to represent famous people. In retrospect, the gags weren't very original: For example, I put a huge blond wig on one, attached two Styrofoam balls to her chest, and called it the Dolly Parton doll. I attached one of those waving hands that people put in the back windows of their cars to the arm of one doll, added a crown on her head, and called it the Queen of England doll. But original or not, it added a visual element to my show, and the audiences seemed to like it.

After the show, I asked Mother what she thought of my act. She shrugged and said, "Well, you looked good."

When we got back to London, Mother continued to act sullen and uncommunicative. My sister Liz finally told me what Mother thought of the show. She'd told Liz it hadn't been worth the trip to Windsor. Liz went on to say that Mother disliked my use of blue humor and thought I'd come down in the world. I couldn't believe that. I used some double entendres in the show, but no foul language. I went back over all my material, trying to see if there had been any portion of the act that might have embarrassed Mother in front of her teenage granddaughter, but I could think of nothing. Finally I had to face the fact that Mother was simply trying to find fault with me.

I wondered if Mother was going to go with me to California after all, and, if she did, if I would be able to stand the negativity. But I didn't confront her about it. I didn't want the trip to end up with the two of us mad at each other. So I swallowed my hurt feelings and kept on my schedule. Mother didn't come to any more of the shows in Windsor.

The worst day of my life

A few days later we went to Liz's house for Lisa's birthday dinner, and the first thing Mother and Liz did was have drinks. By the time the dinner was over they'd both had too much to drink. When we went back to Mother's apartment, I reminded her that she'd promised to go on the wagon for six months and told her I didn't think it was right that Liz had given her a drink.

"We had more than you know," Mother said smugly. "Liz put liquor in my coffee, too."

"I don't think that was very smart of her," I said. "Neither one of you should be drinking so much. You have to start thinking about your health, Mother. You aren't taking care of yourself."

"Smart? You're the one who thinks she's smart," Mother snapped. "You think you're perfect. If you know so much about health, why don't you just write a newspaper article about it?" Then she got a bottle from the cabinet and poured herself a drink.

I could see this conversation was going nowhere, but when I tried to change the subject Mother altered her tone.

"I love you, Jenny," she began. "I think Liz is jealous of you and what you have."

"And just what do I have that she wants?" I asked.

"You have a career where you can sleep all day. Liz has to work hard, and she has so many responsibilities."

I didn't know what my sister Liz thought of me and my career. Ever since Mother moved back to London, my sister and I had been at odds about alcohol. Liz not only brought Mother liquor when she asked for it, she stayed around the apartment and drank with her. I knew about it through Mother's friend Roland who lived across the hall. He got very uptight about Liz's visits, since Mother always ended up drunk.

"Every time Liz comes," he would tell me, "Sophie gets sick."

But I didn't go into any of these complaints. I was always intimidated by Liz, and whenever it was time to address an issue with her, I'd revert to being the younger sister and back down. I just reminded Mother that I worked as hard as Liz did.

"And I don't sleep all day," I said, to defend myself. "I work at night but I'm usually up by ten."

She said I was different and didn't fit in with them anymore. She seemed resentful that I was making something out of my life.

"You think your career and your life are more important than everyone else's. I have to tiptoe around not to disturb you."

Her words hurt, but they didn't surprise me. It seemed as though she was always setting me up to tear me down. I thought carefully about my response, and I tried to keep my voice low and even. I didn't want her to know how much she upset me.

"Mother, I'm sorry my visit has been a problem. I offered to stay at a hotel, but you insisted I stay here. You said it was no problem. You acted like everything was fine. I think it's two-faced of you to do this."

"You think you're so good just because you don't drink or smoke," she spat back. "Everyone thinks you act like you're better than they are. You think you're perfect but you're not."

I couldn't take it anymore. I knew I had to leave. I said calmly, "Mother, I can't stay here. I'm going to pack my things and leave and I'll call you later." I was dying inside. I expected her to say that was fine with her, but instead she begged me to stay.

"Please don't go," she cried. "Don't hurt me like this."

I was confused, but I had to get away. I told her I would just go out for a while and then come back, knowing she would be passed out by then. So I left. I drove around for a while, pulling over when I couldn't see through my tears. I decided that a movie might help

take my mind off what was by far the worst day of my life. I had a
pain in the gut of my stomach. I bought a ticket to see *Blame It On
Rio*. I couldn't tell you what the movie was about but I needed a
place to go. When I got home, Mother was asleep.

I'll be damned if I'll ever come back again, I said to myself as
I crawled into bed. I set the alarm to make sure I was up early, but
I needn't have done it. I didn't sleep five minutes.

When I went in the kitchen the next morning, Mother was sitting at the table. It was 8 A.M. and she was drinking from a cup. My
hands were shaking so hard I spilled my tea when I tried to pour
it. I sat down at the table and waited for her to say something.

"I'm sorry about last night," she finally said, sipping from her
cup.

My voice was shaking as much as my hands.

"Me too," I said. "You said a lot of things." I appreciated the
apology, but I really needed to know she didn't mean it.

"But I meant what I said," she said bluntly. "I meant every word
of it." She sat there staring out the window, and then she turned to
me with a smug expression. "Your father thinks he's better than
everybody else, too. Did you know he had an affair with my aunt,
and she later committed suicide?"

I told her I'd never heard of such a thing, but I had few illu-
sions about Father's activities. She just sat and stared at me, as if I
were a complete stranger.

I was booked in a club in Rochester, New York, that night, so I
packed my car to go. I watched Mother for any sign of emotion, of
remorse, as I carried my things out to the car. In the past, when I
visited or when she went out on the road with me, she'd always cried
when one of us had to go. Even when she was in a negative mood,
she relented and said she hated to leave me and would miss me.

This time there were no tears except my own. By the time I got
to Rochester, I was cried out. I called Mother before my show, hoping she'd thought it over and would take back the hurtful things
she'd told me.

"Did you really mean those things you said?" I asked.

"Yes," she said, in a flat tone.

I hung up the phone and went up onstage to make people laugh.

Not long after I got back to Los Angeles I went to an Al-Anon meeting. I'd thought about attending one for a long time, hoping to gain some kind of insight into my mother and what her escalating drinking had done to our relationship. Maybe I just wanted to know if there ever had been a relationship.

I found a meeting and drove to the address listed, which turned out to be the home of a member of the group. There were a lot of people who all seemed to know each other, sitting around drinking coffee and talking, but they were very open to a new participant so I felt immediately welcome. As I listened to the others talk, I realized that what I wanted more than anything was for someone to say, "If she was drunk, she didn't mean anything she said."

Once I got up the nerve to ask my question, I only got about half of it out. I started crying uncontrollably and felt humiliated. Someone took me off to the side until I could get a grip on my emotions. She told me that if Mother admitted she didn't mean what she said, she would also have to admit she has a problem. That wasn't what I needed to hear. In my heart I knew Mother hated me. I believe that alcohol releases your inhibitions and allows the true personality to come out.

As usual, I tried to erase that episode from my mind and went back out on the road. Many comics do material about their families, and especially their parents, and I'd always heard that comedy comes from pain. But this was too much pain. I didn't even want to think about it, let alone try to find humor in the heartache. The grief I felt about my relationship—or lack of one—with Mother stayed buried when I was on the road.

Luckily, I was getting enough work to keep it buried—or at least covered up.

22

My Date with Seinfeld

Two of the best comics I worked with in those early years were Jerry Seinfeld and Sinbad. I played a date with Jerry at Joker's in Oklahoma City. He was already a name act; every comic on the circuit knew Jerry Seinfeld was going to be a big star. The most impressive thing about his act was that it was squeaky clean, at a time when a lot of comics got laughs the easy way, by doing blue material. (Many of those guys are still on the road, too.)

Like most comics booked together on the road, Jerry and I hung out, got pizza, and went to the movies. (Hey, wouldn't that count as a date? Yeah, that's it—we had a date and then I dumped him, and he only went to Shoshanna on the rebound!) Seriously, he was a very nice guy. We went to the gym together and worked out. I challenged him to match sit-ups with me, and we each did a hundred. According to my diary, we saw *Star Trek III*.

I also got some good advice from him. At the time I was still trying to buy material from anyone I could. I was so naive that after I watched his act I asked if he could write for me. "I'm not looking for free material," I said. "I'm willing to pay." Jerry's advice was to write my own material. He said, "You can do it, you just have to trust yourself. If you're serious about comedy, write your own material. Write every day." I started disciplining myself to write every day, and my act began to improve dramatically.

Jerry was very serious about his comedy; he didn't party all night like a lot of other comics. And with the problems my mother's drinking was causing me, I didn't have much tolerance for drinkers, whether they sat alone at the kitchen table or partied on the road. Some of the comics lived double lives. They'd party and run around on their wives out on the road; then, when we'd fly back to Los Angeles, the wife and kids would be waiting at the airport.

Bob Saget didn't party on the road either, and I always respected him for that, and for his firm belief that the show must go on. We worked together in Tulsa, and it turned out that he caught a bad cold, but he still worked that night. We were sharing a condo, and I tried to help by making him chicken soup. His killer show that night was all the proof I needed that chicken soup really does work. Like Jerry Seinfeld, Bob is an example of a clean comic who transitioned well into television.

Sinbad and I frequently worked together at clubs in Florida, so we'd see each other often on the road. Nobody ever wanted to follow Sinbad, because he is a high-energy performer who never once seems to be doing material. He's an extremely likable guy who simply walks onstage, takes command, and makes you laugh. And I've never heard him do blue material. The first time I saw him work I told the people at my table, "This guy is going to be a star."

I only had one really terrible experience with a headliner. As if having my breast grabbed after I had the implants wasn't bad, this was worse, and it was an incident involving the same man. I was booked again with him on the road, and we were staying in the same hotel, which was not unusual. He told me to stop by his room that night and suggested we walk to the club together, which was also not unusual.

When I knocked on his door, he opened it wearing nothing but a towel.

"I'm not ready," he said. "But come on in."

I came in, and he motioned me to sit on the bed and started back to the bathroom, where I assumed he was going to get dressed. Instead, he dropped the towel, pushed me down on the bed, jumped on it, and straddled me. He shoved his penis right in my face, laughing all the while. It was so shocking to have someone I knew—and was still a bit awed by—shoving his penis at me and acting like it was a joke, I didn't know how to react. I wasn't sure if I should push him off and make light of it, or get mad. I was afraid to get mad, so I pushed him off and simply said, "That's not very funny."

He merely grinned, made another joke, and reached inside my blouse to squeeze my breasts. I pushed him off and got to my feet while he just stood there laughing. It was so bizarre; I knew he wasn't going to rape me, but I realized he must use his celebrity to treat women like that all the time and get away with it. He was smart enough to pick insecure or vulnerable women. I'd like to have seen him try that with Lorena Bobbitt.

· Where are they now? ·

I don't know, nor do I care, what happened to that comic. I'm not divulging his name, so he'll have to remain an unknown comic.

Paying dues

My dream, which was also every other comic's dream, was to appear on *The Tonight Show* with Johnny Carson. We all knew that just one appearance, if you did well, could catapult you to stardom. Unfortunately, they turned me down. Every time I came off the road, I would showcase for the show's talent booker, Jim McCawley, and every time he would say, "You're not ready." He was probably right.

I continued to pay my dues on the road, working my way up from opening act to middle act, writing constantly. I traveled from town to town, appearing at all the clubs that were suddenly booming across the country: Yuk Yuks, Chuckles, Giggles, Jokers, the Funny Firm, Zanies, the Laugh Factory, the Joke Factory, the Laff Stop, Punch Line, Comedy Castle, Comedy Connection, Comedy Stop at the Trop. The newly expanded comedy circuit went on and on.

Some living arrangements on the circuit were even worse than those I'd encountered in my band days. To save money on hotel rooms, club managers often bought a condominium with two or three bedrooms and put the comics up there. Unfortunately, many of these condos were filthy. Even when you least expected it, you found yourself in a dump. I opened in Savannah for Richard Jeni in 1984, and thought my accommodations at the condo would probably be fine, since Richard was staying there too. When I got to the condo I was ushered to an attic room that looked like it hadn't been cleaned in twenty years.

I went downstairs to Richard's room, which wasn't much better. Both rooms were infested with cockroaches. After a fruitless conversation with the manager, who assured us that nobody had ever complained before, we decided to rent rooms at a nearby hotel and pay for them ourselves. It cost me most of my week's pay. (There were many other weeks on the road when I spent most of my paycheck on clean accommodations.) As was the norm, Richard and I hung out all week, went to the movies, got pizza, and worked out together. Since we didn't have a car, we moved the furniture in his room and used it as our gym.

I shared condos with lots of other comics, most of whom I was meeting for the first time. I'd come into town, go to the condo where the other comics had just arrived, and say, "Hi, I'm Jenny Jones. Nice to meet you. Which one's my room?"

Usually, I'd clean my room, unpack, and then check out the kitchen. By the first evening, some of my roommates walked around in their underwear, some did drugs, some brought women back after the show. Once in Sacramento my comedian/roommate started bringing in his luggage, followed by a large box with a scale in it. Don't be surprised that I had no idea why; I had never seen cocaine until I went on the road in comedy clubs. He was dealing drugs from our condo. But I didn't complain; I needed the work.

Because I never knew what I'd encounter on the road—a gentleman like Richard Jeni or a drug dealer like this other man—I started carrying my gun with me. I have a great respect for firearms, so I didn't pull it out of my purse every time I was nervous or scared. In fact, in the years since I'd purchased it, I had only drawn it twice.

I had just done a set at the Deli Smoker, in Sherman Oaks. Another comedian and I stopped by Ralph's, a market on Ventura Boulevard. We were in one of the aisles and heard a man shout, "Open the cash register, bitch." Then someone screamed, "They've got shotguns!" Adrenaline pumped through my body, as I pulled my loaded pistol from my purse.

I knew I wasn't going to stop the robbery—if the men carrying those shotguns saw me with a gun, half the people in the store might be killed. So my friend and I slipped behind the meat counter and down a staircase at the back of the store. We crouched down behind some boxes, and I took the gun out and aimed it at the stairs. If I'd seen anyone except a police officer come down the staircase carrying a shotgun, I was prepared to fire. After about twenty minutes we heard the police upstairs and slowly made our way out.

I never traveled without my gun. When I flew, I packed it in my suitcase, unloaded, with a handful of bullets, and until I went through Newark airport in July of 1984, I was never even questioned about it. I just checked my luggage with the airline and got on the plane.

I'm not a criminal. What am I doing in jail?

I had just worked Nashville, Atlantic City, and then Long Island, where I first met Rosie O'Donnell. She was a regular at the Long Island club and said it was good to meet another female comic. At the time there were just a handful of us, and we were never booked together because we were considered "novelty" acts. From Long Island I was headed home, flying out of Newark on People's Air, a now-defunct discount airline that saved money on airport personnel by having passengers check all their own luggage.

I had completely forgotten that my suitcase would be X-rayed, but even if I had remembered I wouldn't have been too worried. After all, once in Sacramento, I was running late and had to have my suitcase X-rayed before carrying it on. My gun was lying right in the middle and nobody noticed.

I sent my bag through the X-ray machine, wondering if the gun would be detected and, if so, what would happen. I didn't think it would be a big deal, since the gun was registered. It didn't take long for the Newark police to show me just how wrong I'd been. All of a sudden, four police officers surrounded me. I was handcuffed and taken out to a squad car, where they read me my rights.

"You don't understand," I told the policemen. "I was assaulted. I carry that gun for personal protection. It's not loaded."

"No, *you* don't understand, lady," was the answer.

They put me in the backseat of the squad car and hauled me off to jail. It was very embarrassing to be handcuffed in front of all those people, and for once I was glad to be relatively unknown.

On the way downtown all I could think about was losing the money I had. I kept remembering horror stories about people going to jail and, when they were released, finding whatever money they had arrived with was mysteriously missing. I was a working comic who was often paid in cash, and I had almost $1,000 on me from the last three weeks' work. It was money I couldn't afford to lose. I managed, though handcuffed, to ease the cash out of my handbag, under the back of my skirt, and into the top of my panty hose.

After I was photographed and fingerprinted, I was taken to a room and interrogated by two officers. I was still fairly confident that I could talk my way out of the mess if I could just explain about the assault. But before I could get a word in, one of the men asked if I was carrying any money. "Only about twenty dollars," I said.

"You are going to be searched," he said. "Your suitcases have already been searched, and there will be a policewoman coming to strip-search your body. If you are carrying drugs, we're going to find them."

Drugs? I hadn't even considered that they might think I had any drugs. A horrible scenario began to unfold in my mind. They were going to find $1,000 in cash hidden on a woman carrying a gun and think I was a drug runner. So I admitted I had lied about the money and tried to explain why I was carrying so much in cash. The officer was not impressed by my sudden candor.

"You already have two very serious charges against you," he said. "One, you were carrying a handgun at the airport. And two, we found illegal hollow-point bullets in your bag."

I didn't know anything about the legality of bullets. I'd been told those bullets would stop someone in his tracks, so I bought them. I was taken to a cell, and while I sat there crying, I kept thinking, I'm not a criminal. What am I doing in jail?

Someone else must have wondered what I was doing in jail too. Once my baggage had been thoroughly searched, the police officer came back to talk to me.

"We found some vitamins in your bags, that's all," he said.

I just nodded, still crying.

"You won't be searched any further," he said. "Look, we've decided maybe you shouldn't be here tonight," he continued. "Maybe you should get a room at a hotel. We'll let you do that if you pay your bail and promise to show up in court tomorrow morning."

I finally stopped crying long enough to explain that I'd rather stay in the cell overnight because that money had to last me a long time. I couldn't afford the hotel and cab fare.

"We'll have drug addicts and prostitutes coming in here later tonight," he said. "I think you better go to a hotel. Just pay your bail and be in court tomorrow."

"How much is bail?" I asked.

"Seven hundred and fifty dollars."

I stayed at a nearby Holiday Inn, and the next morning I appeared before a judge, who agreed that I wasn't a drug dealer or an international terrorist. But it turned out that New Jersey has the strictest handgun laws in the entire country. After a lecture about carrying guns, the judge returned my bail money and let me go on to my next job.

That was not the end of it. I was investigated by the Federal Aviation Administration, assigned a public defender, and put in a Pre-Trial Intervention Program. After months of paperwork, phone calls, and explanations, I was put on probation—a good alternative to jail, I might add. And as it turned out, I ended up being assigned to a great probation officer, Joann Palwick, who let me send post-cards to her from whatever casinos and clubs I was working. She knew I wasn't exactly a threat to society.

23

Under the Knife Yet Again

By August of 1984 the Vogue implants were so hard I didn't dare let anyone hug me or even brush by me for fear they'd be horrified by the two rocklike bulges on my chest. Once again I underwent surgery, this time insisting the doctor use the Meme implants I'd wanted in the first place. This fourth surgery seemed even more painful than the others, the most pain coming whenever I tried to sit up. My chest burned as if it was on fire.

Unfortunately, I compounded my painful situation by calling an alcoholic comic friend and asking him to help me out. He showed up drunk and stayed that way. He was the kind of person who was used to people taking care of him, not the other way around. Every time I asked him to help me to the bathroom or bring me a fresh glass of water, he acted annoyed. I wound up doing things for myself, and after a few days I went back on the road.

I was booked for a week in Fresno and I wasn't feeling well the first couple of nights, but I didn't relate it to the implants. After all, the last time I'd been implanted, I left town with my stitches still intact and had them removed by a doctor in Birmingham, where I was working. This time I noticed that my right breast had started to swell by the third day, and within a few hours it had gotten so large I became alarmed and called the doctor. As soon as I described what was happening, he said, "It sounds like internal bleeding. Get back here right now." I canceled the rest of my week and immediately drove back to Los Angeles, straight to the doctor's office. "You didn't get up and start doing things too soon, did you?" The doctor asked.

Well, yes, I had to admit I had.

I had emergency surgery that night to stop internal bleeding caused by increased blood pressure. I promised myself these implants would be the last, whether they turned into stone or not.

This time when I went home I phoned my old friend Terri from the Cover Girls, and she nursed me back to health, never letting me so much as make a move without her OK. Terri's the only person I know who won't even scramble you an egg without first removing that goopy gooey white thing that is attached to the yolk. I guess I should have called her in the first place, since she turned out to be an exacting caretaker.

Diagnosis: leukemia

Soon after my surgery, I received a call from Roula that Father had been diagnosed with leukemia. Father said it wasn't as serious as it sounded. "It's called chronic lymphocytic leukemia, and the doctor says if you're going to have leukemia, this is the one you want. It progresses slowly."

Father seemed take the news of his diagnosis fairly well, because he soon decided he wanted a face-lift. It seems so odd to think of your father being vain about aging, but the lines and sags on his face upset him terribly. He made an appointment with a plastic surgeon in Florida, but when the doctor examined him, he told Father his poor health made elective surgery impossible.

"But this leukemia comes and goes," Father protested.

"I'm not talking about your leukemia," the doctor said. "It's your heart."

The next month, Father and Roula came to Los Angeles to visit. We went sightseeing in Catalina and San Francisco, and even though he was concerned about his heart and had trouble walking, Father had a great time. He mentioned that with me on one coast and him on the other, he and Roula were spending a lot of money traveling back and forth. He hinted that he might like to live in Las Vegas, especially now that his health was failing.

"But I'd need a down payment for the house if I move closer to you," he said pointedly.

Setting myself up

I wanted to stay close to Mother, but as her drinking progressed and I refused to be her enabler she had less and less to do with me. I tried everything I knew. I phoned her frequently—if I hadn't, I'd never have talked to her because she didn't call. I continually asked her on the same kinds of trips I went on with Father and Roula, but she seldom accepted the invitation. If I suggested a cruise, she said she was afraid of the water. If I asked her to fly to Las Vegas, she always had another excuse. As soon as airplanes banned smoking, that was her reason.

She seemed to delight in throwing her drinking up to me. September 27 was Mother's birthday. This time I decided not to set myself up for rejection, which seemed to bring her a strange joy, and just called to say happy birthday. As soon as she answered the phone, I knew she was drunk. I couldn't always tell, but this time it was obvious. She was slurring and not making a lot of sense. I said, "Mother, are you OK?"

"I'm fine," she answered. "I'm just having a drink for my birthday."

But I knew it was more than a drink, or even a few drinks. Her tendency was to binge for days at a time without eating. "When was the last time you ate something?" I asked.

"I haven't eaten for a week," she answered.

All I could do was ask her friend Roland to check on her and encourage her to eat, even if she wouldn't stop drinking. She would never have stood for an alcohol intervention and certainly wouldn't take that kind of confrontation coming from me. Nobody wins in a relationship with an alcoholic.

Insights from the past

That September I had a rare opportunity to glimpse into my father's psyche. The talk about his health had alarmed me, and I started to realize I might lose him. So when I appeared on *Press Your Luck* and won a trip for two to the Far East, I invited Father and Roula to be my guests. On *Press Your Luck*, my third and final game show appearance, contestants played a board-type game on a large screen. You'd hit a big button, and if you got no "whammies" you won prizes like trips, furniture, cars, and appliances. If you got a "whammy" you'd lose the prize.

I traded the trip for two for three discount travel packages, paid a small difference, and we were on our way to Tokyo. The first thing Father wanted to do was get a massage, since he thought massage plus Japan equals geisha girl. How Roula felt about his erotic plans was of no concern to him. He didn't ask her, and she didn't object. He fully expected an erotic massage from a young beauty. What he got was a middle-aged woman who dumped buckets of cold water over him and brushed him hard with a broom. The masseuse called it invigorating. Father called it painful, but he took it well. In fact, we laughed harder listening to his description of the massage than any of us had in years.

The food posed an immediate problem, since Father was no more interested in Japanese food in the eighties than he'd been in Italian food in the forties. He was thrilled to find a McDonald's where he could order Chicken McNuggets. A hotel clerk told us about a wonderful music production we should attend called Kabuki. We thought it would be like a Las Vegas review or a big Broadway musical, expecting costumes and dancing. Instead, we found ourselves in the audience of a long-drawn-out version of Japanese opera. It wasn't even music to us, since the singing is all in a monotone. I'm sure it was wonderful if you could understand what was going on, but we were completely in the dark. We were right in the middle of the theater, too, so it was impossible to sneak out. Father was the first to doze off. I decided to let him sleep. Roula was next. I was about to go under too, except that Father's snoring kept me awake.

From Tokyo we traveled to Seoul, South Korea, where Father found the food even more distasteful. "This looks like eyeballs," he said. We finally found a nice Korean buffet, where you could pick and choose, and ate all our meals there.

But in the long run, we had a wonderful time. The shopping was great in Korea. Father bought a white jade and silver ring, and he had a pair of shoes custom made. They measured his foot by having him stand on a piece of white paper, while they traced around with a pencil, and said, "Come back in the morning for your shoes." It was pretty amazing.

We traveled on to Hong Kong, and it was there one night that Father turned reflective. Tired from a day of shopping and sight-seeing, we returned to our hotel room and fell asleep early. I woke up about 5 A.M. and saw Father sitting motionless on the side of his bed. His head was slumped down and he made no sound. I thought he was dead.

I slowly approached him and tentatively touched his arm.

"I'm sorry, I thought you were—uh—" I said, startled when he awakened suddenly.

"I'm not dead," he said. "I was just waiting for my nitro pill to work!"

Roula heard us talking and woke up, but when she saw everything was all right she went back to sleep.

Father asked me to sit on the bed with him a moment. Since he'd already broached the subject, he decided to talk about his death.

"I'm not afraid to die," he said, "even though I don't believe in God."

That astounded me. Father continually talked about how he had prayed to God when he was a prisoner of both the Germans and the Russians. He was always referring to God's hand being in his business when things were either good or bad. And now, after all that talk, he said he was a nonbeliever. Maybe he decided to stop believing in God when God "allowed" my mother to have an affair with a Muslim.

It was a monologue at this point, him talking and me listening. I certainly didn't bring up the fact that he had talked of praying to God many times in the past. I would never have questioned him on such a serious subject, especially when he was referring to his own mortality.

Finally he turned the monologue into something of a dialogue by asking me a question.

"What do you know about my family?" he asked.

I had to admit I knew nothing about his family. His nightly hardship lectures always started when he was taken captive by the Germans as a young man. There was no feeling of family, ancestry, or permanence. I could remember envying people who were going to a family reunion with grandparents and uncles and cousins.

"Tell me about the Stronskis," I said.

"My father hated me," he said, without hesitation. "He never said so, but I knew it."

I felt a chill. I too had experienced that feeling from time to time with my mother.

Father continued. "My father was injured in World War One, hit in the face with shrapnel and forever disfigured. Maybe that was why he was such a hard man. All I remember from my childhood was my parents fighting, nothing else."

"Maybe it was the war he hated," I said, trying to offer him some solace. "Maybe it wasn't you."

"It was me," he answered. "When I was drafted in 1936 and left for the army, I extended my hand to my father. He refused to shake it."

That admission ended the family reminiscences. It was one of the few times I'd ever heard him come anywhere close to soul searching, and his search was short-lived. I asked him a couple of questions about the Stronskis, but he said he was tired and wanted to sleep. I told him good night and went back to bed.

I didn't seize the opportunity to really know my father for many years. Back then, Father's persona was still so powerful that I couldn't see him as a normal human being whose own life might have been adversely affected by a cold, unfeeling father. Nor could I imagine what a world war and facial disfigurement might have done to the young soldier who was my grandfather. Who knows what went through my grandfather's mind when he refused to shake his son's hand as he went off to war? It's possible he hated to see him in the same danger he had once faced. It's just as possible that my grandfather was trying to thwart the pain he would feel if his son died or was disfigured in battle. And it's possible he was just an unhappy and loathsome man who hated his son. I can see those possibilities now, but I didn't then.

All I'm doing is getting older

We flew back to Los Angeles and the first thing Father asked me to do was find him a sexy massage girl. I went through the motions to satisfy him but had no luck. Roula said nothing.

Father and Roula went home and I left for Canada for a one-nighter at Yuk Yuk's in Toronto. I called Mother to see if she wanted to go with me. Although she seemed negative about my career and about me, she agreed to drive to Toronto with me.

I was just there to do an unpaid showcase for the club manager in the hopes of getting bookings. I had never even seen the club before and had no idea what kind of audience to expect or whom I would have to follow. I really wanted to impress Mother, but showcases are always a gamble — as was being around Mother.

My prayers of desperation were answered, and I got a standing ovation; it could easily have gone the other way. I knew it went wonderfully, and nobody could tell me otherwise. Well, almost nobody. I knew Mother might tell me I was bad, and while one part of me knew better, another would be devastated.

"You were good," she said when we settled into the car for the ride back to London in the pouring rain.

I breathed a sigh of relief. "Thanks, Mother," I said. I thought the friendly atmosphere was conducive to a "Let's get Mother healthy" talk. I'd been worried about her ever since her birthday, so I tried once again to broach the subject of her health. At least this time I avoided the drinking issue. All I cared about was that she was at least eating some nutritious food fairly regularly. I'd just started talking about my concerns when she stopped me.

"You think you're better than everyone else," she said, and stared out the window.

"Mother, what have I ever done to make you say that?" I asked.

"You don't have any problems in your life."

I considered the fact that my father had leukemia and a bad heart a problem. I considered the fact that my mother was an alcoholic a problem. But I knew Mother wasn't referring to my feelings about her or Father.

"I've got problems, Mother. Most of the other comics I know are starting to make it big, and all I'm doing is getting older."

She shrugged and repeated herself. "You don't have any problems."

I didn't talk anymore. This could lead to another night like the time Mother told me everyone thought I was "above myself," and I couldn't face another of those encounters. So I shrugged it off. It was very easy to do that with Mother, because she so easily drifted off to her own strange and isolated place. I drove through the rainy night thinking about what she'd said.

I didn't have any problems? It was almost laughable.

24

More Makeup! Bigger Hair!

I had been doing stand-up comedy since 1981, and I still had to showcase to try and get jobs. I was living on the road in roach-filled condos and watching my peers on television. I managed financially only because I lived so frugally. I made my own clothes, cooked at home, and didn't dine at expensive restaurants.

I had been turned down by *The Tonight Show*, *Letterman*, and *Merv Griffin*. It seemed like everyone I started out with was beginning to make it. Jerry Seinfeld and Gary Shandling certainly weren't doing showcases at Yuk Yuk's in Toronto. Bob Saget was hosting *America's Funniest Home Videos*. Kevin Nealon and Dana Carvey were on *Saturday Night Live*. Television exposure is vital for comics, and I couldn't seem to get booked on anything.

And then there was Roseanne Barr.

I'd never even met Roseanne, much less worked with her. But I was very much aware of her, because we were both incorporating our experiences as women into our acts. Word started drifting through the comedy clubs that she was awesome. I'd smile and say, "That's nice," but underneath I didn't want her to be good, because her act was succeeding and mine was struggling.

The first time I saw her on *The Tonight Show*, I was working in a club in Salt Lake City. Between shows I noticed that all the comics and staff were crowded around the television. I eased up behind them, and there Roseanne was on the show I most wanted to do, the show that said I wasn't good enough. I'm ashamed to say

I hoped it wouldn't go well, but when I saw her Domestic Goddess routine, I knew she was not just doing well, she was a star.

I couldn't help making the comparison. Here I was, trying to be glamorous, talking about male/female relationships. And there was Roseanne wearing baggy shirts and minimal makeup, looking unkempt, and talking about male/female relationships. She killed. She absolutely killed.

I applauded wildly in spite of myself.

Father and Roula were always asking how my career was going, and it wasn't going well. Sometimes their disappointment was harder to deal with than my own. On my thirty-ninth birthday, I visited them both and father tried to cheer me up by cooking a rabbit.

I knew one thing I needed: a manager. I was always approaching managers about handling my career or calling up other comics and asking them for their advice. When I was first starting out I had gotten Jay Leno's telephone number from a mutual friend and called him just as he was sitting down to dinner. I knew Jay casually, but we certainly weren't pals, and I was mortified that I'd interrupted his family's dinner. I apologized and said I'd call back, but he couldn't have been more gracious. He didn't say, "Who gave you this number?" or even "I'll have to get back to you." He listened politely while I explained how I'd been doing everything from booking myself to designing my own promo materials. Then he said, "I'm not sure you really need a manager at this stage. It sounds like you've been doing a pretty good job on your own."

I appreciated Jay's confidence in me, but after three years under my own management, my career was in limbo. I approached Don Rickles's manager, Joe Scandori, hoping that with his connection to a superstar comic he could piggyback me into some television guest spots. He was big time, completely out of my league, but I either didn't fully understand it or else I was too desperate to care.

Joe came out to the Ice House to see me work. I was so determined to impress him I put together an outrageous new look, which included a very brightly colored jumpsuit, contrasting bright belt, and gigantic and, yes, brightly colored earrings. My new theory was: The more they remember your look, the more they'll remember your comedy.

"I don't have the time to work with you," Joe said after the show. "But take my advice and get a new look. You look like a clown."

Want a career? Get sexy

Joe suggested I talk to a guy he knew named Rick Marcelli, who'd managed David Copperfield and Shields and Yarnell. Rick came out to watch me work at the LA Cabaret in Encino on March 23, 1985. He brought a friend of his for a second opinion, a film location manager named Denis McCallion. Rick said Denis was one of those naturally funny people, who probably should have been a comedian but preferred behind-the-scenes work.

"He'll know a good comic when he sees one," Rick said.

Denis was a warm, friendly guy who didn't have the usual Hollywood-hype personality. I liked him immediately. I hoped he liked me enough to encourage Rick to take a chance and handle my career.

I'd worked hard on my stand-up, always taping my shows and studying them afterward. And I'd followed Jerry Seinfeld's advice about writing every day. Rick asked me to meet him the next day. But he was surprised at the way I looked. Onstage the previous night, I wore my—yes—brightly colored pantsuit, but I went to meet him the next day in my street clothes, a short, tight minidress and high heels. Rick said the minute he saw me in my street clothes the first step was clear.

"Dress this way onstage. Show your body more," he said. "Wear sexier clothes, more makeup, and bigger hair."

I had all the elements according to him: the blond hair, the face, and the body. I just wasn't using them to my advantage. He also believed I might have a shot at guesting on some sitcoms and encouraged me to take acting lessons.

Rick's first priority was to get me an agent. A personal manager's job is to manage your career and help you make the right choices. Although many managers do help you get bookings, it's not part of the job description. An agent's only job, on the other hand, is to get you work. Chances are, you're better off to get a manager first. A good manager can get you an agent, but an agent is not so likely to find you a manager.

So Rick started sending out my tapes. I videotaped my shows as often as I could, and then I'd go to an editing facility and edit all the best pieces together for a compilation tape. We worked on a new résumé and photos, and Rick sent press kits out to ICM, Triad, William Morris, all the big agents. He even set up showcases so they could see me perform, but in the end Rick didn't have much better luck than I'd had.

I didn't enjoy seeing myself on these clips, just as I still don't like to watch myself on television. I'm too critical about everything—the way I look, the way I say something—and it's not worth the aggravation.

My first television break came from an unexpected source. I had opened for Mac and Jamie, a terrific comedy team, at Joker's in Oklahoma City, and they called one day and asked me to appear on their new variety show, *Comedy Break with Mac and Jamie.* I was so excited I invited Father and Roula to come from Florida, and Denis tagged along with Rick. I suddenly realized, "Hey, I have an entourage! This is the big time!" Charlie Callas was also on the show and was very gracious about taking a picture with Father and Roula. He started acting silly with us, and we laughed till we cried.

25

Star Search

At Rick's suggestion I had been taking acting lessons, and I finally got my first audition, for a guest spot on *Night Court*, playing Bull's girlfriend. I was much too nervous to do an adequate reading, but at least my first one was over. I read for countless television series and movies after that, and once in a while I even got a callback. That was the case when I was up for a part on *It's a Living*. I was called back several times by producer Tony Thomas, but the part finally went to Sheryl Lee Ralph. But callbacks were the exception, and I racked up an endless string of rejections from shows such as *Cheers* and *Dream On*.

Auditioning for TV shows wouldn't pay the rent, so I still had to work the road. I opened for Kevin Nealon at the Punch Line in Atlanta and often crossed paths with Dennis Miller. Dennis and I share a little mutual history of rejection. We both auditioned for *The Tonight Show* on the same night at the Comedy and Magic Club in Hermosa Beach, and we both got turned down. Word was that the booker thought Dennis was too much like David Letterman and would never make it, and that I wasn't funny enough.

About a year after I started working with Rick, he decided there was one way to get television exposure that we hadn't tried: *Star Search*. Not only did the show offer national television exposure, it offered a $100,000 prize to the winner. What he didn't know was that I had already tried and been turned down the last two years in a row. Nineteen eighty-five was the third season on the air for *Star*

Search, and they didn't appear to be using many women comics. I had no reason to believe they would accept me this time.

Besides, I had made good progress in the past year and a lot of people, including Rick's friend Denis, tried to convince me not to audition again. They said I was a working professional and could be perceived as an amateur if I did a competition show.

But I didn't see it that way. I was still being turned down by *Letterman* and *The Tonight Show*. I was getting club work, sometimes even headlining the small clubs, but being on the road was demoralizing. I believe that to succeed in show business you need to know when to make money decisions, when to make career decisions, and when to take risks.

Star Search was all three.

The exposure was a career risk. It could do wonders for my career, or it could set me back if the industry perceived this as an amateur show. If I should win (a highly unlikely outcome, if you asked me) I could walk away with $100,000, definitely a money decision. Or I could do the show, get no laughs, no money, walk away a loser, and have a bad hair day on top of that. There were risks.

I decided to go for it for one simple reason: I didn't want to wonder for the rest of my life what might have been. Taking a risk didn't scare me. I had come back from failure before, and I could do it again. So I gave Rick the go-ahead, and he presented my demo tape to the *Star Search* producers, who said the magic word: "Yes." I don't know what made the difference this time. Maybe my comedy was better; more likely, it was because Rick was aggressive.

The minute he phoned me that I had been chosen to appear, I phoned my parents with the news. Mother was a fan of *Star Search* and seemed pleased to hear I'd been accepted. Father and Roula were so excited that Roula sent me Father's gold cross to wear on the show for good luck.

Give 'em something they've never seen before

I still had one qualifying audition after I'd been tentatively accepted. I had to perform my act at the *Star Search* audition facility, located in Hollywood. This was where the show's producers could screen your material for anything they considered inappropriate for television, double-check the time it took you to get through your act, and make sure that your audition tape truly represented your live show.

I'd rather have been auditioning as anything but a comic. It's one thing to sing or dance in front of a table of producer types, it's quite another to do comedy that they've already seen on your tape. The silence was deafening; I was shocked when they didn't change their minds about booking me. Of course, they'd done this before with dozens of comics. They knew what they were looking for.

There was no turning back.

Rick said, "It's time to pull out all the stops. You have to knock 'em dead when you walk out in front of the cameras. Give them something they've never seen before."

Rick was talking about glitz, and I didn't have the money to buy it. My money kept going for silicone. So I got out my sewing machine and went to work.

There was no need to look farther than the International House of Silks and Woolens on Third Street in Los Angeles. When you see those beautiful sequined gowns at the Academy Awards, chances are the fabric came from this place, because it's frequented by Hollywood's biggest designers.

And Rick needn't have worried about how short my dress would be, because the fabric was upward of a hundred dollars a yard. I turned out to be my mother's daughter when it came to saving money on fabric. I had a simple minidress that I thought would make a good "knock 'em dead" dress if it were made up in sequined material, so I took it apart and used it as a pattern. Then I took my pattern to the store and laid it out right on the material, so I wouldn't waste an inch of fabric. What few scraps of material I had left went to make a matching belt.

My first appearance was scheduled for December 18, 1985, at the Aquarius Theater in Hollywood. It was a very long day. I wasn't scheduled until the afternoon, yet they had me in makeup at 9 A.M. We had a scheduled time for blocking, where they show you where to stand and explain where to walk if you lose, where to walk if you win. Then we waited to go on.

Each contestant had a dressing room, but once the taping started we all waited in the green room, watching the other performers on the monitor. I was a nervous wreck. I hadn't done much television, and watching the entire production was overwhelming. People with clipboards and headphones raced all over the studio, which was thick with fog from the smoke machine backstage.

When I was asked to come backstage and prepare to go on, my knees were visibly shaking and my hands were cold.

Ahead of me was a two-minute window in which I had to impress a very small group of people: four judges, to be exact, who could change my life. I stood backstage, trying to breathe deeply and relax, but I wound up inhaling the artificial smoke and started to choke. They gave me some water so I could get back to being terrified.

In some ways, I was beyond being nervous. I didn't really think I could win, but there was still a lot at stake. It was a show that everybody watched: industry people, club owners, and fellow comedians. Would my entrance in this sequined little homemade number grab their attention?

Wait a minute! There was no entrance! They went to a commercial break and told me to walk out and stand on my mark to be ready for the cameras to roll. The reaction I hoped to generate from the audience by making my big entrance, that would lead right into the first laugh, was gone. Oh, they did react when I walked on, but that soon died down and I was left standing there looking out at the audience with nothing to do.

The only thing I could think to do was to let the audience know how uncomfortable and nervous I was. I clasped my hands and rolled my eyes. What I was saying was this: *Please help me out, Please laugh. Please like me!*

Suddenly Ed McMahon walked out and introduced me.

"Ladies and gentlemen, here is a very funny lady from London, Ontario, Canada. Please welcome *Jenny Jones!*"

> *I'm honored to be the first female comic this season on* Star Search.
> *I think you're better off with a female comic. I believe we're more dependable. If we don't feel like performing, at least we can fake it.*
> *I want to talk about my favorite subject tonight—men. I think sometimes men are confused about women and what it is we actually look for in a man. So I'm going to tell you what I find attractive on a man. Cash.*
> *I went out with a cheap guy once. Dinner at the Sizzler. It was the worst. He forgot the coupons. We had to go back. He took me to a drive-in movie. I didn't see the movie—he forgot to let me out of the trunk.*
> *The truth is that I don't really date that much. I'm always afraid I'm going to wind up with some weird guy who wants something kinky. I went out with a man once and he asked me to mother him. I didn't know what to do, so I spit on a hankie and wiped his face.*
> *I think the only kind of man I don't like is a married man that asks out a woman. That really bothers me. Especially when they lie. They tell you they're single, then pick you up in a Winnebago with a swing set on the top.*
> *Thank you very much.*

I was afraid to even hope as I watched the other comic perform. Finally it was over, and we were called back onstage for the announcement. Standing there, I realized that winning wasn't the most important thing about *Star Search*; it was about not losing. I didn't care so much that I came across to the world as a winner; I felt like saying, Please God, don't let me look like a loser.

And then Ed McMahon announced, "Evan Davis, two and one-quarter stars; Jenny Jones, two and three-quarter stars. Jenny Jones is the winner!"

I was stunned, and although I still couldn't equate one win with the possibility of taking home that $100,000 and all the visibility an overall win would entail, I felt like I owned the world. Anyone in the industry who saw this show when it aired would see I was no loser.

And so would my family.

I didn't have long to bask in the glory of the moment, because I had to defend my crown the very next day. I approached this second round with trepidation. It's very common for a comic to kill the first night and then bomb the next time out. Maybe it has to do with the emotional buildup going into an opening night that gives you extra energy the audience picks up on, or maybe it's overconfidence from doing well the night before.

Luckily, I didn't have very long to be nervous, because I was too busy sewing. I rushed back to the fabric store with my pattern and bought some different sequined fabric, went home, and stayed up late into the night until my second dress was complete. This time I used the leftover scraps to cover a pair of shoes to match.

There I was again, shivering backstage in the pretend smoke, even more nervous than the previous day, because among the judges was one of the most powerful men in the business as far as I was concerned: Jim McCawley, the talent booker for *The Tonight Show*. Remember, the one who kept turning me down? If he didn't like me then, why would he like me now?

> *Thank you. I'm very happy to be back. I went to the doctor today. I hate getting undressed in front of him. He's a good eye doctor, though.*
>
> *My parents are really excited about me doing this show. They live in Florida. I could never live there. I hate bugs. Even today I saw one of those big black spiders on my porch. I said, "Oh, please let it be a hibachi."*
>
> *In Florida they have these palmetto bugs. They're like cockroaches this big, and they fly. Normally when you have*

cockroaches you go into the kitchen at night and turn the light on and they scatter, right? Down there they put sunglasses on.

Palmetto bugs are fearless. Nothing scares them. The other day I left my shopping list on the counter. In the morning there were three more items on the list.

I had to kill one once. This thing flew into the house. I was so scared. I had to trick the bug to kill the bug. It took about two hours, but it worked. I made a little trail of honey, and he followed it around the house, into the garage, and up the wall. I hit him with the car.

Bugs never scared me when I was growing up. Other things scared me when I was growing up. Like buying my first bra. I was twelve years old, and I decided I should buy a bra. I went to the department store, and the saleslady was gorgeous. Five-foot-eight, thirty-eight-D. I walked up and said, "I'd like to see something in a bra."

She said, "I bet you would, honey."

I was shaking when they announced my name as the winner of the second round. "Gary Lazer, two stars; Jenny Jones, three and one-quarter stars!" And I almost fainted when I learned that Jim McCawley had given me a perfect score. For the first time, the $100,000 in prize money seemed real. All I could think about was what I'd do with it if I won. I lay there at night thinking, This can't be happening! Even the possibility that I could get this much money—it was beyond my wildest dreams to have enough money just to pay my bills, let alone do anything for other people.

It was very important to me to be able to do something for my family. At the time I didn't understand why. Now I believe the attention and gratitude I received when I did something nice for them filled a void I'd felt since I was a teenager. My parents had divorced. My dad was physically gone. My mother was emotionally gone. And now they were back. If I was good enough, maybe I could hang on to them this time.

I was not important during my volleyball tournament or my

track tournament or my tennis tournament, but I was important now. My father had kicked me out of his house because I wanted to make something of myself. Well, he couldn't do that if I bought him the house. That was my promise to Father and Roula—I would buy them a house in Las Vegas if I won.

Mother wasn't so easy to please. "If I win the money I'm going to buy you something wonderful," I promised.

She didn't respond.

"How about a new car?" I suggested.

"I don't need a car," she said flatly.

"How about a mink coat?" I said, hoping for some small glimmer of interest.

"No, I don't want a mink coat," she said, slurring her words slightly.

"I love you, Mom," I said.

"I love you too," she said, and hung up.

I didn't know if Mother meant that or not, and I wondered what would happen if I bought her a house too.

I had to keep winning.

26

Falling in Love

Star Search wasn't the only excitement that winter, because I also got a choice job in a successful Las Vegas revue at the Maxim: Playboy's Girls of Rock 'n' Roll. In late December, I began commuting between Vegas, for the revue, and LA, where we taped *Star Search*.

The show was a compact all-female revue with a live band, dancers, singers, showgirls, and comics. My new image worked to my advantage. After all, if you hear the word *Playboy* you're going to expect to see women. If they'd had male comics, the audiences would have been checking their watches and yelling, "Bring out the girls!" But a female comic in a sequined minidress was perfect. The Playboy revue was probably the easiest job I ever had. I had all day to do things like go to the mall, watch television, and work on material. Then I went onstage for nine minutes and my workday was over.

This was probably the first time I really felt like a star, and it showed me that no matter how little I sometimes felt I'd progressed, I had come a long way in the last fifteen years. The show was tightly choreographed, well produced, highly successful, and, best of all, my act was well received virtually every night.

Variety reported:

> *Former band drummer Jones has also chored as backup singer for Wayne Newton, but she emerges as a tough-talk-*

ing stand-up schpritzer here.

And the *Las Vegas Mirror*'s critic said:

> *Playboy's Girls of Rock & Roll are all dynamic but, for this reporter's money, Jenny Jones is worth twice the price of admission. She could be the opening act for any of the Las Vegas superstars, and I wouldn't be surprised to see her climb into that exclusive category herself in the not too distant future.*

I was convinced the reason for the kudos was all those weeks and months spent on the road, performing for all walks of people from all across America. Because that's exactly who came to Las Vegas—Middle America. It was a sweet success. My hard work was paying off, literally. I was earning $1,000 a week for working nine minutes a show. It was a great security blanket in an uncertain business. I realized that, for me, security was more important than stardom.

This glitzy revue was just the kind of show my father loved, so he brought Roula and the two of them stayed with me in my hotel room for a couple of weeks. They came to the show each night, wining and dining at the Maxim. Father told me once again how much he wanted to move to Las Vegas for good.

Does this guy have a brother?

Rick's friend Denis had come to a lot of my shows in the year since I'd met him, and I never knew if it was because he was interested in me or because Rick wanted his professional opinion on what I was doing. And Rick never gave me a straight answer about Denis's personal life. Believe me, I'd asked. So I was both surprised and pleased when he finally asked me out, not long after the second *Star Search* win.

I'd gone to MTM Studios to read for a part in *It's a Living*. Denis, who was then a location manager on the *Twilight Zone* series, gave me a tour of the set, then asked me to go to dinner with him. We met at Solley's Deli on Van Nuys Boulevard in Sherman Oaks. We were so comfortable with each other that we just started talking, and suddenly three hours had passed.

I knew that day he was the man I'd been looking for all along.

Denis was so different from most of the men I knew. When I was in music, I hung out with musicians and talked about music. When I started doing comedy, I hung out with comics and talked about comedy. Denis wanted to know about *me*.

I was starved for someone to take a personal interest in me. Most of my conversations over the past several years had been superficial talks with my colleagues or painful confrontations with my mother. Either way, I got very little from the encounters. I later saw that Denis is one of those people who is genuinely interested in others. People are drawn to him. Children like him. Elderly people like him. Even cats and dogs take to Denis. When my women friends meet him, they all ask, "Does this guy have a brother?"

Since he'd met Father and Roula at the Mac and Jamie Show, he inquired about my mother.

"Are you as close to your mother?" he asked.

I tried to sidestep any conversation about Mother, but Denis was persistent. Weeks later, he told me that the minute he brought up the subject of my mother, he saw I had a lot of unfinished business there.

I attempted to explain our relationship. I admitted that we were not really close and that I often felt she didn't like me much. And I tried to explain my frustrations in trying to please her. I told him about the time when Mother was out on the road with me, and I invited her to dinner at an inexpensive café. She refused, saying, "I couldn't eat that food. It's too expensive."

I suggested we get something at the market and take it back to the room.

"No. The food would have poisons and pesticides in it," she said.

That statement from my mother, a woman who smoked cigarettes and drank straight whiskey.

Most of our disagreements were because I was concerned about her well-being. I may not always have been tactful, but at no time in my upbringing had I learned anything about being diplomatic. So when I worried about her health, I said so. I'd ask her to try yogurt instead of sour cream on a potato. She'd tell me yogurt wasn't good for people. I'd tell her how I'd learned to make omelets with egg whites, and she'd laugh at me. "The vitamins are in the yolks." Even when she seemed to be asking me for advice and I did use some tact, it turned out wrong.

"My face is puffy and sagging," she said once. "And look at my skin."

"You know, smoking dries out your skin," I said.

"You think you know everything, don't you?" she sneered.

I decided not to tell her the puffiness was due to her drinking, so instead I offered her a face tightener I'd heard about. It seemed like a mother-daughter kind of conversation.

"Those things never work," she said.

That night with Denis at Solley's Deli, I admitted my relationship with my sister had deteriorated, once I realized she was enabling Mother to go on drinking. Yet if I ever criticized Liz, Mother was quick to tell me that I thought I was better than everyone else and no one liked me.

I remembered once when I was visiting in London on a day off from playing shows in Detroit. I had to decline a dinner invitation at Liz's house. I told Mother I couldn't go because I had to get back to Detroit and work on some new material. When she protested, I told her my career had to come before socializing.

"I suppose you think you and your career are more important than Liz and her work," Mother said angrily.

"No, I don't think that," I said. "All I'm saying is that I have to work and can't go to this dinner."

As I poured out my emotions to Denis, I finally began to cry, thinking about my history of no-win conversations with Mother. I was burning with embarrassment, sitting there in a restaurant with tears running down my face. When Denis saw how hard it was for me, he tried to get me to examine my relationship with my mother and sister from a distance.

"These painful things should be taken out and looked at," he explained.

I did what most comics do when someone touches a nerve. I tried to make a joke of it.

"If you take it out and look at it," I said, drying my eyes, "then I'm leaving."

So Denis let the subject drop for the time being and started talking about his desire to see me again, concerned about whether I'd have the time to see him anytime soon. I thought he meant because of *Star Search* and my career. But it was soon apparent that he thought I had dozens of boyfriends practically hanging out the windows of my apartment.

"I'm willing to be one of your many suitors," he said.

"What are you talking about? I don't have any suitors," I said, shocked.

As it turned out, Denis had been questioning Rick about me too. Rick's responses ranged from "I don't know who she's seeing" to "I think she has a boyfriend," both of which were untrue.

In the weeks to come, Rick seemed threatened by my newly developing relationship with his friend, but he had no choice but to accept it. He had a two-fold interest in keeping Denis and me apart. First, he wanted me to focus on my career. He'd worked with women whose boyfriends distracted them and kept them from focusing a hundred percent. When I met Rick I was unattached, and Rick liked it that way. Nor did he want Denis getting too involved, even though he'd wanted his initial opinion. Rick's contacts and managerial skills were solid, but Denis's instincts were almost always right on the money. Even when he advised against *Star Search*, he had solid reasons—I could have very easily been written off as an amateur by the industry, win or lose. So it would have been easy for him to ease Rick out of the deal if he'd wanted, but Denis had neither the inclination nor the disposition to manage a stand-up comic.

When Denis brought me home that night, I put my purse in front of my chest so he couldn't feel how hard my breast implants were when he gave me a good-bye hug. I didn't know how I was going to tell him about those.

They call me MISTER Fluff

Denis started coming to Las Vegas on his days off to see me, and our romance quickly blossomed. He was naturally funny and had the quickest wit of anyone I'd ever met, which is why I occasionally asked him to critique my act; he always had positive reinforcement to balance the negatives.

The first couple of months of 1986 were crazy, with the highs and lows happening so close together they tripped over each other. I was still traveling back and forth from Las Vegas to Los Angeles, where I continued to chalk up wins on *Star Search*. Ironically, I was winning with the same material I'd auditioned with the previous two years.

Denis often came to Las Vegas, and I knew he had to be either falling in love or crazy, because he'd stay up late with me and then catch a plane back to Los Angeles in the early morning and go to work.

Best of all, for Denis and me it was love with all the trimmings: he sent flowers, balloons, teddy bears, and cards; we danced all night at the top of the Landmark and sometimes talked all night at the Peppermill on the Strip, where we had our first kiss. And like most people falling in love, we made up little nicknames for each other. He called me Baby Cakes and Sweet Stuff. I called him My Precious Little Puppy Fluff. And just to make sure he had to own up to the title, I got him a silver ID bracelet with M.P.L.P.F. engraved on it. Now, when he wears it and people ask him what the initials stand for, he has to say it out loud: My Precious Little Puppy Fluff. But you can call him *Mister* Fluff.

Denis showed me how to enjoy life. At forty years old, I went on my first vacation. We flew to Cancun and snorkeled, rented bikes, and shopped. I parasailed. Best of all, it didn't cost much because I had won the trip on *Press Your Luck.* For the first time in many years I felt safe, secure, and happy with the man in my life.

My career was in as big a whirlwind as my love life. I was invited to tape *Bloopers and Practical Jokes* with Dick Clark. Ed McMahon brought Dick into the makeup room to introduce us, and as they left I overheard Dick tell Ed that I was too pretty to be a comedian. I sat there in makeup, wondering if that was a compliment or a prediction that I would fail.

I flew to New Orleans to represent *Star Search* at the NATPE (National Association of Television Programming Executives) Convention, and as I walked through the airport someone called out, "That's Jenny Jones from *Star Search!*" It was the first time that had ever happened to me, and it again reminded me of the power of television. It turned out to be the first of many trips to NATPE; the next one would be to launch *The Jenny Jones Show* four years later.

I was also reminded of the darker side of celebrity that month, when hotel security at the Maxim arrested a stalker who'd seen me on *Star Search* and was looking for me at the hotel so he could "take me to another planet." He called me at the hotel the next morning from jail and asked me to send him bail money!

I just want to be left alone

I had another disturbing phone call about my new celebrity status. Mother called and said my success on *Star Search* had disrupted her life.

"My phone has been ringing all day," she said accusingly. "Some camera crew even tried to film me. They wanted to know why I'm living in such a small apartment if my daughter is a big rich star."

I asked her if she wanted to move to another apartment or come and stay with me for a while.

"No," she said, "I just want people to leave me alone."

I hung up and thought about my so-called success and stardom. I'd never had any money and usually had trouble getting a major credit card. For a time, the only place I could shop was the Broadway, because that's the only place I could get credit. Thank goodness it was a big department store. But I always had to worry about money, about things like rent and phone bills and utilities. I don't know where Mother got the idea I was rich. She knew that when I'd given her or Father presents, I'd had to save for months.

Mother might have withheld support, but Denis never did. And he seemed to be able to anticipate the times I needed him. On my day off from the Playboy revue I flew into Toronto to tape a television show with Jeff Altman. The next morning I was delayed at customs and missed my flight back. I panicked. I had never missed a performance in my life, as a musician or a comic. I called Rick, crying and upset, and he said, "Don't worry. I'll arrange for someone to fill in. Just relax and call when you get here." I was still upset that I couldn't be there in time, and when I finally arrived at the hotel, around 10 P.M., there was a note under my door.

If you need a hug, I'm right down the hall. Love, Denis.

He was the single most supportive individual I'd ever had in my life, and I was falling more in love with him with each visit. He was also the only person who understood the pain I felt each time I called and found Mother drunk and belligerent. He was the only one I could talk to about the feelings of inadequacy I still felt when I was around my father.

I knew I had to tell him about my implants, otherwise he would find out for himself.

Finally, I got up the nerve and told him the whole story. I explained about feeling so inadequate all those years, having a garage sale to buy the first implants, the multiple surgeries and resultant scarring.

"I know they don't look natural or feel natural," I said. "I'd give anything to have my old body back."

He reassured me that my breasts—large or small, hard or soft, scarred or not—were not what attracted him to me. He was only concerned about how it was affecting me emotionally.

For the first time in my life I had unconditional acceptance. I hadn't had it from my parents, or from either of my husbands, and I didn't know how to react. Since my previous relationships had all failed, I kept telling myself, "This is great for now, but it's probably going to turn bad."

Denis told me he was so much in love he hadn't even been able to eat, but I was afraid to believe it. I even thought about breaking it off before it got any deeper, just to avoid the pain of disappointment later.

27

And the Winner Is . . .

The *Star Search* finals were held February 13, 1986. Denis and Rick both came with me, as did my friend Terri, from the Cover Girls. Father and Roula made me promise to call as soon as the taping was over. They sat by the telephone for hours, waiting to hear if I'd won—and if they'd be moving into a new home in Las Vegas. A few of my peers called to wish me luck, including Rosie O'Donnell. I appreciated the call, because I hadn't seen her since Long Island.

I was nervous about this, the big showdown. All I could think was that there were two and a half minutes between me and a fortune. A hundred thousand dollars was more money than I'd ever had in my life. It seemed like a million to someone who'd sweated out paying the rent and making the car payments. And as any comic knows, it's not easy to do an effective monologue in two and a half minutes.

Until the finals, all the performers had been very cordial to one another. We'd chatted and schmoozed through the early rounds. But on February 13, the atmosphere changed. The tension was thick, and we didn't talk much. Everyone was just pacing around, afraid to think about winning and even more afraid to think about losing.

Losing on *Star Search* is crushing, since the show doesn't have a consolation prize. It's not like a boxing match, where even the loser wins something. The day of the finals I heard that a couple of performers were considering making an agreement up front that no matter who won, they would split the money 50-50, so they'd at least come away with fifty thousand.

My competitor in the finals would be Evan Davis, the same comic I beat on my first appearance. He was very good, and I knew it could go either way.

My confidence was boosted by knowing I had competed on *Star Search* five times and had won every time. It also meant making my sixth dress. I had noticed that royal blue looked good on television, and I hoped it would be my lucky color. I was becoming a familiar customer at the fabric store by now, and this time I bought the most expensive fabric ever.

I later learned that Evan thought the dresses gave me an unfair visual advantage, and he asked the show's producers if he could appear in a sequined dress as well. If they'd let him wear it and go on after me, he'd probably have won.

I've been working in Vegas a lot. The thing that gets me is these guys with more chains on than a snow tire. You know, refugees from the disco. They are all in Las Vegas. I'm sitting in a casino after my show and this guy walks up. He's wearing enough polyester to ignite a forest fire, OK? His shirt is open, and his chest hairs spell out: "Let's have lunch." Italian guy. Tony Testeroni or something.

I don't even know this guy and he said, "That's a very nice perfume you're wearing. What's it called, Evening at My Place?"

I said, "No. It's called Fat Chance."

He said, "I don't get it."

I said, "That's right."

He had a great comeback, though. He said, "So what are you—celibate?"

I said, "What are you? The alternative?"

I don't date that much, but people try to set me up for blind dates. I had one blind date. Let me try to describe this guy. It's very sad. You know when a guy's trying to grow a mustache and he can't? He had nine hairs on his upper lip.

His eyes bugged out; he looked like a catfish in a suit. I'm telling you. I don't mind talking about it. I opened the door and he said, "Come on, we're gonna to be late."

I said, "Why? Do you have to get back before low tide?"

It wasn't just me that saw it. The waiter at the restaurant saw it. He brings over his shrimp cocktail and says, "It's OK, we checked it for hooks."

But things have changed. Dating has changed. Morality has changed. Some of the guys aren't really hip to this yet. I was out with a man the other night. He actually said to me, "Am I the first one?"

I said, "Yeah. Today."

What Ed said: "And the winner is—Jenny Jones!"
What I heard: *"You get the money!"*

It was the first time a woman comic had ever won. I was so overwhelmed I had trouble breathing. (Thirteen seems to be my lucky number. I won *Star Search* on February 13. On February 13 six years earlier, I won big on *The Price Is Right*.)

As soon as I got offstage, I ran to the pay phone and called my family. Father and Roula started crying. Even Mother was excited. We'd celebrated some of the earlier wins at Martoni's, a great old Hollywood restaurant that served the best gnocchi ever, so we all went out for a big celebration dinner. I paid for the dinner with my new credit card. After all, every time I won I was paid AFTRA scale plus a thousand-dollar bonus. As we left, Rick leaned over to me and said, "Be careful about this sort of thing. It can get out of hand."

I didn't tell him then, but I'd already decided to pay him a $5,000 bonus on top of his 15 percent commission, as a way of thanking him. When my $100,000 check arrived, I sat down and made out a check to Rick Marcelli for $20,000 and then thanked him for being my manager and getting me this opportunity. Then I started paying bills. It was such an extraordinary feeling, knowing that I could pay everything and for the first time in my life be debt free. Of course, the same day I received the winning check, I was also told I'd have to audition for *The Tonight Show* again to see if I was funny enough to appear.

Rick and I weren't the only ones who made money on *Star Search*. Every time I returned to Vegas after taping a *Star Search* segment, one of the musicians would ask me who won, naming every category: singers, dancers, actors, etc. The shows usually aired about two weeks after they were taped. I later found out that he was taking bets, all nice and legal in Nevada, from people who thought the shows were live.

If I wasn't good enough for mainstream television, at least I was good enough for the big rooms, because I was offered my first job opening for a star in one of the big rooms. I left the Playboy revue to open for Kenny Loggins at Harrah's Tahoe. Wayne Newton was also playing in town, so Denis and I caught his show. It was great seeing Wayne again, but he still does the longest show in Nevada. I was exhausted and actually fell asleep on Denis's shoulder while we sat in a booth in the darkened theater. All of a sudden, Denis shook me awake.

"Stand up, Jenny!" he whispered. "Wayne's introducing you to the audience!"

I jumped up, sleepy-eyed and dazed, just as the spotlight stopped at our table. There was only a smattering of polite applause, from people who knew I'd won *Star Search*. But I appreciated the kind gesture on the part of my old boss.

Hangin' with the man

I laugh and cringe when I watch old *Star Search* tapes. My delivery was stiff and the material contrived. But whether I was good or bad, being the first woman comic to win on *Star Search* changed the course of my career.

I was immediately offered a development deal with ABC. It sounded better than it actually was, because it offered a minimal amount of money for a long-term commitment. What "development" really means is they want to keep you away from the competition until they figure out if they can do anything with you. Rick suggested we turn it down. I've always wondered what would have happened to my career if I had signed with ABC.

Like any comic, I knew I couldn't make it big without TV exposure, the more the better. I was in a bad position, though, since I went out on the road immediately. I tried to get back to LA to audition as often as possible, but casting is immediate, and I missed a lot of television opportunities because I was earning a living on the road.

All the *Star Search* winners were invited to perform at Radio City Music Hall. Denis came to New York with me, and we turned the week into a sightseeing junket, going to the Empire State Building, taking buggy rides through Central Park, and playing on the park's swings like kids. By this time I knew that, whatever else happened in my life, I had found my permanent partner.

I was interviewed by national media, and even by Dr. Ruth, and appeared on shows like *Good Morning America*. I was a natural for *The Dr. Ruth Show*. Before you go on the air, the show's producers ask you to give them some lines from your comedy act. Then they write questions for Dr. Ruth to ask that will relate to relationships, men, or sex. For example:

> Dr. Ruth: So, Jenny, what kind of things do you look for
> in a man?
> Me: Cash.
> Dr. Ruth: Well, Jenny, do you think that moral standards
> have changed since you were a young girl?
> Me: Oh, yes. I was just with a man the other night, and
> he asked me if it was my first time. I said, "Yeah, today."

I got what I considered the opportunity of a lifetime that April, when Sammy Davis Jr.'s manager called Rick and offered me $2,500 a week to be Sammy's opening act for two dates in Florida. Sammy Davis Jr. was a legend. I'd read Sammy's book *Yes, I Can,* and had such an admiration for what he overcame, working in casinos that wouldn't even allow him to walk through the front doors. From the compassion and understanding that came across in his book, I had guessed he was for real, not just as an entertainer but as a person. And once I worked for him, I knew my guess was right.

Sammy later told me that he had requested me personally after seeing me perform on *Star Search*.

The first booking was in Sarasota at Van Wezel Hall. I couldn't wait to meet Sammy. I went to rehearsal that afternoon, and since I wasn't sure what to do, I just walked up, introduced myself, and said hello. He could not have been more gracious. "Nice to meet you." he said, as he shook my hand warmly. "I saw you on *Star Search*. You were funny."

"Thank you," I managed to get out. "It's an honor to work with you."

When I asked if he had any specific requests of me, topics I should or shouldn't do, he simply said, "Just do your own thing. I'm secure with what I do." You moron! I thought to myself. Did you really think anything you do is going to impact Sammy Davis Jr.'s show? He was adored by his fans. He could have opened his show with slides from the fishing channel, and they still would have loved him.

Some headliners aren't so trusting. When I later opened for Tony Bennett, his son, who managed him, came around to my dressing room and said, "Dad doesn't want you to do any Italian jokes." I said that was fine.

Guess who's coming to dinner

My second date with Sammy was at Ruth Eckerd Hall in Clearwater, where Father and Roula still lived, and from the moment my father heard, he started pushing me to invite Sammy out to his house for dinner.

"Dad, I can't do that," I protested. "Sammy Davis is a huge star! I barely know him."

That didn't stop John Stronski. He kept at me until I considered lying and telling him that I'd asked Sammy and been turned down. I thought Sammy would think I was a complete idiot if I asked him to come dine with my father and stepmother.

On the other hand, I knew Sammy liked home cooking so much he brought along a trunk full of pots and pans and spices and cooked on the road! That's when he wasn't playing Pac Man, which he did for hours backstage.

I didn't want to lie to my father, so I decided to issue his invitation. From what little I'd been around Sammy, I knew that when he turned me down, he would be a gentleman about it. And I didn't think he'd consider me a fool for asking. Either way, I'd get my father off my back. So one night I approached him after the show.

"Mr. Davis—"

"Sammy," he quickly corrected.

"Uh, Sammy, we're playing Clearwater next week. My father wanted me to invite you to dinner at his house. He's a wonderful cook, but I'll understand if you—"

"Sure, I'd love to come," he interjected. "What time and where?"

The minute I phoned my father with the news, he and Roula started cooking. There were several days to go, but they would cook and freeze to have everything ready. They'd been planning to have a party for me on that Sunday anyway, to meet all their friends.

"All I ask," I told them, "is that Sammy not be hounded by fans. Please be sure his dinner is over and he is gone before we start the party so he can dine with us in privacy." I believed he was genuinely coming for the home cooking and not to make a "public appearance."

Sammy was supposed to arrive at four, with dinner from five to seven, and then our party would start at eight. But Sammy and his entourage, which included driver, conductor, and bodyguard, were late and didn't arrive until close to six.

Sammy loved the meal they'd prepared for him: salad, borscht, cabbage rolls, pierogi, roast leg of lamb, and Greek spinach squares.

Father and Roula really knew how to cook, and Sammy seemed to enjoy it.

I don't think a black man had ever been in a house owned by John Stronski before, and given my father's racist nature, I got very nervous when Sammy started talking about being black in the South. I had no idea what my father might say or do. He wouldn't have meant to be insulting, but he was certainly capable of it. Sammy talked about his once-controversial marriage to Mai Britt and then about the number of interracial couples he sees today in every audience. He said it was startling yet reassuring to see these couples happily walking along the beach, unhassled. I was gratified that all my father did was agree with him.

We hadn't even started dessert when it seemed like the entire Florida chapter of AARP began ringing the doorbell. Each time, Roula would jump up and run to the door. How do you act normal when you're saying these words: "Would you mind waiting in the den over there? Sammy Davis Jr. is here and hasn't finished his coffee." By the time Sammy finished his coffee, about thirty people were waiting in the den, and they'd all brought cameras expecting to take pictures of me. Sammy had no way to exit except to walk past them. They went crazy, begging for photos with the superstar.

"Sammy, I'm so sorry," I said. "This was not supposed to happen."

He just smiled at me. "You're gonna owe me for this!" he joked, and graciously posed for all the photos. He then headed for his limousine, tightly followed by all thirty-five of us. There will never be another Sammy.

The next day, Father called me aside and told me he was having some financial problems and couldn't make his house payment that month.

"How much is it?" I asked, wondering what was going to happen once they moved to Las Vegas. I knew Father's propensity for lavish dinners and big impressions. If he tried to impress Las Vegas, he'd be broke in a month.

"The house payment is three hundred and fifty dollars a month," he said.

"I can help you with that," I answered, knowing that was the answer he expected.

A few days later as I was preparing to leave town, I sat down to take care of the house payment. "I'll just send you a check every month. How much is it exactly?"

"Five hundred dollars," he said.

"I thought it was three fifty," I responded, feeling confused.

"It's five hundred with utilities and phone."

I didn't like the way that felt.

Sammy must have liked either my comedy or my dad's cooking, because I was asked if I could open for him at Harrah's in Atlantic City later in the year.

Like Sammy said, *Yes, I can!*

Dribs and drabs

That May I invited Mother to come visit me in Los Angeles. I was hoping to convince her to take the car and fur coat I'd offered when I won *Star Search*, but she didn't seem to want anything to do with my prize money. She didn't want to hear how my career seemed to be picking up, nor did she want to know much about Denis. She wanted to talk about peanut butter and jelly sandwiches.

"I used to get so sad for you," she said, "back when you started out in those bands and didn't have any money. Sometimes all you had to eat were peanut butter and jelly sandwiches. I saw you live on those for a whole week."

"It wasn't so bad," I said. "I hardly remember those times. I'd rather think about now, when things are going well. *Star Search* changed so much for me, Mother."

Her tone darkened immediately. "They showed *Star Search* on TV last week," she said. "You looked tired, and you didn't say anything funny."

"Mother! The audience didn't laugh at all?" I was being a bit sarcastic.

"Just in dribs and drabs," she said.

Why was she doing this to me? In retrospect, I've wondered if Mother could only relate to me when times were hard and I was struggling because that's all she'd ever known. The more success I attained, the more resentful she became. I thought maybe a change of scenery might help, so I took her to the place she loved, Las Vegas.

She had a good time, mostly playing the slot machines. She seemed to lose herself in the noisy clatter of all those levers. I was used to her negativity and I wouldn't let it spoil our visit. After she went home to Canada, I called, and she thanked me for the trip. She seldom, if ever, called me.

In my entire adult life, she may have called me five times.

Mother had only been gone a few days when I got bad news about my father. Roula called to say he had started chemotherapy. We knew it was only a matter of time before he'd need chemo, so none of us was surprised. At first he said he didn't want the lifesaving treatment if it meant losing his hair. I couldn't believe he could let his vanity take priority over his health. The thought of dying, however, seemed less acceptable than hair loss, so he reluctantly began treatment.

Expecting to die together

When I wasn't working the big rooms, I booked myself into clubs. *Star Search* had brought me some notoriety, and I had a chance to work on new material on the club circuit. Denis joined me later that month when I was working in Fort Myers, Florida. The road was boring to me until Denis came along. We always found fun new things to do, and this time it was parasailing. A couple of young guys on the beach had all the equipment. When they told us we could go tandem, we paid them and started getting hooked up.

"Are you sure this is safe?" I asked one of the guys, not remembering ever having seen a couple flying through the sky.

"Oh, absolutely," he said. "You just have to make sure to keep running until you're in the air."

Denis and I listened carefully to all our instructions as they strapped us together with ropes and pulleys. I was in the front. Then we were tied to a speedboat, and as soon as we got the signal we started running. I'm not sure what happened next, but I fell. I couldn't keep up with the boat. We were still on shore and my legs just gave way. I pulled Denis down on top of me.

The boat, which was accelerating to about twenty-five miles per hour, was dragging us into the water. The weight of Denis on top of me was pushing my body into the sand and rocks. We were dragged underwater for at least fifty yards, unable to communicate, expecting to die together. When the boat finally stopped, we were both choking on water and barely able to stand up. Our knees sustained the most damage, especially mine. Luckily we survived with no broken bones or permanent injuries.

I was luckier with the parasailing accident than I was with my breast implants. Not only were they becoming hard again, they were also misshapen and unmatched. I decided to see a different doctor. Just looking in the mirror made me cry, and I was determined to find someone who could help me. Denis knew I was upset and offered to go with me, but I refused. I guess I thought the less he knew about the problem, the better chance I had of still being attractive to him. I drove to Beverly Hills to see Dr. Harry Glassman, who is Victoria Principal's husband. After the examination, I anxiously waited to hear how he could fix my body.

"There's nothing I can do," he said.

I was devastated.

This was a plastic surgeon to the stars. I had been sure he was going to fix me. I started crying in the elevator. As soon as I stepped outside, I ran into Denis. He had followed me over and was waiting for me—"just in case," he said, "you needed a hug."

I've never seen dead people smoke before

In July I headed for Atlantic City to open for Sammy again. When I arrived at Harrah's I was told my room was on the sixteenth floor. Sammy had taken the entire floor for himself: his band, entourage, and opening act. What fun! It felt like a dormitory, with people's doors open all the time, and I often ran into Sammy in the hall.

The audiences knew and loved Sammy, but they didn't know or love Jenny Jones, especially in Atlantic City, where I didn't seem to be able to get a chuckle, let alone a laugh. I'm not sure what it is about Atlantic City, but it can be a tough crowd to play. To make matters worse, the room at Harrah's had heavy fabric and drapery that absorbed a lot of the sound. On those rare occasions that I did get a laugh, it never made it to the stage.

Also, there were a lot of New Yorkers in the audience, and maybe I just wasn't hip enough to play to them. New Yorkers can spot a Midwest personality, and despite the fact that I'd grown up in Canada and spent years in LA and Vegas, I was still very much a midwesterner. My spirits were briefly lifted by a visit backstage from Joann Palwick, my former probation officer. New Jersey, after all, was her jurisdiction.

Every night my twenty minutes crawled by like twenty hours and I felt like I'd just written my professional eulogy, right there in front of Sammy Davis Jr. We had some dates booked together at Harrah's Tahoe in a few months, and I was terrified that Sammy would cancel me as his opening act.

The good news was Sammy didn't fire me. The bad news was I was booked back in Atlantic City four months later to open for the Pointer Sisters. Needless to say, I had mixed emotions. I still hadn't recovered from my death-defying stint there with Sammy. But while going back scared me, it wasn't about to stop me.

The Pointer Sisters were on the same plane out of Los Angeles, so I introduced myself to the girls and they invited me to ride to the casino in the band bus waiting to pick them up at the airport. To my great relief, my shows went very well. We were at Caesar's Palace, which might have drawn a different type of crowd from Harrah's. I didn't try to analyze it too much. After five years of doing stand-up, I knew that sometimes there was no explanation for a difficult audience.

On closing night the ladies called me into their dressing room and gave me a present, a red Gucci handbag. I was amazed. No other act I'd ever worked with had given me anything, and it never occurred to me that they would. That series of shows seemed to break my Atlantic City jinx. I lost some of my fear of the audiences, loosened up, and, in fact, have worked there many times since.

I was thrilled about opening for big stars like Glen Campbell, Andy Williams, Tony Bennett, Eddy Arnold, Neil Sedaka, and Nell Carter, because when you open for a star you stay in nice hotels, get substantial pay, have your name on the marquee, and are usually treated well.

Working with Neil Sedaka and Nell Carter at Harrah's Tahoe was an easy job, since I only had to do eight minutes a night between their shows! One Sunday afternoon, Neil even took me out on the boat Harrah's had provided for him. The invitation was a shock, because headliners seldom socialize with the opening acts. Nell said she had seen me on *Star Search* and liked my comedy, and I appreciated her taking the time to say so. I remember she had trouble breathing, in the high altitude of the Tahoe mountains.

Not all the stars were approachable. When I opened for Dionne Warwick, she never said much to me, and I was disappointed because I was truly a fan of hers and have all her albums from the sixties. What surprised me most is that her voice is as powerful and clear as ever, and yet she smokes constantly. She'd take a final puff just before walking onstage, and her assistant would wait in the wings to hand her a lighted cigarette the minute she walked off. I guess she liked my act, because I did several dates with her, including an outside venue in Brooklyn in front of sixteen thousand people. That one wasn't comedy, it was survival.

I was earning from $2,000 to $5,000 a week, but my television career was stuck. I tried every angle to get television work. For example, I convinced a publicist who worked with Bob Hope to bring him to see me at the Ice House in Pasadena, hoping he'd like my act and invite me to do one of his television specials. Nothing came of it, but Bob did come back to the dressing room and pose for a photo.

He was given five to ten years to live

Father's leukemia had progressed, and he needed his first transfusion in July. The next month Roula called, sounding hysterical, and told me that Father was undergoing quadruple bypass surgery (in Canada, due to insurance considerations). I flew to London that night and went immediately to the hospital. I could barely stand to look down at the man I had considered invincible. His coloring was gray, and the skin on his face stretched taut. He had staples in his neck. When his eyes fluttered open, he looked frightened. Despite his self-absorption and rigid personality—or perhaps because of it—I never wanted to see him in a powerless state. He was given five to ten years to live.

He started to regain his strength within a few days, and I guess Roula decided he should celebrate, because she slipped a bottle of cognac into the room and poured some in his tea one morning. I was flabbergasted. First there was my sister Liz slipping liquor in Mother's coffee; now Roula was sneaking cognac to Father while he was recovering from a bypass! I thought the whole family had lost all sense of propriety. Even Father grimaced when he tasted it. Luckily, a nurse smelled the liquor and chastised Roula for bringing it in, thereby saving me from what would have been a nasty confrontation with my stepmother.

Facing a parent's mortality sometimes causes you to do some

soul-searching about your own life, and I did just that in the months to come. I was making a good living, but I wasn't sure I wanted to spend the rest of my career on the road or how long I could keep getting bookings. I was already forty years old. And wouldn't you know, just as I was wondering if I was wasting my time in comedy, Rick Marcelli quit as my manager, saying he'd opened all the doors but no one was buying.

Was he ever right! Once Rick departed and I started managing myself again, I was hit with the overwhelming rejection he'd spared me by being the middleman.

I did get some television spots on my own, including a local TV show in San Francisco with Rich Little and Ned Beatty, and George Schlatter's *Funny Firm*, which I taped with several of my peers, including Arsenio Hall. I also taped *Puttin' on the Hits* along with Reebie Jackson and Greg Louganis. But despite those few successes I was hitting an inordinate number of brick walls.

On and off the midway with Mother

That Labor Day weekend I was asked to appear at the Western Fair in London. It was a personal thrill, because while I was growing up the Western Fair was the biggest event of the year. I couldn't wait for the carnival rides and cotton candy.

"I'll do it," I said, "as long as I can ride the Tilt-a-Whirl."

And they thought I was kidding! Not only did I get to go on my favorite ride of all time—twice—but with the manager's help we took Mother around to all the attractions in a wheelchair. By now, she couldn't walk very far because of poor circulation, mostly due to smoking.

We had fun out on the midway, and once again I thought the ambiance of the day was a sign that the visit with Mother would be positive. I didn't have long to wait to be proven wrong. She came to watch my opening night show, but when I signed autographs afterward she turned away. I would have been proud for her to see people asking for my autograph, but she went off to have a cigarette. The next day I came to visit, and the first thing she said was that Liz had told her I hated playing the Western Fair and wouldn't have done it if I hadn't signed the contract.

"Mother, that is a complete fabrication," I said, shocked. "All Liz and I talked about was Father's deteriorating condition."

Mother rolled her eyes and smirked. "Well, maybe I just made it up," she said.

I decided not even to mention it to Liz because I knew she would either deny it or not remember saying it.

After I got back to Los Angeles, Father called to say that Liz had called complaining about me. "She says she is sick of hearing about you and your success," he said. "She says it isn't fair to your mother. Sophie has to spend money going to the beauty parlor now that you put her in the public eye."

I started to protest, and Father cut in.

"Liz also says you refuse to buy your mother the car you promised her."

Where did all that come from? I wish I knew.

I'm forty years old—what happened?

In October, I had another date to play with Sammy, this time at Harrah's Tahoe. I had not seen him since that awful date in Atlantic City and hoped his confidence in me wasn't shaken. I stopped in his dressing room (which he always decorated with family photos) to say hello, and he welcomed me back to his entourage, never mentioning anything about my last performance. I figured he was probably waiting to see how I did opening night.

When I got to town I noticed that Jay Leno was playing down the street, and decided to pay my respects and congratulate him in person on all his success. Between shows I went to his dressing room to visit with Jay, and interrupted his dinner, as I had done a few years earlier. Once again, he was gracious about it, inviting me in to chat while he ate. I mention this because I think sometimes people wonder if certain stars are as open and friendly in person as they seem to be when they are on stage. Jay Leno is.

After my second show, I was invited up to Sammy's suite. It was nice to feel important again, and "hangin' with the man" was definitely the way to feel important. We sat and talked for a long time, and finally I broached the subject of Atlantic City.

"I don't know why you even hired me again after that fiasco," I said. God love him for his answer. One thing about Sammy Davis Jr.: his trademark line, "Love you, babe," wasn't just an empty phrase. He meant it.

"That's a tough room, Jenny," Sammy said. "I knew what you were going through, and that's why I left you alone. You think it hasn't happened to me? Look, if you ever have questions about this business, you ask me. Pick my brain, 'cause I've been out there a long time." Then he smiled. "You're a dichotomy, Jenny," he said enigmatically.

I didn't ask him to explain what he meant, but I thought about it off and on over the next few months. I wondered if he saw the deep conflict between my surface confidence and my profound insecurities. I went from total command of a stage, making people laugh, to seeing my mother and feeling impotent. I went from running my own career and making my own decisions to being completely intimidated by my father. Sammy had watched me interact with my father. My intimidation was probably evident.

Perhaps the dichotomy he saw was the same one Dick Clark saw. And maybe it was holding me back from success in television. If I was "too pretty" to do comedy, maybe, when a part called for a funny woman, they wanted a funny-*looking* woman and didn't consider me. Or if the part called for a pretty woman, they looked for a pretty woman and not a comedian. That was my theory at the time.

Whatever the reason, when the year ended so did most of my bookings.

I had no agent or manager and was so desperate I accepted a booking at Houlihan's in Los Angeles for $150, where I performed with fellow comedian Jon Melichar. It was depressing to stand onstage at

Houlihan's, fighting for the audience's attention, while remembering I had actually shared a spotlit stage with Sammy Davis Jr.

I also went to Canada for the pilot of a game show called *Bafflegab*, hosted by newcomer Pat Bullard. One night I sat alone in my apartment watching *Saturday Night Live*, featuring Kevin Nealon, Dennis Miller, and Dana Carvey.

"I'm forty years old—what happened?" I asked myself.

28

Engelbert Humperdinck

I needed steady work, and with that goal in mind I signed with a new manager, Rick Bernstein, who had managed the career of Steve Landesberg. Right away I landed an opening spot with Andy Williams at Harrah's Reno. What was Andy Williams like? Your guess is as good as mine. We said hello on opening night and good-bye on closing night. That March I got a job opening for Kool & the Gang at Caesar's Palace in Vegas and was stunned when their manager told me they might have more work for me in the coming year. That was great news because I needed a salary I could count on. My *Star Search* money wasn't going to last forever.

I'd heard that Engelbert Humperdinck was in the market for a comic. "Engelbert is good to his people. Johnny Dark was with him for four years." So said Bonnie, my friend and former catering assistant who now sold real estate in Vegas. I changed my plane reservation to stay in Vegas and go to the Hilton to the Engelbert Humperdinck show. Bonnie's husband, Chris, knew Engelbert's drummer and got me invited to Engelbert's dressing room, the same facility once used by Elvis himself. The room was filled with flowers and gifts and people, but the most decorative thing in the room was the star, one of the handsomest men I'd ever seen. All I had a chance to say was, "If you ever need an opening act, I've had a lot of experience." I gave him a video tape and a press package and went back to LA.

I wanted this job as badly as I'd ever wanted any job in my life.

*S*tarting my new career as a comedian in 1982.

*J*ay Leno always had time for aspiring comics. We met
at the Improv in Hollywood, 1982.

*B*ob Hope came to see me perform at the Ice House in Pasadena, summer of 1986.

*B*uddy Hackett stopped backstage when I was opening for Engelbert at the Westbury Theatre, summer of 1987.

*O*pening for Jerry Seinfeld in Oklahoma City.

*O*pening for Pat Paulsen in Sacramento.

*O*pening for Bob Saget in Tulsa.

*W*ith Sinbad at a *Star Search* taping in 1986.

*M*y homemade sequined dresses sparkled on TV. We considered
making this book bigger to incorporate the hair.

*W*inning on *Star Search* with Ed McMahon . . . and winning in love with Denis.

THE '86 GRAND CHAMPIONS

KENNY JAMES
Male Vocalist

CHRISTOPHER & SNOWY
Dancers

JENNY JONES
Comedy

PEGGI BLU
Female Vocalist

DEVIN DEVASQUEZ
Spokesmodel

TCHUKON
Vocal Group

SCOTT THOMPSON BAKER
Leading Man

CYNDI JAMES-REESE
Leading Lady

*S*ammy Davis, Jr. came to Father and Roula's house in Florida for dinner.

*O*n tour with Engelbert Humperdinck in Hawaii, December 1987.

*W*hoopi visits backstage at Universal Amphitheater, June 1987.

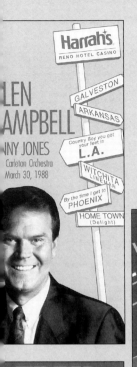

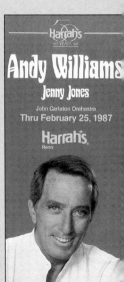

*O*pening for Tony Bennett in Atlantic City, March 1988.

*T*he Girls' Night Out logo said it all.

*O*pening for Smokey Robinson at Bally's, Atlantic City, December 1987.

1971

1975

1980

1983

986

1988

A mini-history of head shots from the past.

*O*ut for pizza with mother in Playa Del Rey, around 1984.

*P*hoto taken by police before I was jailed in New Jersey, July 1984.

I was smiling at Denis moments before our parasailing mishap in Fort Myers, Florida.

I had to wade through the flowers in my office on September 16, 1991, the day *The Jenny Jones Show* debuted.

*R*oula getting ready to appear on Jenny Jones to meet Mr. Right.

*M*y assistant, Dana. Is she gorgeous or what?

*T*yler on the job with Ed.

*T*he evolution of my hair since I started my talk show.

*F*un on the job—Ed, Debby, and yours truly. I still think I would have made a good chicken.

In a matter of days I got the call. Engelbert was opening in two days and needed an opening act. "Where?" I asked, bubbling with excitement. "Reno? Tahoe? The Amphitheater?"

"No. You're going to Atlantic City."

Once again I prayed the Atlantic City audience would be kind to me, and once again those prayers were answered. But by the second night, I'd noticed something odd—the front row looked the same. It consisted of the same women in the same seats, just wearing different clothing from the previous night. And they remained there through closing night, when rumors were flying backstage that I'd be offered a contract.

After the show, Engelbert called me aside and asked me if I would do the rest of the year. I was ecstatic and immediately called Mother with the good news.

"I thought you were coming here to tape *Bafflegab*," she said.

"Well, I had to cancel that."

"I don't know why you would cancel *Bafflegab* to open for this singer."

That was my mother.

Our next booking was Las Vegas. Opening night came, the curtain went up, and I walked on. I was so stunned by what I saw I almost stopped in my tracks. The front row in Vegas was filled with the same women as Atlantic City seated in approximately the same seats, wearing new outfits. I inquired and learned that the women I saw night after night formed a core group of fan club members who followed Engelbert's show religiously, especially in 1987, his twentieth anniversary tour. They were women in their forties and fifties, some of whom had been fans since Engelbert first started out twenty years earlier. I'd never seen anything like it. Not with Wayne Newton, or Sammy Davis Jr., or any other star with whom I'd worked. I think it was because he was such a romantic singer that he brought romance—realistic or not—into their lives. I could understand the need, too.

The various fan clubs had names like Engelbert's Cleveland Gypsies, Enge's Birds of Paradise, Enge's Flaming Hearts, and the Humper Dears. Being loyal fans didn't get them free show tickets or hotel rooms or transportation, and those women spent a lot of money traveling around to see his shows. Engelbert knew all of them and appreciated their fanatic devotion. They even decorated every one of his dressing rooms before the shows, which explained the unusually festive atmosphere I'd seen at the Hilton. They blew up balloons, placed flower arrangements on all the tables, and left a stack of gifts for him, mostly handmade: embroidered towels, cookies, cakes, and other baked goods.

After the show Engelbert often invited them back to the dressing room, where they showed off photo albums filled with pictures of Engelbert posing with these women at various performances throughout his career. He graciously examined each handmade cake or embroidered bathrobe and personally thanked the woman who'd brought it. And he posed for more pictures to be placed in those treasured photo albums.

I'd never worked before a primarily female audience, especially not the same one every night, but Engelbert, or Enge, as he was called, talked to me about them and told me not to worry, just to do my best.

"I think they'll like you," he said reassuringly. "And if they do, they'll be your fans forever."

I saw a lot of those women, at every venue from Vegas to Parsippany to Cohasset to the Catskills. When the tour bus arrived and we'd check into the hotel, they'd be waiting in the lobby.

"Is Engelbert with you?"

"What time will he be getting here?"

"How is he?"

I didn't have the heart to tell them he'd already gone in the back door and up to his room.

On those rare occasions when Engelbert did walk through the lobby where the women had been waiting for hours, they kept their distance and respected his privacy. They even knew his wife and children. If he stopped and talked to them, they loved it; if he was in a hurry and swept through the lobby, they just waved.

They always stopped by to see me after they finished decorating Engelbert's dressing room, and I could usually count on getting some cookies or a little cake, maybe some flowers, if Engelbert's dressing room was too small to hold all the arrangements they'd brought. I started looking forward to seeing them, and I made sure I always had some new material so they'd never get tired of my act. And I found myself writing material specifically for women, a concept that would have a mind-boggling impact on my future.

Touring with Engelbert allowed me to work some of the best theaters in the country: Radio City Music Hall, Irvine Meadows, the beautiful Chicago Theatre, and Universal Amphitheater in Los Angeles. In fact it was before our opening-night show at the Amphitheater that I made my usual stop in Enge's dressing room, waded through the flowers, and was stunned to see Whoopie Goldberg standing there among the well-wishers. It turned out that Whoopie's mother was a huge fan of Engelbert's and wanted to meet him. And I was a fan of Whoopi's. So I approached her and asked if she would mind taking a photo with me. She couldn't have been nicer. I'd met a lot of performer-type stars, but it was pretty cool to have my picture taken with a movie star.

The thing I admire most about Engelbert is his ability to stay current. His band is young and contemporary, his look is constantly changing, and he continually updates his show. He happened to see me wearing my traveling clothes—a pair of pants, a casual shirt, and flat-heeled shoes. My hair was looser, and I was wearing very little makeup. Engelbert kept staring at me with a pensive look in his eyes, and finally he approached me. "You really ought to think about doing your show dressed like that," he said. "It's much more contemporary than the sequins."

It was good advice. I didn't realize just how much my glitz was putting me into a dated Vegas-type category.

I didn't pay sufficient attention to what Enge had told me, but I usually did put good advice to work. For example, Buddy Hackett stopped by once and gave me some pointers. We were working a club in New England with a stage-in-the-round that turned slowly as you did your show. I had never worked in the round before so I performed in the center, thinking more of the audience could see me. After he watched me work he pulled me aside and told me to go right up to the edge.

"You're not connecting," he said. "Don't be afraid to go out there and get close to the audience. And get rid of the spotlight."

He was right. I started working the perimeter, and without the spotlight I could see the audience. It was much better.

Mother's Day, and after

Mother softened a little about my opening act job when I invited her to attend Engelbert's grand opening at the Las Vegas Hilton on Mother's Day. I sent her an airline ticket to Vegas, rented her a wheelchair, bought her a beautiful beaded blouse to wear to opening night, and vowed that this visit would be a positive experience for both of us. I was surprised she chose such a bright and colorful blouse, since it did not match her personality. I offered to take her shopping for more clothes, but she declined.

"We entertain ourselves by watching television and playing games, not by spending money," she said. "And I don't want to go out shopping. I don't know why you always have to be doing something."

I remember standing there in our hotel room and thinking, She doesn't like me at all, and there is nothing I can do to change it. Still, I had promised myself I wouldn't let this trip turn negative, so I let it drop. I knew that my high energy made her tired, so I chalked her comments up to that.

Only one thing I did during that trip really pleased her. Since the florist was closed that evening I made her a Mother's Day corsage out of my dressing room flowers. Maybe it was because she knew I'd made it myself, or more likely because she knew it hadn't cost any money, but Mother was genuinely touched by the corsage.

"I'm glad I came, Jenny," she said, with tears in her eyes.

I arranged front row seats for the show, and Mother loved Engelbert, even more so when we visited in his dressing room and he charmed her. I could see why his fans adored him. He really knew how to make a woman feel special. Once she'd seen the show, she actually seemed happy. She always loved the glitz and glamour of Las Vegas, especially the slot machines. Maybe that's why she never enjoyed my work in comedy clubs, because after seeing the Cover Girls on the Strip, everything else seemed dismal.

I didn't see her drink anything but coffee during her entire stay. I flew back to Los Angeles with her so she could catch her flight back to Canada. She cried when we said good-bye at LAX and told me she appreciated everything. The next day I was shocked when she called.

"I called to say thank you," she said. "It was the best trip of my life."

But as gratifying as her comment was, I knew her approval was always subject to her whims, and those whims were never more evident than on my birthday that June.

Mother took a train to Port Huron, Michigan, to help me celebrate. The band offered either to take us out to dinner or have a barbecue at the motel where we were staying. I picked the barbecue, because it sounded like fun, and I thought Mother would enjoy it.

Mother seemed to have a good time, and I even wondered if her trip to Las Vegas a month ago had somehow caused us to turn a corner. Maybe we could get back to being friends, like we'd been briefly when I first left home and started playing in bands. But as soon as we finished our barbecue and went back to the motel room, Mother started in on me. It didn't take long to know she had a private agenda attached to this trip.

"Liz is getting married again," she said, "and she asked me to ask you to give her five thousand dollars toward a down payment on a house."

"Five thousand dollars is a lot of money, Mother," I said.

She shrugged. "That's no more than you did for John and Roula."

"I'll have to think about it," I said. Liz and I hadn't spoken much over the past twenty years.

"Well, why don't you give her two thousand as a wedding present and loan her five thousand," Mother countered.

Now the amount was up to seven thousand and Mother knew

I was not likely to be repaid. Finally she got a smug look on her face. "Your father told Liz that if she ever wanted money just to call you. He said you've got lots of money."

So there it was out in the open. If Father condoned the idea, it was OK. I never asked him about it because either way, it didn't matter. I sent Liz the money and wondered how we had all grown so far apart. (Could Mother's affair still be playing a part in our family relationships? I remembered a line in my diary as recently as 1984 that read, "Called Father who said Liz accused him of getting rid of Mother and the kids so he could have an affair with Roula. Now they're not speaking.")

Every time I phoned my mother that summer, she was depressed. Her circulation problems were worse than ever, and the doctor told her she might even lose a toe. I tried to talk her into quitting smoking, or at least trying to cut down, but she wouldn't even discuss it.

"I don't want to prolong my life," she said during one conversation. "I don't enjoy anything anyway. All I do is buy groceries and do laundry. And I only get eight thousand dollars a year to live on."

Well, what can you say to that? I asked her if I could help in any way. Did she want money?

"No, thanks. I don't need it."

Did she want the car I'd been wanting to buy her?

"No," she said. "Where would I go?"

Engelbert was devoted to his mother, and when she became ill that September he canceled the last few days of our Vegas engagement and immediately flew to England. Jeffrey Osborne filled in for Enge, and I was supposed to continue on as Jeffrey's opening act, but at the last minute they hired Byron Allen.

I used the off time to do *Super Dave* for Showtime, which taped in Toronto. Also on the bill were the Smothers Brothers and Gallagher. Who would have guessed that Gallagher would one day bring his Sledge-O-Matic on *The Jenny Jones Show*?

Here's a new car—now do you like me?

The next time I decided to go to London and check on Mother, I went bearing gifts—new clothes and soft shoes that wouldn't hurt her bad toe. She accepted them without comment and started complaining about Father and Roula.

"They're nothing but freeloaders," she said accusingly. "You'll never get rid of Roula, and you have no obligation to her once your father dies."

I didn't have much to say about her grievances, since I knew any discussion involving what I'd done for Father and what I hadn't done for Mother and Liz was a no-win situation. I did ask her if she'd changed her mind about the car, and she said no. When I had to leave, I tucked a few hundred dollars into her purse.

I called her a few days later and asked her if she'd found her little "surprise."

"Oh, it wasn't much of a surprise," she said. "But I've been thinking. Why don't you buy an apartment here in London and let me rent it from you?"

I was stunned. Every time I'd broached the subject of moving her into a nicer place, she'd balked.

"I thought you said you'd never move," I said.

"I never said that."

I told her that the next time I went back we would look at some property. A few days later she phoned to say she'd changed her mind and wanted the car instead. "That's wonderful!" I said. "We'll go shopping for a car as soon as I can get back." The next day Liz phoned to say she could help Mother buy the car and suggested we have the title put in her name. I declined her offer of help, went to London, and paid twelve thousand in cash for the new car.

Mother was truly excited about her new car but nervous about driving, especially since we purchased the vehicle in the evening, and by the time the paperwork was done it was dark. So I drove us home, and we waited until the following morning for her to test it. While she drove slowly through the neighborhood, it occurred to me that she'd not driven in years, and I wondered if too much time had elapsed for her to relearn the skill. And then a much more somber thought occurred to me. *What if she gets drunk and then drives?* I found consolation in the fact that she drove very slowly, mostly in the right lane, and she did not plan to drive at night. A new car was not the only thing Mother was excited about. She was falling in love.

It's better than what I had in the old country

It took a long time for Father and Roula to decide on a home in Las Vegas. I felt it was because they wanted a bigger, more ostentatious home than my budget would allow. The price range I felt safe with was around $100,000. Their previous homes were sprawling and very nicely furnished, and all the ones in my price range didn't impress them. Then Father decided he wanted to build. He said, "I want to show off. After all, you're a star and should have something to be proud of." I offered to give him $10,000 down and $800 per month, which was still all I was willing to invest.

One day Roula asked me how much I was making with Engelbert. "Five thousand a week," I said.

"Then you should have twenty thousand in a month," she responded.

I didn't waver, and finally they agreed on a two-bedroom condo in a beautiful golf course community. Here's a quote from my diary on the day we made the down payment:

> *I put a deposit on the condo but knew in my heart they wanted a mansion. I asked Dad how he liked it, and he said, "It's better than what I had in the old country." That hurt me so much I will never forget it. Once we finalized the deal, Roula cried and Dad said, "It's small."*

Father and Roula moved into their new place in December of 1987. They sold their house in Florida, hired movers, and came to

California. From there Denis and I drove them to Las Vegas in my sports car. The drive from LA to Vegas can seem pretty short, it's only 280 miles, but this one seemed to go on forever. Roula and I sat cramped in the backseat with a small refrigerator between us. My right thigh was numb from the cold enamel and lack of circulation. As we finally headed into Vegas and the bright lights of the Strip got closer and closer, I was feeling more and more distant from my family.

Father, too, was preoccupied with finances. Maybe a bout with pneumonia caused him to start thinking about his own mortality, but he became obsessed with getting his memoirs published. Since he didn't know any publishers, he told me he was thinking about cashing in his mutual funds to pay a vanity press $14,000 to publish his life story. When I discouraged that idea, he asked me for names of Hollywood producers who might want to turn his story into a movie. I didn't know any Hollywood producers, but I told him I'd see what I could find out.

Not long after that, Father called and asked me to sign a legal document swearing that I'd take care of Roula if anything ever happened to him. He said Roula always felt that she was "nobody's mother" because they had been unable to have children. It hurt to think that Father believed I'd ever turn my back on my stepmother, but I signed a handwritten piece of paper for him.

Fears of flying and failure

The downside to touring on the road is the actual travel. I don't like to fly or to drive in any vehicle unless I'm at the wheel. It's an idiosyncrasy that a psychologist might label a control issue, and one that caused the only serious contention I ever experienced with Engelbert. One night, when one of the roadies was driving the bus and I tried to rest in a back seat, I thought the bus was not only going awfully fast but was also veering more than it should. I went up front, and it was obvious that the driver was high; I asked him to slow down, and he just laughed.

It was scary enough to think about what would happen if the bus simply ran off the road on one of those sharp curves in the Catskill Mountains. But those buses have the power of eighteen-wheelers. If we crashed into a car, the people inside it wouldn't have a chance. I didn't know what to do. I sat up front with the driver all night, prepared to grab the wheel if necessary, and when we arrived at the next venue I told Engelbert what had happened.

He approached the roadie, who told him he was only driving fast because I had challenged him to make it to the venue in record time. I tried to explain to Engelbert that there was absolutely no way I would ever say something like that. I am a careful, nervous driver. I'd rather drive than be driven because I never exceed the speed limit—and I go even slower if road conditions warrant it. But Engelbert believed his roadie. What hurt the most was that Engelbert thought I was lying.

That would never have happened in the Cover Girls. No one would have been summarily written off as a liar.

To Engelbert's credit, he knew I didn't want to ride with that driver any longer and he said I could travel in the private plane with him. It was only a four-seater, but he squeezed me in. I was exonerated some months later when the driver was exposed—by another roadie—as not only a drug user but a drug dealer. Exonerated or not, my confidence was shaken after that incident. No one had ever called me a liar before.

I toured with Engelbert the remainder of his twentieth anniversary tour. When it was over, nobody called about the following year, and suddenly I was back looking for work.

By now I felt like a seasoned pro, confident that I could work any room, any type of audience. That confidence would come in handy because my next booking was opening for Smokey Robinson in—you guessed it—Atlantic City. And what could be worse than facing that fickle audience again?

Doing it on New Year's Eve!

I didn't even want to imagine what a New Year's Eve audience in Atlantic City would be like. And opening for Smokey Robinson would be a major change after my past year of Enge's female crowds. On opening night I was onstage in the Bally's showroom, about twelve minutes into my act, when the stage manager whispered through the curtain, "Smokey's not ready. Do an extra five." I segued into another piece of material that I knew would add five minutes, and then headed again into my closing bit. Just as I was about to wrap it up, I heard the same guy whisper through the curtain.

"Smokey's still in his dressing room. Stretch some more."

So once again I switched gears and added material. I didn't want to waste my ending, because you always want to finish strong.

A few minutes later, the guy behind the curtain said, "Keep going."

I didn't want to keep going! The audience was getting restless and annoyed. They weren't there to see me, and I no longer wanted to see them. So I went into my last bit, said, "Thank you very much," and walked off.

Smokey was chatting with his backup singers, as if nothing was going on at all.

He smiled and thanked me for opening for him, and talked to the backup girls a few more minutes while the band kept vamping. He finally went onstage. I don't think he was being contrary or throwing his stardom around. He's just a casual guy. I joined him onstage at midnight, and we had champagne with the audience.

With that sip of champagne I also celebrated the end of my secure livelihood.

I spent days sitting around the condo, crying, cooking, and eating. I should have paid more attention to what Engelbert Humperdinck had told me. I was still making my own stage clothes, but my image wasn't working. Talent bookers considered me a Las Vegas act, dated by too much hair and too many spangles. Glitz is good in Vegas, but it doesn't necessarily work in the rest of the country. I didn't figure that out for some time, and kept pouring myself into those little minidresses, trying to find ways to make my hair even larger.

I thought my booking prayers were answered when Rick Bernstein got Triad to represent me, but months went by and still nothing happened. One day I saw an industry publication called *Just for Laughs*, with a listing of agencies and their clients. I immediately looked at the list of comedians who were signed with Triad to find my name, but it wasn't there. Triad hadn't even bothered to put my name on their list. Tears started running down my face, and I called Rick right away. He called Triad and asked why my name was missing from the roster. Triad's comedy department told him I just wasn't happening, brushing off Rick's inquiries with cruel finality.

"Jenny Jones hasn't got a career."

29

Father Is Gone

I spent most of 1988 auditioning for anything and working any job I could get. I booked a one-nighter in Florida with Sinbad, taped *Dick Clark Live*, and opened for artists like Tony Bennett and Glen Campbell. I spent my summer touring with Dionne Warwick and then Gregory Hines. I was a last-minute fill-in for *Evening at the Improv*. I read, unsuccessfully, for *The Fabulous Baker Boys* and was also a last-minute fill-in on *Hollywood Squares* because Martha Raye had canceled.

The invitation to tape *Hollywood Squares* couldn't have come at a worse time, because when they called me that morning I was lying down with an ice pack on my lower back. Every once in a while my back would just go out for a week or so, and ice was the only way to deaden the pain. This was my second day of immobility, but I was not about to turn down a national television appearance.

"Can you put together five changes of wardrobe and be here in two hours?"

"No problem."

Denis helped me off the couch, and as I pulled clothes out of my closet he packed them into a bag. I showered (he offered to help me do that too), and we were on the way to the studio. At some point during the drive I realized I had no back pain. In fact, we taped a week's worth of shows that day, so I needed to change clothes quickly between shows. I would switch my panty hose and wardrobe, put on those high heels, and race back to the set. Anyone who's had lower back pain knows the hardest things to do are get into a car, put on socks or panty hose, and—especially—wear high heels. Within an hour after I came home, my back pain had returned, and it lasted the rest of the week.

Ever since then I've firmly believed that you can postpone pain and illness and sometimes totally eliminate it. As with a lot of other things in life, if you believe it, you can make it happen. I know I've come to work many mornings with menstrual cramps, but they're not convenient when I have to work, so I make them go away until later in the day.

I taped *Hollywood Squares* several times, in awe of some of the big stars. Who could have known that some of them would soon be appearing on *The Jenny Jones Show,* stars including Richard Simmons and Toni Tennille, who was nice enough to loan me a pair of earrings when I appeared with her on *Squares.* I got to thank her again when The Captain and Tennille appeared on *Jenny Jones.* And who could have known I'd soon be appearing on *The Joan Rivers Show?*

During our meal break, Joan gave me some good advice about appearing on *Hollywood Squares.* Being a comic herself, she suggested that I write my own responses to the questions and not use the jokes that were written by the writers. (Also, a stage manager on *Hollywood Squares,* John Zook, was to become the associate director of *The Jenny Jones Show.* Small world, show biz.)

That year I was subpoenaed to provide information regarding some work I had done for my ex-husband, Buz. He had operated a business producing educational audiocassettes, using famous voices like Tommy Lasorda, Pat Boone, Vincent Price, and Billy Dee Williams. Buz hired me about two years after our divorce to help out in the office, but I had little involvement in his affairs. Without warning, the business closed down, and the next thing I knew, federal investigators were at my door asking a lot of questions. I gave them what they wanted and was never contacted again. After working with my ex-husband, the thought of Mother working at Sophie's with Roula and Father didn't seem so bizarre.

Family matters

"Malignant" and "terminal" are vile words. I was to hear them often over the next year, and they never became commonplace, never lost their malevolence. It started in October of 1988, when Mother called from the hospital in London, where she had just undergone a painful biopsy for a spot on her lung. Mother said she thought the doctors were misleading her, that there was no spot on the X ray and they put her through all that pain for nothing. I called and spoke with her physician. He said she told him she had felt no pain, and anyone could see the spot on the X ray. The tumor was malignant and had to be removed. Mother insisted they postpone the surgery for a week because I was on *Hollywood Squares*.

Liz and I both flew to London for the surgery. I went to the hospital on the day of her operation, but Liz wouldn't join me, saying it wasn't that serious. I assumed she had her own reasons for wanting to be alone. I continued to visit Mother every day and felt helpless seeing her connected to tubes and then doing painful breathing exercises. She finally said she was bored, so I offered to rent her a television. "I have no time to watch TV," she snapped.

Six months later Father's health began to deteriorate rapidly, and Roula asked me to come to Las Vegas. I don't think I fully understood how sick he was until I arrived, to find a gaunt, weak old man who clung to me and began to sob. I had never seen my father dependent before that day.

All Roula seemed to know was that his liver was failing, and since his test results were written in medical jargon they were meaningless to me. I tried to call his doctor, but he never called back, and I found myself wondering if Father had somehow alienated him. As sick as he was, my father was still capable of being belligerent.

I called a doctor in Los Angeles and read the report over the phone. He translated the language to layman's terms. My father had fluid in both lungs and the abdomen, an enlarged liver, prominent lymph glands at the aorta, and vomit around the lung and heart sacs. The doctor said it was bad but, not knowing Father's complete medical history, he was reluctant to speculate more. Armed with that information, I called his family doctor in Canada. He was very diplomatic and cautious, but it was clear he believed that Father was terminal, with two or three months left at best. The question is, he said, does John want to die in the hospital or at home?

I could only stay until the end of the week, but even in those few days I could see what Roula faced in taking care of Father. He was quarrelsome, combative, and not always coherent. Everything Roula and I did was wrong. I tried to help him with some paperwork, and he shouted, "Do you think I am stupid?"

I tried to give Roula a break every few hours by sending her on some small errand, and the minute she was out of the door Father was berating her. He criticized her housekeeping, and said she continually lost his things. Then he went back to something that happened over a year ago. "I asked her to bring me an orange," he said, "and she brought me a whole orange—and a knife! She expected me to peel it myself!" He said he didn't know what would happen if he died, because Roula couldn't function without him. He said she couldn't even draw his bath properly; it was always either too hot or too cold. "How could she be so inconsiderate?" he asked. "Isn't she here to serve me?"

I let the servant reference pass, reassuring him that Roula loved him and would do anything in the world to make him happier or more comfortable. "Oh, I know that," he said grudgingly. "I love her. I just don't like the way she does things." He continued to list her shortcomings. At that point I felt sorrier for Roula than I did my father. She was put down and berated by him every day of her life. The scars of physical abuse would have been no less damaging than this kind of psychological damage. I wondered if he had ever hit her.

"I can't walk, I can't have sex, and I can barely talk. I am living for nothing," he said.

"As long as you are alive, that's what's important," I told him.

"That's easy enough for you to say," he declared.

"I think you should check into the hospital until you get your strength back," I said. "If you can just build up your energy, you might be able to fight this."

Father said he didn't need strength or energy. He wanted to pray. After that trip to the Far East, when he proclaimed himself an atheist, I had no idea to whom he planned to pray. And neither did he, as it turned out. He began his "prayer" by repeating his lack of faith. "I don't like preachers and churches. I don't believe in God or heaven," he said, lifting his face up toward the heaven he didn't believe in. "When you die, you just die."

After he finished his disavowal of all things religious, he pulled a body-building type of photo of himself at about age twenty from his drawer and handed it to me. "Look at me back then, Jenny. And just look at me now. Why does this have to happen to people?"

I couldn't answer him, because I was asking myself the same question. I couldn't stand seeing him scared and hurting.

He shoved the photo back in the drawer and sat staring at the wall for a bit. Then he turned and asked me if I had any good news about my career. I had to admit it was in something of a holding pattern. "This isn't the time to talk about me and my career," I said.

"You need to come up with something different," he said, in a sad, flat tone. "Otherwise you'll never make it."

I promised to do my best.

The right to know

That night, Roula and I argued at length about what to tell Father. I thought it was obvious from what he had said that he believed he was going to die, and I felt he should be told that his doctors agreed. But Roula remained steadfast in her desire to keep him in the dark because she feared he would give up. I believed he should have been allowed to make that choice for himself. And I believed he needed permission to die. But Roula didn't want him told, and against my better judgment I complied with her wishes.

We did agree that Father should be in the hospital. I couldn't help but think that if he'd been there all along, he might have had treatments that could have given him a slightly better quality of life. When Roula and I talked with him about it, he seemed only interested in the new recliner he'd purchased shortly before he took a turn for the worse.

"I hate this new chair," he complained to Roula. "It hurts my back. The old one we put in the garage never hurt my back."

"Well, let's go get the old one," I said.

"No! It looks ugly."

"Then throw a blanket over it, Father! How can you be worrying about a ratty chair when you ought to be in the hospital?" I couldn't believe that with all that was happening, his main concern was whether his chair looked ugly! It shouldn't have surprised me. His whole life had been about show.

He sank down in the new recliner and pouted. To Roula's and my relief, he did agree to check into the hospital. I said I'd visit him soon. Father knew I was booked to work on a cruise ship in a few weeks.

"What about that cruise?" he asked. "You're still going, aren't you? I'm not that sick, am I?"

"No, no," I said quickly, "of course I'm still going. I'll see you when I get back."

"OK," he said, seemingly satisfied with the plan.

I had managed to handle things fairly well until I drove them to the airport the next day, as they headed for Canada for Father to be hospitalized. We took him to the gate in a wheelchair; he was too weak to walk that far on his own. Before boarding he stood up and slowly went over to the window to look at the plane. As always, he was well attired. How like Father, still to be dressed smartly in pressed pants and a sport coat; he didn't have his health, but he still had his pride. I followed him, afraid he might fall, and noticed he had lost so much weight the bones in his back and shoulders were pushing through his jacket.

I started to cry and walked away so he wouldn't see me.

As soon as Father was checked into the hospital, I phoned his physician to try and get a better picture of his prognosis. The doctor said

Roula was making life very difficult for the nurses, she was so afraid someone would let it slip that there was no hope for his recovery.

"And are you sure there is no hope?" I asked.

"There are five stages to leukemia, and your father is in the fifth stage. I give him six months at the most."

Well, I thought, six months is better than two or three months, which he'd predicted earlier.

I spoke with Roula at the hospital, and Father's bad disposition remained the same, though I couldn't blame him. She said his testicles had swollen so badly that for the first couple of days in the hospital he wouldn't allow anyone to touch them when he was bathed. He relented when a nurse explained that they were trained to wash sensitive areas, and that his condition depended on his staying sanitary.

I could hear Father asking Roula for the telephone. When she handed it to him, he could barely whisper.

"Jenny, would you please send me a picture of yourself so I can put it on my wall?" he asked. "I want everybody to see my daughter the celebrity."

Tears rolled down my face as I assured him I would send one.

"And Jenny," he went on, his voice gaining some strength, "make sure it's the one where you're standing with Bob Hope."

A couple of days later, Liz and I were discussing Father's health when she told me that Mother was indifferent to Father's situation.

"Maybe that's just her way of dealing with it," I suggested. After all, she had few good memories of her former husband, and she'd recently had cancer surgery. On the other hand, Mother tended to be indifferent to most everything.

I planned to cancel my upcoming job on the cruise ship. But Father's doctor called and told me he was responding to treatment and might even be up and around a little by the time I returned. I wasn't sure what to do, but I decided to go. Just before boarding the ship with Denis in San Juan, I phoned the hospital, and Roula told me Father was running a little fever but other than that his condition was the same. I spoke to him, but his voice was hoarse and the conversation very brief. "I'll see you soon," I said. "Bye, Father."

Four days later we docked in Miami, and as soon as I could get to a phone I called the hospital. Roula told me Father had lost some weight.

"How much does he weigh?" I asked.

"A hundred and twenty-five pounds." She was whispering as though she didn't want him to hear. I was shocked. He normally weighed close to two hundred pounds! I didn't know how this could happen so rapidly. I immediately wondered if he really was OK, as Roula had said when I left, or if she didn't want me to know the truth either.

"He's lost weight but he's not doing badly," she said, insisting that it wasn't necessary for me to cancel my job and fly to Canada. I tried to talk to him, but he sounded groggy. Roula said it was the medication. I decided to finish the cruise.

Two days later, Denis and I were exploring the ship and had decided to try playing shuffleboard when I heard my name being paged. I thought it was the office calling with my show time for that night.

When I got to a phone, the ship's operator said, "Elizabeth Stronski is calling from London, Ontario. You can take the call in your room." I ran back to the cabin, praying that she merely wanted to give me an update on Father's condition.

"I have a shock for you," she said. "Father is gone. He died at five A.M. of pneumonia."

She explained that Father Tony, a Catholic priest, had come earlier in the day to ask him if he wanted the last rites, and Father had said he did. So much for his atheism. Father Tony was actually the second attempt at last rites. A Greek Orthodox priest had come at Roula's request, but when he learned that Father was a Roman Catholic he refused to perform the rites. Roula's brother, Tom, became enraged and physically threw him out of the room. I told Liz that Denis and I would fly back as soon as we could make arrangements to get off the ship.

"There's no need to do that," she replied. "He donated his body to medical science. We aren't having a service."

I still feel torn about not being with my father when he died. The last time I saw him in Las Vegas, he said, "I want to die with Roula holding one hand and you holding the other."

In a way, though, I'm glad I didn't have to see him again in his ravaged condition, and I am happy he didn't have to linger in his misery. Yet I would have liked to talk with him one last time, and I think he should have been told he was dying. I thought he might be expecting to get well, right up until the priests started appearing in his room. What must he have thought when they started talking about last rites? Did he wonder if we'd known and hidden it from him?

If he'd known he was dying, he might have asked to see his daughters when he felt himself slipping away, and I might have made it back in time to be with him in those last moments. There may have been things he wanted to say to us, things he wanted done. I couldn't forgive Roula for not telling him the truth.

Father died in May of 1989, just two weeks before his seventy-fifth birthday. Afterward I remembered the story he had so often told us over Sunday dinner of when he was a young man and a psychic predicted that he would die at the age of seventy-four.

30

Hitting Bottom

Father's death in 1989 took the wind out of me and probably contributed to one of the worst periods of self-doubt I've ever experienced. I didn't want to be a struggling comic for ten more years, yet that appeared to be my future. For the first time in five years I couldn't pay my rent. Even the cruise ships didn't want me back. What if I'd had my chance and I'd blown it?

Rick Bernstein had done as much as he could, and he and I both knew it. He had even said to me a few months earlier, "If something doesn't break soon, you may have to accept the reality that you just don't have it." And he was my manager. I knew he was right. I had been turned down by some of the best: ICM, William Morris, the Comedy Store, Rollins and Joffe, the Spotlight Agency, Irvin Arthur, Shapiro-West, Arthur Spivak, *The Tonight Show*, *Letterman*, Brillstein-Grey.

I remember going to the comedy awards thinking I needed to be seen and photographed. As I made my entrance in front of the paparazzi, they asked me to step aside so they could get a better shot of Mary Hart. I remained humble.

The most difficult and humiliating rejection came when I was hired by NBC to do a pilot for a comedy series. I was elated beyond belief. This was my dream come true. The show was called *Nurse Bob*, and I was hired to play one of the leads, along with Tim Thomerson and Norman Fell (another future *Jenny Jones* guest). NBC had big plans for the show. Brandon Tartikoff even came to the first rehearsal. Three days into rehearsal, I was fired. Once again, I had disappointed everyone.

To say my career in stand-up comedy was an emotional roller coaster would be an understatement. The ups and downs are evident of my diary entry of March 26, 1989: "For the first time in my life I'm no longer convinced that I can do anything. Maybe I had my chance and blew it. I don't want to be a pathetic struggling 'young comic' for the next ten years. But I refuse to live with limitations for the rest of my life. If I accept limitations, I reject my dreams."

The next day *The Arsenio Hall Show* called and invited me to appear. My confidence was so low I assumed someone had canceled at the last minute. Then Arsenio called me personally to discuss my appearance, but I kept thinking it was a joke. In the end, I did appear and thought I did well. The next night I had a spot to do at the Improv so I went a little early so everyone could tell me how well I did on the show. I figured I could use a few kudos. When I arrived at the door, though, the doorman said, "Can I see your ticket please?"

I decided it was time to tell Rick I was leaving, so I went to his office and sat down, prepared to drop the bomb, until I found I was but one of several bombardiers that day. We started chatting. The first thing he told me was that his assistant had just quit. He said she just kicked the fax machine and left.

"As if that's not bad enough," he continued, "Alexandra just told me she wants a divorce."

"Rick, I'm so sorry," I said, shocked. I had recently been to his wedding.

"I can't believe they both happened today, but life goes on," he said. I could see the pain in his eyes. "So, what's up?"

"I just came by to see if you wanted to have lunch."

Several weeks later I did leave Rick and once again started trying to find representation. After many phone calls and dead-end leads, a friend suggested a woman named Judy Thomas. We were told she didn't have an office but worked at home, partly because her husband was ill. So I called her, talked for a while, and she agreed to speak with me. It seemed almost too easy.

Denis and I drove to her apartment on Sunset Boulevard and knocked on the door. We heard a voice shout, "Come on in!" We stood there uneasily for a couple of minutes, and the voice shouted out again, "I said come on in!" So Denis pushed open the door, and we walked into the most bizarre apartment I'd ever seen. Things were stacked and strewn everywhere—boxes, books, magazines, show bills, you name it. A man sat watching television from a chair in the far corner, but he barely glanced at us as we made our way through the darkened room. In the middle of the room was a bed, and on it sat a large woman wearing a muumuu surrounded by stacks of papers, files, and notebooks. She had a telephone receiver tucked under her chin while she talked, a cigarette in one hand and a glass of scotch in the other. The way she was sitting I could only see her torso. I was relieved when she stretched out her legs.

But from what I could gather from her phone conversation, Judy talked a good game. She sounded like most of the fast-talking managers I'd been around, name-dropping, reassuring, promising, and cajoling. She hung up the phone, stubbed out one cigarette and lit another, took a swig of scotch, and said, "You must be Jenny Jones."

I stood there thinking I might as well kiss my so-called career good-bye. But nobody in those steel and glass offices downtown wanted to work with me, and I knew she had represented Brad Garrett, so I signed on for a project-by-project basis with the management company Judy Thomas ran from the middle of her bed.

It turned out that Judy's name-dropping wasn't a sham, she really did have a lot of good contacts, industry people she'd done business with for years and who would still take her calls. But I think most of them were just being kind for old times' sake, because during the six months I was with her I seldom saw any results beyond the seemingly friendly chats. She did get me some bookings, but there were usually attendant problems.

I learned quickly to double-check her instructions, since she often sent me to the wrong club, told me the wrong night, or quoted the wrong price. The volumes of scotch she consumed while she did business probably contributed to her lack of efficiency.

One of the bookings she got me was a pilot that I taped with another struggling comic, Tim Allen, at Penrod's in Miami, which was a nightclub popular with spring break partygoers. Tim and I each did monologues on a stage set up on the beach, and then we got into a hot tub together to do a comedy sketch. The whole thing was just a venue for viewing pretty college girls in bikinis, but I needed the $1,500. Thank goodness it never aired.

I lasted about six months with Judy. I had hit bottom, but, like an addict or alcoholic, I was the last one to know there was a problem.

Taking stock

It was time to either give up or take action. I chose action. At the time it was hard to think positive. On September 27, 1989, I wrote in my diary:

> *I feel totally worthless. The clubs don't want me. The agents don't want me. I have no value.*

I decided that my twenty-five-year investment in my career had to be worth something, but if I was going to survive I would have to reinvent myself. That process began with an honest analysis of Jenny Jones.

I made lists.

I am 43 years old.
I am perceived by the industry as not being hip.
I am not afraid of hard work.
I can take a good idea and make it come to fruition.
I need a good idea and a new look.

Next, I began to analyze my material. I watched tape after tape and decided my act seemed dated, just like my look. First, I changed the easier of the two: my look. I got rid of my spike heels, threw out the extra-hold hair spray, packed away the sparkle and the minidresses, and stopped wearing heavy makeup. Wearing less makeup was the hardest thing to do because I used to feel nicely hidden behind all that eyeliner; now I was exposed. It actually felt good to be natural, except for those fake breasts I was carrying around.

I then made my new contemporary-looking self sit down with all my material and went through it line by line. I divided all the bits into categories:

Dated Stuff/Never Do Again
Funny Stuff/Keepers
Good Ideas/Try

The more material I categorized, the bigger the Dated Stuff pile got and the smaller the Funny Stuff. Then I started noticing something. In the "Good Ideas" pile were tons of things that were funny to me, a woman, but I hadn't tried them out because I knew the men in the audience wouldn't find them amusing. I thought to myself, If I had an all-female audience, we'd have a great time with this material.

Why hasn't anyone thought of this?

That simple thought changed my life. Why couldn't I have an all-female audience? I thought. I'd done all my own promotion up until then. If I advertised my show as being "for women only/no men allowed," I knew they would come. Because I would come if I saw that ad. When women get together for girl talk, we can laugh for hours without having to explain ourselves.

I was encouraged by the fact that Engelbert's audience, which was mostly female, always laughed at my material. Just as I could see men's eyes glaze over when I did a bit about bad dates or leg waxing, I could see that the women always got it.

I went over all my material, stripping away jokes aimed at the men in the audience and adding more about women's experiences. I decided to try a more informal structure than most comics offered, creating a pajama-party atmosphere where the audience became a part of the act. I spent hours honing the lyrics to a song I planned to use as the show opener: "I Got a Bad Attitude," a song about PMS. It began to take concrete form; I could envision myself starting out with a song, doing about fifteen minutes of stand-up, incorporating some props, and then involving the audience for the rest of the show. Maybe, I thought, it would be enough of a novelty idea to draw crowds.

When I explained it all to Denis, he got a peculiar look on his face and slowly shook his head. "What's the matter?" I asked. "Don't you think it will work?"

"I think it will succeed beyond your wildest dreams," he said. "I think the concept is far bigger than you imagine."

I respected Denis's opinion, but I also realized he loved me and wanted to help me come back from my slump. I wondered if his heart was dictating his opinion. So I asked for a second and third opinion. First I called Bob Fisher, who owns the Ice House in Pasadena. He certainly knew comedy, so I asked him to meet me at Art's Deli in Studio City.

"What do you think, Bob?" I said. "Will it work?"

"It's hard to tell, because nothing like it has ever been done before." I was hoping he wasn't just sparing the feelings of an old friend, but he suggested I try it out. The next opinion came from David Stewart, who was managing Ray Combs.

"I'd definitely try it out," he said. "It could work."

To get a woman's perspective I called a friend of Denis's, Helen Gale, a former producer and personal manager. She also encouraged me to try it out.

I started putting together a press kit. I decided to call it "Girls' Night Out" and designed a logo using the international NO sign with a woman's leg crossing out a male's silhouette. The big question was, Where to try it out?

If it bombed and word got out, whatever was left of my career would surely be over. I decided to take it as far away as possible and chose Canada. So I called Yuk Yuk's in London, where I knew I wouldn't be turned down. If I could get a decent crowd response and a little good press on my home turf, I knew I could build on that bit of success to secure more bookings.

I negotiated with the manager that I would work just for the door receipts, and he could make money on the drink sales. That way there was no risk to him. I tried not to think about the risk to my career. I kept my fingers crossed that I'd make enough money to get back to California after the show.

I pasted up a flyer, printed a couple of hundred, and sent them to the club. Then I started working eight to ten hours a day putting together a show, writing material, and working on publicity angles, props, and music ideas.

I offered to do all the advance work, and sent the local paper a press release that read, in part:

> *It's an outrageous night of comedy and fun designed especially for women. It's somewhere between group therapy and a pajama party where we talk about everything from leg waxing to multiple orgasms. You can get up and share your pet peeves or just come to laugh like you never have before. No drag queens, please.*

Girls' Night Out

The club sold all two hundred and fifty tickets in one day. When I arrived at the club to do my show the manager said he'd been forced to turn down over a thousand women wanting tickets and admitted to scalping his wife's four tickets for $200. He had to shut the phones down because they wouldn't stop ringing. Newspaper and television reporters hovered at the door but were not allowed in.

I didn't expect that kind of response. In fact, it was scary because I didn't really have a show yet. This was just a test run. I expected to start slowly and build. But the sellout shored up my sagging self-image, and I went onstage with the confidence of a kid who doesn't know anything about failure. The audience clapped wildly when I started singing, to the tune of Patti LaBelle's "New Attitude":

> *My period's due, it's three days late,*
> *I wish men had to ovulate.*
> *I made a list of all the people I hate:*
> *I've got a bad attitude.*
>
> *And now there's zits on my face,*
> *I'm really depressed,*
> *And no one understands that I've got PMS.*
> *I'm feeling bad from my head to my shoes,*
> *And I'm so bloated I don't know what to do.*
> *I want to call up nuns and be rude:*
> *I've got a bad attitude.*
>
> *Out of control, my emotions are fried,*
> *And I've got cramps like I'm gonna die.*
> *Life's a bitch and so am I:*
> *I've got a bad attitude.*
>
> *I'm wearing a Stay-Free, a Maxi, a tampon, a Playtex,*
>   *and a Depends just in case,*
> *I'm having cheesecake, cookies, chocolate, M&M's, a quart*
>   *of ice cream;*
> *I'm gonna stuff my face,*
> *And then I'll make a double-fudge layer cake disappear*
> *And finish with a Midol and a six-pack of beer.*
>
> *Out of control, I think I hate men,*
> *I'll probably never have sex again.*
> *Let 'em beg to see me in the nude:*
> *I got a bad attitude.*
> *I want to break wind and be crude:*

I got a bad attitude.
I'm gonna get my ass tattooed:
I got a bad attitude.

The response to the song was staggering. Then I went into the stand-up.

Thank you so much! We've got so much to do, we gotta get going! First of all—the men's room is open tonight for all of us. Feel free to use it and leave the seat down. Second, get comfortable. Take your shoes off and put your feet up.

This is very open show, so if you've got something to say—say it! Come on up and take the microphone out of my hand. I'll come out there looking for you, too.

Anybody here know what a real labor pain is? That's when you find out that the guy who does the same job as you is making three times your salary.

OK, let's be honest, who's faked an orgasm in the past week?

"I did, last night!"

Well, let's hear you do it again!

What's your pet peeve?

"Old men with hairy backs wearing Speedos."

Anybody else?

"Ex-husbands who call from their Mercedes to say they can't pay the child support."

More?

"Men who think you really want a tongue shoved in your ear."

"Men who name their penises!"

So, anybody got a pet peeve about male gynecologists?

"Yeah, it's like going to a mechanic who never owned a car!"

I got the first of many standing ovations that night. Denis had been right—this idea was bigger than I'd ever dreamed. When I received my final standing ovation, I was overcome with emotion. The anxiety of not knowing what was going to happen was finally over. My career was back. I'd be able to pay the rent. I did it, and Mother was there to see it all happen.

When the room finally cleared out I sat at Mother's table, which of course was right up front, and said, "What did you think, Mother?" I knew full well there was no denying the overwhelming success of the evening.

"I couldn't even see you from here," she said. "You spent all your time in the back of the room. And I don't know what the big deal is about this women's show. It was so noisy, I couldn't hear anything anyway." She said my singing had improved but she hated the club.

I wouldn't let her spoil my moment, because also in the audience were some old friends of Father, whose words touched me. "Your father would have been very proud of you tonight." I wished he could have been there, but then I remembered: We wouldn't have let him in!

With the success of the London show behind me, I was able to get bookings almost as fast as I could dial the telephone. I made the show a no-risk deal, always asking for the door instead of a fee, with the venue taking the bar. I booked on Sundays or Mondays, when the club was usually closed or having an amateur night. Virtually every club I contacted wanted the show, so I booked them all. Now all I needed was a show.

I insisted on an all-female staff and decorated every room with balloons and funny signs to create a party atmosphere. I made up role-reversal games, like *The Dating Game*, with women taking on the male roles. One time a woman stuck her entire handbag inside her pants to duplicate a man's emphasis on penis size. We also had a lot of fun with game-show takeoffs. In one takeoff of *The $25,000 Pyramid*, I asked, "What do these three things have in common: a laundry hamper, a toilet bowl, and your G-spot? Answer: Things men can't hit with a target!"

After each show I sold Girls' Night Out T-shirts at the stage. It was really a great time for me. I spent all my time working on the show: writing new material, pasting up flyers, working on my mailing list, and booking myself into new venues.

It didn't take long before local television news shows were asking me for permission to film Girls' Night Out, but much as I loved the idea of the immediate publicity, I always turned them down. The mystery about what exactly happened at the show was as much a part of its attraction as the No Men Allowed rule. But female reporters were welcome. I'd tell them to wear casual clothes, comfortable shoes, no makeup, and no panty hose. I even told them not to shave their legs.

The shows got more outrageous as time went on. Everybody participated, and no topic was off limits. The age range was astonishing, from girls just barely old enough to get in the club to women in their seventies. The women were open, irreverent, and funny.

I asked outrageous questions and got outrageous answers. One time in Denver I asked if anybody had ever really located her G-spot. One woman got out a piece of paper, drew a map of its location, and passed it around the room! Another time, a seventy-five-year-old woman said her pet peeve was a man who exaggerated the size of his penis. The younger women in the audience just died laughing when that sweet little old lady started talking about men's equipment.

What a drag

I was serious about the show being for women only, and with a few exceptions we kept it that way. A lot of guys tried to come in drag, and since the spotlight was always in my eyes, it was hard to spot them. So the audience would help me out by pointing out the queens and demanding they be exposed. One night a woman walked through the back of the room, headed for the rest room. As soon as she went in, the audience members started saying that a drag queen who looked like Tom Hanks had infiltrated our party. I grabbed my wireless microphone and headed in after him to make the bust. The entire audience could hear me.

"Come on outa there, fella!" I said. "We know you're a guy, and we want you to know you are busted!"

The women in the audience were just roaring.

The toilet flushed, and that caused another big round of laughter from the audience. Then the Tom Hanks look-alike stepped out of the stall, still adjusting her skirt, and in a very icy feminine voice said, "I beg your pardon?"

I went back out to the stage, mortified.

"Big mistake," I said sheepishly.

I apologized, when she came back to her table, and got her name and address so I could send her flowers the next day. I truly felt terrible and never made that mistake again.

Men did make it past our scrutiny. After a show at Zanie's in Chicago, two women—or so I thought—approached me, and just as I started to thank them for coming, one of them said, "I'd like you to meet my husband, George." He was in one of the best drag outfits I've ever seen. He'd fooled everyone, looking so fine that he could have passed for female under a spotlight.

As it turned out, a lot of people liked Girls' Night Out. I couldn't keep up with the demand as I toured and sold out city after city. Within a month I had to hire an assistant, Brad Rivers, and a publicist, Dijon Aragon. I was setting attendance records in club after club—even the Montreal Comedy Festival—and being written up in magazines like *People* and *Time*! One day Dijon called me with exciting news. After all those years of trying to get booked on national television shows, I had a big one: *20-20* had called. They wanted to do a story on this overnight sensation with her "talk show" type comedy act.

I found out later that I only got the feature piece because another story was canceled at the last minute. But it didn't matter to me that it was a stroke of luck because my luck was about to change big time.

Wanted: On-Air Personality
Interested in people, curious, nonjudgmental,
humorous, and sympathetic.
Must not mind wearing panty hose every day.

Oh, the power of television! My segment on *20/20* aired on a Friday night. The following Monday my phone started ringing at 9 A.M. and didn't stop until after 7 P.M. I didn't have a manager or agent, so I fielded all the calls myself. Producer after producer called with offers of my own series, talk shows, game shows, production deals, and commercials.

I was astonished at the reaction.

Over the next weeks and months, I met with some of the people, listened to their offers, and tried to pretend I understood their television jargon. The person who impressed me the most was Jim Paratore, an executive with Lorimar Television, who offered me a daytime talk show. All right, I said, I'll do it on one condition—that it be different. I came from music and comedy, where the more original you were, the more successful you became. So after much discussion they agreed that we would offer an alternative to the issue-oriented programs; ours would be a fun, light daytime show. Things were happening at a very fast pace that summer, and I knew my life was about to change, but as to how much, I didn't have a clue.

31

My Kind of Town

The first change I learned about was geographic. I assumed the show would be taped in Los Angeles but was asked how I felt about moving to Chicago. With its abundance of production facilities and its ability to attract large studio audiences, Chicago had launched both the *Donahue* and *Oprah* shows.

I loved Chicago. My first impression of the city had been memorable. Several years earlier I'd flown in to perform stand-up comedy for the Metropolitan Life Group at the Drake Hotel. It was just before Christmas, and when my taxicab pulled onto Michigan Avenue the view took my breath away. The street was lined with beautiful skyscrapers and classic old buildings, and every tree along the Magnificent Mile was filled with tiny white lights. There were horse-drawn buggies sharing the roadway with the cars, and the weather was crisp and wintry cold, just like Canada.

It was an indelible first impression, and I happily agreed to relocate, especially since we had been experiencing more and more earthquakes in Southern California. Next to flying, earthquakes are second on my list of fears.

Jim Paratore also explained to me that with the large amount of production in Los Angeles, it wasn't always easy to get good audiences. That made sense; I myself had been solicited several times on the streets of Los Angeles to come and be part of a studio audience. I wanted to know more about my new prospective home, so I tuned in to the weather channel. (Nobody said my dream would be perfect.)

Mother sounded excited for me when I gave her the news, though I doubt if she grasped the magnitude of a nationally syndicated show. But then, neither did I. Her first response was "What time will it be on?" That question could have been interpreted one of two ways: (a) "I can't wait to tell the neighbors so they can watch" or (b) "I hope this doesn't interfere with my day." I chose the first way.

Roula, as expected, cried. They were tears of joy for me and sorrow for Father. Denis, who was about to sign a five-year contract with Disney Television as a production executive, gave me his blessing to move to Chicago, and we agreed to continue our relationship by long distance and see each other on weekends. It was a whirlwind, surreal experience for the first few months. I continued to fulfill my Girls' Night Out bookings, traveling all over the country. Every time I sat next to a stranger on a plane I wanted to scream, "Guess what? I'm getting my own talk show!"

Jim introduced me to dozens of promotion, marketing, publicity, and sales people who suddenly became part of my new life. There were photo shoots, video shoots, and interviews, including full-page ads in trade publications like *Broadcasting* and *Electronic Media*. When I saw my first big ad, which read "America's Hottest Traveling Talk Show Is Coming to Television," I still couldn't accept that it was me, feeling strangely separated from this new Jenny. Perhaps it was an unconscious act of self-preservation, so that if the "celebrity" Jenny didn't succeed, the "regular" Jenny wouldn't be a failure too. When the show became the fastest-selling talk show in television history, one of the subsequent ads read, "Jenny Jones Is Turning the Tide in Television Talk."

My reaction? Fear. I wondered how I could ever live up to their expectations.

Fasten your seat belt, it's gonna be a bumpy ride

I am a self-admitted control freak and a firm believer that "If you want something done right, do it yourself." That belief had served me well up until this point, but it soon became obvious that my role in *The Jenny Jones Show* was to be limited. In the summer of 1990 I flew to Chicago to tape the pilot, which is essentially a sales tool providing a sample of what the television buyer will be getting. By the time I arrived, the operation was in full swing, with a bustling staff of producers, writers, audience coordinators, and assistants.

I was escorted to my office, a bare room with a desk and a phone. I put down my purse, sat at the empty desk, and tried to figure out what I was supposed to do, since everyone was working on the show but no one was working with me. I wandered around the series of busy cubicles and offices. I was sure there must be something for me to do.

I met the woman who was hired to produce the pilot, Bonnie Kaplan. The first indication that I was not a full partner was when Bonnie asked me to leave her office so the producers could have a topic meeting. I walked out, confused.

This was not what I expected.

We taped three different shows over two days to put together the pilot. Our guests were all talkative and articulate, including actor Corbin Bernsen, model Carol Alt, and soap opera star Kim Zimmer. It was no effort to get them to talk, thank goodness, because back then I wouldn't have had any idea how to coax someone into opening up. I remember one of the producers trying to tell me about the "focus" of an interview. I thought, Focus? I'll be lucky to get through this without throwing up.

I was a nervous wreck, but I did get through the tapings, reading cue cards and doing what I was told. The tapings worked more because of the guests than the host. I said, "Tell me your story," and off they went. I wish I could tell you what the guests on those early shows had to say, but I was so nervous during the interviews I remember very little about them.

When the work was over, I was convinced I'd blown it and nobody had the nerve to tell me.

"You must be exhausted," said Jim.

"I am. So what do you think?"

Here's what he said: "You did a good job."

Here's what I heard: *It was awful. You have no talent.*

I was sure I was so bad they'd have to scrap the whole thing. I had to know the truth.

"Do you think it's good enough to use?" I asked.

"Oh, definitely, when it's edited." He was convincing, but I still wondered if he was just being kind. If the pilot wound up being any good, I thought, it would be due to the editor's good work, not mine. Every insecurity I'd grown up with and tried to bury came charging straight to the top.

I never felt that Bonnie had confidence in me, and I turned out to be right. I later found out that she predicted I would never make it—I wasn't good enough or smart enough—and the show would fail. It was just the kind of challenge I needed to shove those old self-doubts aside and try to prove her wrong.

Selling it was the easy part

Once the pilot was edited into a presentation tape, we went off to the NATPE convention in New Orleans in the hope of selling the show. When I previously represented *Star Search* at the same convention, I didn't have a clue what NATPE was all about. This is a trade show held each January, where television syndicators try to interest station buyers in their shows for the upcoming season. Every distributor is represented: Warner Bros., Disney, Multimedia, Paramount. They all have elaborate booths, and the stars of the shows make appearances to take pictures and sign autographs.

It's a giant entertainment schmooze-fest, and that week was one of the most exhilarating times I've ever had. I'd leave the booth a few minutes, and when I got back one of the salesmen would say, "We've got three more cities!"

Little did I know, selling it was the easy part.

Warner Bros. had purchased space on the side of the convention center and erected huge paintings of the stars of their shows. When I drove to the building and saw it—my face was twenty feet tall—I would have given anything for my father to have been in the car with me. He would have been stopping people on the street, saying, "That's my daughter, the celebrity!"

Ed McMahon stopped by the booth to say hi. He didn't mention his idea to me at the time, but a couple of months later I read in *USA Weekend* that Ed believed Jay Leno should pick a woman as his second banana, and Ed's picks were me or Rosie O'Donnell.

Among the talk shows being launched that season were *Realities* with David Hartman, *Up Late* with Ron Reagan, *The Gossip and Fame Show*, *The Chuck Woolery Show*, *The Maury Povich Show*, and Geraldo Rivera's *Now It Can Be Told*. There were some very well-known names in that list, yet our show sold faster than any of them.

By the second day of NATPE we had clearances in 70 percent of the U.S. market; the president of Warner Bros. domestic television distribution, Dick Robertson, said it was the fastest-selling show he'd seen in thirteen years.

That was great, but the pre-show hype was scaring me to death.

The Phil Donahue caper

I was being touted as some sort of "talk show goddess," and I was terrified that they'd all find out I wasn't. "Scared little girl" would have been a better description, because I had no understanding of the inner workings of talk shows and no good way to obtain the knowledge. If you want to be an accountant or a teacher or a lawyer, you can go to college to acquire the necessary skills. Sometimes you can intern to get on-the-job training. But there's no college course called Talk Show Host 101; I'd have to create a curriculum for myself.

Then I started thinking about how I'd learned things I needed to know thus far in my career. When I was getting into music, I bought records or went out to hear bands, and I'd learned to do stand-up comedy by watching other comics, so when I heard Phil Donahue was taping in Los Angeles for a week, I decided to go on a spy mission.

Although I wasn't on the air yet, I'd had my share of television exposure as a comedian, and they had already run ads for the up-coming talk show. I was afraid someone would spot me, so I pulled my hair back into a bun, got a pair of phony glasses, and wore a very conservative white blouse with a Peter Pan collar. (I'd always heard you shouldn't wear white on TV and hoped that would keep the cameras away from me.) I went to the studio and chatted in line with the other audience members, telling them I was just in town for a visit, omitting any mention of my role as talk show spy. They ushered me in and I took a seat in the back, where I thought I would be safe.

What I hadn't counted on was the fellow seated next to me—a Canadian tourist determined to be on American television. He had his hand in the air throughout the show, like the kid who knows all the answers in junior high. When Phil came into the audience and stood right next to me, my heart pounded harder than it had dur-ing my first night of stand-up at the Improv. Surely he had seen my face in the trades. I prayed he wouldn't recognize me, while at the same time I strained to see what was on those blue cards in his hand.

Phil went to several people in the audience, and I kept my head down like the junior high kid who knows *none* of the answers. Then he came right to the Canadian guy next to me and stuck the mike in his face. At one point I was sure Phil had noticed me and I thought, That's it. I'm dead. It's over. He knows. But I was wrong, because he finally walked on to another part of the audience and I could breathe a sign of relief.

It was the closest I could come to a talk show lesson, and I wasn't able to learn much except to satisfy my curiosity. Even his blue cards remained a mystery.

I can't remember the topic that day, something about celebri-ties, but I do remember Phil's black Reeboks. Many times since that day, I've stood out in my audience wearing panty hose and heels and envied him those tennis shoes. Several years later I felt kind of silly about my caper when Rikki Lake called us to book a seat in our audience. She was preparing to go on the air with her own show and wanted to check us out.

I just hope this is my last operation

In the middle of all the excitement over my upcoming talk show, I heard about a new implant called Misti Gold, made with a non-silicone polymer, which was having great success among women with a history of hardening. When my doctor told me my breasts could be 50 percent softer, that's all I needed to hear. I made an appointment for my fifth set of breast implants.

Denis begged me not to put myself through another surgery simply to have soft breasts, but I wouldn't listen. I wanted to do it before I went on the air, even though the timing was bad.

I had recently broken my shoulder in an ice skating fall. Denis and I had gone skating at the Ice Capades Chalet in North Hollywood. I had grown up skating every weekend and loved to glide around the ice. I even had my own skates, which I had purchased at a garage sale.

I hit a rut in the ice and fell full force on my left breast with my arms up. The whole time I was falling I felt like I was in slow motion. As soon as I landed, I knew something was wrong. Denis was taking a break so someone helped me to my feet but my arm didn't want to come down. When I forced it, I felt excruciating pain as it strangely popped into place.

Denis drove me straight to the hospital where I found out that I had dislocated my shoulder and broken the ball of the bone. I spent the next six weeks with an immobilized left arm.

The frustration of not being able to do things during those weeks brought me to tears many times. Try doing these things with one hand strapped to your side: Washing or combing your hair, manicuring your nails, putting on pantyhose, putting on a pair of pants, making a sandwich, putting in pierced earrings. God bless Denis. He did it all for me.

I was in the process of physical therapy and was almost able to raise my arm all the way up. I knew I would not be able to raise either arm for two weeks after implant surgery and that would be a big setback, but it was worth it to me.

A week after my surgery I went in for a post-op checkup. The doctor told me everything looked fine and to come back in a month. He left the examining room, and his nurse accompanied me to the door.

"Everything looks pretty good," she said, referring to my new scars.

"I just hope this is my last operation," I said.

"I heard both your implants were ruptured."

"Excuse me?"

"Oh, didn't the doctor tell you? They were both badly ruptured."

No, the doctor had not told me. In fact, when I had rushed to see him the day after my fall at the ice rink because I landed squarely on my left breast, he had checked both breasts and said, "They feel fine. No ruptures."

The truth is, no one can tell by just feeling, or even by a mammogram, if an implant is ruptured. The only way to see a rupture is with an MRI.

A week later, I started my shoulder therapy all over again. I also developed a mysterious red blotch on my chest. When I had it checked out, the doctor said he had no idea what was causing it and summoned a colleague for a second opinion. They seemed to view it as a curiosity but couldn't explain it. He treated me with antibiotics and an antihistamine, and after about six weeks it was gone. I should have been concerned about what the ruptured implants were doing to my overall health, but we had scheduled a trial run in Las Vegas, and I focused all my attention on learning my new job.

I had pushed for Vegas as the location because it had been my second home. Plus, Roula was there, and while that played a small role in the decision, there were bigger issues. The show would air only in Las Vegas, which was not a metered market, so we could avoid being under a ratings microscope while taping a six-week trial. And since we had access to stars, we booked some celebrities: Phyllis Diller, Rip Taylor, and Kenny Kerr from Boylesque.

This job was more difficult than the pilot, where I'd been walked through every step. In Las Vegas, we taped every day and I did homework every night. There were briefings and comedy writing sessions (I was always welcome at those), but that was about the extent of my involvement. They tried out different producers and directors during the six weeks. Roula came to almost every taping and had the time of her life.

I hate to burst your bubble

One of the topics we covered in Las Vegas was plastic surgery, specifically implants: chin implants, calf implants, and, yes, breast implants. One of the guests that day was Sybil Goldrich, an opponent of silicone breast implants. She was booked, I presumed, to provide a touch of conflict to my lighthearted approach to a table full of silicone props. So the audience could see, I picked up a breast implant on the show as if I had never seen one before, making up bad jokes. Then Sybil walked out and said, "I hate to burst your bubble, but these things are dangerous."

I knew that implants could cause problems, that they might harden and you could lose sensitivity. But the things Sybil talked about were far more serious: lupus, scleroderma, rheumatoid arthritis, and other autoimmune diseases. I just thought she was a fanatic. I couldn't believe implants could cause all that.

Two months after we taped in Las Vegas, the Misti Gold implants were hard. My breasts were completely numb, and I had a raised ridge on my right breast. This time when I went to my doctor, I told him I wanted them out.

"If you do that, you'll be suicidal in two weeks," he said.

32

Control Freak,
Meet Corporate America

When we finished in Las Vegas, I didn't feel ready to go national with this show, but we were going to anyway. Hosting a panel show with ten or twelve guests, while also including the audience, reading cue cards, obeying time cues, and remembering what everybody said is not easy. It may look easy, but believe me it's not. I begged for two or three additional weeks of practice. No dice. I was headed for Chicago.

In June of 1991, I packed up my belongings and moved to an apartment in downtown Chicago. It was a modest two-bedroom, two-bath, and I felt so insecure about my future there I rented furniture. It was just a block from the NBC Tower, where we would be taping the show, and I could walk to work. Denis helped me get settled and helped calm my nerves when I first got there.

The apartment was on the twelfth floor, and even though I knew an earthquake was unlikely it still made me nervous. It was a week before I could stand at the window and look down. Between that and anxiety about my new job and my regular nightmares, it was a long time before I had a good night's sleep. Insomnia has been a problem for me as far back as I can remember, but it was never worse than those first two months in Chicago.

But I didn't mind moving to Chicago because it always reminded me of where I grew up in Canada, also near the

Great Lakes, and midwestern people are friendly just like Canadians.

I wanted to get acclimated to my new city, so Denis and I took an architectural tour on a double-decker bus, went to Taste of Chicago, an annual summer food fest held in Grant Park, and explored the grocery and health food stores in the area. Since I'd been warned that life as I knew it would change once people recognized my face from television, Denis and I crammed a lot of activities in before the show went on the air. I continued to cook my own meals and do my own laundry in the apartment building. I remember sitting down there in the empty laundry room, listening to the dryer whir and thinking, I feel like I've been sentenced and am living my last days of freedom. (But not everything changed; I still do my own cooking and laundry.)

My first day at the NBC Tower was an odd experience. Not surprisingly, the staff was up and running. They were all hired without any input from me, except for my assistant and the executive producer, Stu Crowner. I had been invited to meet Stu in Los Angeles, where we were neighbors, before he was hired and relocated to Chicago with his family. Now I got settled in my office and was ready to work. My state of readiness turned to uneasiness. Nobody asked me to attend any meetings. Nobody asked my opinion about anything. They just smiled, waved, and sailed on by. The numbers of people passing by my office seemed endless.

The executive producer, Stu, supervised the entire production. Next were supervising producer, segment producers, and associate producers; then there were promotion coordinators, publicists, production supervisors, post-production supervisors, editors, production assistants, script supervisors, writers, audience coordinators, receptionist, travel coordinator, operations manager, researchers, and assistants; and this did not include the crew: director, associate director, technical director, stage managers, lighting director, audio supervisor, audio technicians, chyron operator, TelePrompTer operator, cue card person, stagehands, lighting technicians, video operator, prop person, tape operator, audience warm-up, and makeup, hair, and wardrobe supervisors—and I've probably left somebody out.

At first I had no idea what all those people were doing when they scurried around, and it was terrible to feel so left out of everything. I'd gone from handling things myself—writing my own material, choosing my own material, booking the jobs, preparing press releases, designing flyers and advertisements—to wandering around, among all those people, and asking if anybody needed me for anything.

They didn't.

Drop your pants and set your hair on fire

I expected to be in on meetings, to be a part of the creative process; in fact, I was excited about the idea. I wasn't afraid of working; I thrive on it. I couldn't stand not knowing what was going on. If I didn't understand how a television show worked, how could I contribute anything?

I wanted to understand everything from chyrons (those words across the bottom of your screen that identify topics or people) to the budget. The budget was a big issue. I remember the first time I asked to see a copy of the budget. I was just curious, maybe I could learn something.

The response was deafening silence. You'd have thought I said, Drop your pants and set your hair on fire.

I soon learned that I was considered "talent," and talent doesn't get involved in things like budgets. Whenever I asked questions I wasn't supposed to, they would say, "You shouldn't worry about those things," or "Don't get involved in station business," or "There's no reason for talent to hear about research. Just concentrate on hosting." Confrontation does not come easy to me, so I accepted that that's the way it was done.

For every show, I was told the topic and given a script. Since comedy was something they couldn't deny me, I was allowed to work with the writers and contribute material.

Then came the script meeting. Again, everything was new to

me and I had nothing to compare, so unless someone told me different, I had to assume this was the way all talk shows were done. A meeting would be called in Stu's office, starting about 5 P.M. The group surrounding the big table consisted of Stu, the director, segment producers for that particular show, one or two writers, a script supervisor, a prop person, and I can't remember who else. We'd go through the hefty script, page by page and line by line.

We'd start by going through the opening comedy bit. We did some elaborate comedy sketches, word for word, and if it didn't work in the room it was rewritten.

Then we rehearsed each one of the questions that was written, followed by the anticipated answer: question, answer, question, answer. Then we went over our bridge, which was a mini segment, or sometimes a comedy bit, that transitioned to the second half of the hour. Then more of the same: my questions, their answers. By now, it was usually 8 or 9 P.M. and we were tired and hungry. Someone would send out for food and we kept going. We still had the closing comedy bit to rehearse, hoping it would work in a room full of short-tempered people with low blood sugar.

Thank goodness for one of our writers, Jayne Hamil, who always kept me laughing as we suffered through these marathon meetings. She was smart enough to bring food, and on one particular occasion she brought a potato. She placed it under her chair, and into about the fourth hour I leaned over and whispered, "Did you know there's a potato under your chair?" Without missing a beat she said, "Have we been here that long?"

After the final comedy routine was done and we were all exhausted, I went home to start my homework. Some nights, it was midnight before I got home. Any changes that were made were noted by the script supervisor, who then left the meeting to rewrite the script by morning.

We all regrouped first thing in the morning to block and rehearse all the comedy sketches, which often included other actors and props. Blocking means knowing where to stand; I was lucky to be standing at all, since I'd usually been up late memorizing lines and reading all the pre-interviews of the guests. I never came to work without doing my homework, so I was usually functioning on three or four hours of sleep. If I had cramps, I made them go away. On the weekends I brought home all the viewer mail to read.

Stu didn't trust me to waver from the script, insisting I follow it precisely as written. Even as time went on, and some of the other producers would say, "Let her roll with it," Stu would respond, "I don't trust her yet."

If I switched from question two to question four, he held up a cue card prompting me to question three. I didn't understand how I could be funny or spontaneous when I was just reading dialogue someone else had written, and I said so frequently. Stu countered by calling the script "planned spontaneity."

I liked Stu. He'd been a producer for Mike Douglas, and he loved the light comedy-driven-style talk show. But he came from an era when shows were tightly scripted. It worked then. I didn't think it was working for me, but since I was "talent" my opinion didn't count for much.

You've got to be better, Jenny

In the beginning they tried out hairdresser after hairdresser, attempting to find someone who could work with my thin, fine hair. Sometimes I ended up doing it myself. (Little did I know that bad hair would end up getting me some of my first bad press.) And it wasn't just the hair that had to be redone. Our first few shows were a mess. I thanked God we weren't live because we had to redo a lot of things, and I knew everyone was disappointed in me. Almost every day the studios executives would call. "You've got to be better, Jenny."

They would call me at home late at night. They criticized me during the day on commercial breaks in the middle of tapings. They came down on me in front of the staff telling me how many mistakes I was making. Always, "You've got to be better, Jenny." They said if I didn't get better I'd soon be back in clubs doing Girls' Night Out. All I could do was cry.

I had never felt pressure like I felt during the weeks leading up to our first day on the air. In addition to trying to concentrate on the actual shows, I was trying to do everything possible to help with the pre-launch publicity, one day taping thirty-three interviews with various radio and television stations. On September 16, 1991, the first *Jenny Jones Show* aired. Despite their growing disappointment with me, David Salzman, one of our executive producers, and Jim sent flowers and good wishes. Jim even threw in a Strip-O-Gram, trying to bring a note of levity into a very tense day.

Our very first guest was Dan Carlson, who shared his secret for growing giant vegetables: his wife, Marge, whistled to them.

The Neilsen rating system, which monitors the viewing habits of a key group of Americans, allows you to know, overnight, how many people are watching your show. That can be a good thing or a bad thing. In my case, it was bad.

The only thing worse than waiting for ratings to come in is hearing that they are low. A year and a half of preparation, anxiety, and hard work had come to this. I sat by the phone, waiting to hear from Scott Carlin, who at the time was senior vice president of distribution for Warner Bros., the morning after we went on the air. He promised to call as soon as the overnight ratings were in. The phone finally rang.

"Hi Jenny."

I could tell by the tone of his voice the news was not good. "How did we do?" I asked, not really wanting to know.

"Well, people are watching the show, but not a lot of them."

My first thought was, Bonnie Kaplan was right. I don't have it. My next thought was, There is one person who will enjoy hearing that my big premiere was a bomb—Mother.

I didn't tell her about the low ratings because I didn't want to hear her say, "And you actually thought you had talent?"

Pressure mounted when the ratings didn't pick up, and we started doing postmortems after some of the shows to figure out what was going wrong. But I already knew: me. I was familiar with post-show conferences, like those Wayne Newton held after his shows. But nobody there was pointing a finger at anyone. Now I felt the finger was always pointed at me, and I didn't know what I could do to get better at my job. Thank goodness Denis was coming up on weekends to give me moral support.

33

Meet the Press

On October 3, 1991, a *Chicago Sun-Times* columnist pointed out the downside to *The Jenny Jones Show*'s initial immediate sales success. Unlike *Oprah* or *Donahue*, he said, we wouldn't be able to work out our bugs quietly. He was right on the money with that assessment. He pointed out that our director had been dropped from the show and replaced, a writer had been fired, and we had set problems that sometimes caused delays.

Yes, that was all true. We were working out problems, just like any other show or start-up operation, and we were doing it on national television. Maybe the director doesn't work out; people are hired and fired until the staff gets established. Sometimes the audio system doesn't work. On one show the TelePrompTer broke. Things happen.

The final problem, as he saw it, was the firing of a dozen or so hairdressers. We did audition a lot of hairdressers until we came up with a person who could work with my hair. But it was more sensational to say they all were fired and I was difficult. (Maybe he knew my mother.)

At first the critics took me to task for trying to be different. Another *Sun-Times* writer said the show was a "June Cleaver" kind of format. Whereas *Donahue* and *Oprah* were going for on-air confessions, probing the lives of incest victims, *Jenny* was "trotting out puppies and kittens."

Others said we suffered from a lack of identity. "[*The Jenny Jones*

Show] doesn't know if it wants to be funny, folksy, poignant, or breezy. . . . If it's not celebrity driven or issue driven, what is it?" A national magazine called us "spunky" but suggested that my calling a male psychologist who appeared on the show "hot looking" was inappropriate.

On October 14, a weekly newsmagazine noted that Phil Donahue, who once described talk shows as group therapy, had revolutionized the genre two decades earlier by involving the studio audience, shifting from celebrities to real-people problems. Donahue, they said, brought heft, relevance, and emotion to a genre that had become a show-biz confection. Now, the news magazine added, the genre had become a circus. They said I was trying to balance my show somewhere in the middle, coming off as a nineties Dinah Shore with homey, lightweight subjects.

I was hoping the critics would support our determination to bring something different to daytime, with multiple topics and comedy sketches, but because they couldn't categorize it they chose to criticize it. (Later on, when we switched to a traditional single-topic format, they criticized that too.)

By November, our ratings were still low, so in an attempt to survive the crucial November sweeps period, we took the show on the road. It was the only time The Jenny Jones Show ever taped outside of our Chicago studio. We went on location to Los Angeles, to do a week of shows with the stars of All My Children and The Young and the Restless. I sat backstage with Susan Lucci for an interview, and on a sofa right on his set with Eric Braeden. By now I'd had a few months of experience and felt rather proud of my interview skills; in fact, the Los Angeles producer told me I did a great job. When the week was over, David called to tell me that same producer told him I was incompetent.

Television is no business for the faint of heart.

She's funny, she's fresh, she's kidding herself!

On November 20, *LA Times* critic Howard Rosenberg said we were the best of the season's new shows: "no one else is funnier or fresher."

But the day after Howard Rosenberg sang my praises, David Salzman invited me to dinner and sang a very different tune. I was elated when I walked into the restaurant, since the soap segments had gone well and the *LA Times* had given us a positive write-up. We hadn't even been served our salads yet when he told me the show was in jeopardy. The problems were numerous:

> Some producers wanted to quit.
> One producer was angry with me for mentioning that I didn't like "depressing" topics.
> They were making budget cuts.
> Our ratings were bad.
> A lot of people connected to the show thought I was doing a terrible job.
> I needed to be more involved with the audience.
> I needed to be a better interviewer.
> I needed to be funnier.

And that was before the salads!

Being told I wasn't good enough was sounding very familiar. Who did I think I was? Mother had said it. And she would revel in my failure. I didn't want her to win. I didn't want her to be right.

I couldn't remember the last time Jim or David paid me a compliment, and when people are watching you, just waiting for you to make a mistake, criticism only makes it more difficult. The minute someone says, "You've got to get better," your voice tightens up, you start stammering, and you make mistakes.

In addition to my perceived lack of stage presence, I was also allowing guests to talk too long.

Furthermore, he added, I didn't understand what power the star of a television show wields, so I needed to keep my mouth shut. When I questioned the way things were run, it intimidated people, and that didn't make for a smooth-running ship.

I went back to work and tried to keep my mouth shut. I was raised to be a people-pleaser, and I hate confrontation. But I was also the person who took the hits when the media trashed the show and our ratings were bad. One day a bunch of the execs were having a meeting in Stu's office. "Shouldn't I be included in this?" I asked, peeking my head in the door.

They looked at me as if I were a Martian exposing himself.

"No need, Jenny," they said. "We're just meeting about—uh— marketing."

Later, someone told me the meeting was about content.

On December 30, 1991, *Electronic Media* cited our low ratings and said we'd be closely watched at the 1992 NATPE convention. The problem remained: What is the right formula for this show to be a hit?

One of the ways we tried to make the format work was by booking more celebrities. Ivana Trump did the show and talked about having a new boyfriend, the guy she's now divorcing. She seemed so open and likable, I found myself thinking, Well, she's not that different from any of us here in this room. Then I noticed a yellow diamond roughly the size of North Dakota on her hand and was reminded that we probably had very little in common after all. We booked Gloria Steinem and Suzanne Somers, who later became one of my competitors. I think she was surprised to learn we'd once been neighbors. Jane Seymour painted a pretty water color on the show, which is still displayed on our office wall. I even got to dance with Tommy Tune.

Marlo Thomas came on the show and was a compelling guest. She talked about her father, Danny Thomas, and began crying on the air. As I watched her cry I envied her those emotions, because I realized at that moment that I had never cried over the loss of my own father.

Usually by November, a new show gets word on whether it's

canceled or renewed. It was December, and we'd heard nothing. By Christmas, I was living my life one day at a time, waiting to get word on my future, wondering if I should go back to booking Girls' Night Out. In the meantime, Martha Stewart did a holiday crafts show and Brooke Shields appeared on our Christmas show.

Bad reviews and low ratings weren't the only things making me sick with worry. The ridge on my right breast had become so large I could actually see it in the mirror. A couple of years earlier when I had some publicity pictures taken it was not visible, but the photographer noticed it on all my negatives. I knew what it was but I convinced him it was a flaw on the film. The fact that it looked bad didn't concern me as much as the fear of what that loose silicone was doing to my body.

But my physician didn't seem concerned. "I don't think it's dangerous," he said, when I went in to have it checked. Every time I picked up a magazine or a newspaper, I read more distressing news about the dangers of breast implants. I didn't want to bet my health on a doctor's telling me he didn't think it was dangerous.

I'd had occasional problems with my white blood cell count in the past, but I didn't connect the implants to the cell count then. Only recently had I been hearing stories about the possible effects of silicone on the human immune system.

I decided I wanted the implants out and consulted several doctors, one of whom said, "You'll look like you had seven kids and breast-fed every one of them." Can you imagine? This man supposedly deals on a professional level with women every day, and he views us in such contempt! Another doctor told me removal would cause serious deformity. "You can't take out the marbling from beef," he said. "To get all the silicone out of your body we would have to take out tissue. You would be considerably deformed." Confused, I decided to leave the implants in place. That same doctor called me in Chicago a few weeks later, saying he'd be in town for a few days and asking me to have dinner with him.

I declined. I happened to mention this to another breast implant recipient from California, who told me he had asked her out as well.

At first the doctors had me convinced I was the only breast implant recipient having problems, but as more information started coming out, I realized there were others. As the newspapers printed story after story about the FDA hearings on the dangers of silicone breast implants, I thought about Sybil Goldrich when she said, "These things are dangerous." I knew she was right, and I was scared. I remembered her saying they had found silicone in her liver.

I knew the implants had been the biggest mistake of my life, but I had no idea what to do about them. I wanted to call Sybil, but she didn't know about my implants, and I was too embarrassed to tell her. I wondered if I should go public and free myself from this terrible secret so I could get the help I needed. As it was, I was sneaking in and out of doctors' offices, hiding behind my sunglasses, hoping no one would recognize and expose me. I believed it was only a matter of time before someone from my past decided to sell "before" and "after" pictures of me to the tabloids.

I also believed that with my visibility I might be able to keep other women from making the same mistake I did. It often takes a disaster happening to someone you know to get your attention. My audiences knew me. Maybe they would listen.

The first person I talked to about it was Denis.

"I'll stand by you, whatever you decide to do." His answer didn't surprise me.

"But what will people think?" I said. "What if they hate me for it?"

"Don't worry about what anybody thinks," he said. "Go with your heart."

I appreciated his support, but I was still afraid of the consequences. I wondered if admitting publicly that I'd had five sets of breast implants would destroy what was left of my career. I'd worked too many years to sabotage myself. I needed advice—a professional opinion. And I knew just whom to ask. She was a celebrity I admired very much. I suspected she would be both candid and insightful about the reaction I could expect.

I started tracking her down, calling around until I got her manager's phone number. I knew it would be a challenge to get this very famous woman on the phone. It was almost as hard to get through to her manager.

"Who's calling, please?"

"This is Jenny Jones."

"Jenny—and is that J-O-N-E-S?"

"Yes, Jenny Jones. I host a national talk show."

"What is this regarding?"

What I wanted to say was, "I need to talk to his most famous client about my breasts."

What I said was, "I—uh, I—uh . . . I can't exactly, uh—"

This was more painful than my last surgery.

"Can I take a message and have him call you back?"

I decided not to wait by the phone. A few days later I tried again.

"This is Jenny Jones again, and I host a national talk show. I need to speak with Mr. X about a personal matter, and it will just take a minute. Could you please ask him to talk to me?"

He took my call. I explained that I had a very personal matter about which I needed advice from someone in the business, and his client was a woman I admired and respected. I swore to him that I wanted nothing more from her than advice and gave him my word that our conversation would remain confidential. He was silent for a moment. I wondered if he was laughing at me or considering my dilemma.

"I'll call you back," he said.

A few days later he phoned and didn't say much, except to tell me to call at 7 P.M. that evening. I wondered if she would be there.

"Hello, this is Jenny Jones."

"Hold on, please."

"Hello." It was her. I recognized her voice. I tried to remain calm.

First, I reassured her that I only wanted advice and that I would never divulge her name. Then she listened as I told her my story.

"Would it be a mistake, professionally, to come forward? Will it ruin my career?" I asked.

Her answer shocked me. "I can't believe you're asking me this question. I have the same implants, and they've been making me sick!"

That was all I needed to hear. Women had to be told, and I was going to tell them.

I came out of the implant closet on February 24 on the cover of *People* magazine. Then I taped a show on breast implants and invited Sybil Goldrich. We received over four hundred phone calls the day it aired.

I felt like the weight of the world was off my shoulders. Obviously, magazines, newspapers, and television news shows contacted me about my admission, and I certainly used those press opportunities to warn other women of the dangers of breast implants. *People*'s story was titled "Body of Evidence."

"I want to urge other celebrities to come forward," I told the magazine. "My goal is to say to anybody who is considering implants: Don't do it. It's not worth the risk. Learn to love yourself. If I could have learned that, I wouldn't have had to suffer eleven years of torture."

Only three people were kind enough to write me letters applauding my honesty: my personal physician and two celebrities, Roseanne Barr and Dr. Robert Schuller. I thought about how much those letters meant to me when Ellen DeGeneres came out on her show, and it prompted me to write her a letter in much the same vein.

I did do a lot of press in the weeks after I went public including an appearance on *Donahue*. I didn't go through the embarrassment of announcing to the world that my breasts were misshapen, felt like rocks, and might be poisoning me for nothing. I wanted women to know what could happen. I spoke about my ordeal whenever I could. I was invited to speak to a women's health group. I accepted the invitation but they canceled a few days later because of the number of complaints by plastic surgeons.

Some of the interviews I did were via satellite, which means you sit in front of a camera and talk to one city after another, using an earpiece to hear the questions. It's very strange, because you can't see who you're talking to, their facial expressions or hand gestures—anything that might help you feel like you're connecting.

Most of the questions were standard: "Tell us your story" or "When did you first start having problems?" But when I was switched via satellite to a station in Florida, a very puzzling thing happened. The woman who was interviewing me turned hostile and started insulting me, saying that I didn't know what I was talking about and that implants were completely safe.

I was stunned but stood my ground. "I have all the research I need to show that breast implants can be dangerous," I countered. "I'm living proof of it."

She continued to be abusive, and when we signed off I felt almost as if I'd been assaulted. Two days later I found out that her husband was a plastic surgeon. But that wasn't the end of it. The station got so many complaints about her behavior toward me that they demanded she apologize. I heard she has since been terminated.

As soon as I went public, a columnist wrote in the *Sun-Times*, "Jones and her handlers have orchestrated a shrewd media campaign designed to cash in on her private suffering. Never mind that Jones could have gone public at any time if her only goal were to help others. Instead, she conveniently waits until the sweeps to strike her deal with *People* and generates tons of fawning, sympathetic publicity."

I hadn't told Mother about the problems I'd been having with my implants or about the multiple surgeries. I called her to see if she'd read the *People* article, and the first thing she said was, "How did you get the cover?"

It hurt that anyone thought my going public had anything to do with ratings, but the hurt lessened every time I read a letter from someone reconsidering the idea of breast implants or was stopped on the street by a woman who had experienced the same pain and shame. Later that March, I flew to Los Angeles to do the Easter Seals Telethon with Pat Boone, and on the return flight a woman approached me on the plane. She simply took my hand and said "Thanks." As embarrassing as my revelation was, I knew it was worth it. I was heard. I made a difference.

34

Making Peace with My Body

By April 1992, the show still was not renewed for a second year and I fully expected to be unemployed soon. According to my diary, I was "living a lifetime a day waiting for word on my future." Then Jim Paratore called to say there was a glimmer of hope. "If we are more compelling and do less comedy, I think we'll be renewed," he said. He asked me if I was willing to do a more serious show. The answer was easy: yes. I had reinvented myself more than once, and I could do it again.

I waited for the phone to ring like the guy on death row waiting for the governor to call, wondering if my life would be saved, and when the call did come and Jim told me we were being renewed, I was thrilled. Somebody believed in me. Statistics show only one out of ten syndicated shows makes it past the first season. I felt lucky to be that one.

The number of letters I received from women with breast implant problems only strengthened my resolve to have my implants removed, even though my problems were not as serious as some of the other women's. I was convinced they were dangerous, and I didn't want that silicone in my body any longer. I just had to find the right doctor.

I will be forever grateful to all the women who wrote to give me advice and names of support groups and doctors. The doctor's name that I received more than any other was Dr. Lu Jean Feng in Cleveland. Many women told me she was a compassionate and skilled surgeon. I flew to Cleveland to see her. I called Sybil Goldrich, who recommended Dr. William Shaw at UCLA in Los Angeles. It turned out that Dr. Feng was trained by Dr. Shaw, and I had complete confidence in both physicians. I chose Dr. Shaw because I still had my Los Angeles residence and a comfortable place to recover.

On May 8, 1992, I checked in to UCLA Medical Center to have my breast implants removed. *20/20* wanted to bring a camera into the operating room, but I declined. Denis was completely supportive of my decision and went with me to every doctor visit. He cried when they wheeled me in, not for the loss but for the years I'd spent in agony in my misguided quest for womanhood. It took three hours for Dr. Shaw, chief of plastic surgery at UCLA, to remove the implants and the encapsulated scar tissue around them. He then lifted and reshaped the remaining breast tissue and cut away the excess skin, so that what was left of my breasts would not look like "basset hound ears," as one doctor had predicted.

Recovery from this surgery was far worse than I had expected. Or maybe I just forgot how bad the pain always was. I threw up twice on the way home. I'd been told that drainage tubes had been inserted, but I had no idea how painful they'd be to remove. (If you ever have to have drainage tubes removed, take a pain pill.)

I scheduled the surgery after the end of the tape season to allow plenty of time to recover. I expected to be on the phone within a few days, but I was not up to it. Denis waited on me for days and came with me when it was time to remove the bandages. I remember looking down and saying, "They're bigger than I expected."

"That's just swelling," Dr. Shaw said. "You'll be much smaller in a few weeks."

I wasn't emotionally prepared for my chest to be flatter than it had been back in 1981, before I had my first set of implants, so Dr. Shaw suggested I see a therapist. He recommended a psychologist who specialized in mastectomy cases. My case certainly was not as traumatic as having to deal with cancer, but it was also about accepting a different body than you had before. I agreed to see a therapist for several months afterward. I wish I could tell you I now love my body, but I don't. I have made peace with it, thanks to some counseling, but there are still days that I get angry about what I did to myself.

Letters continued to pour in from implanted women who had severe health problems, and I knew my problems were minimal compared to what some of those women were going through. It was demoralizing to hear, but it made me realize that there was a continuing need for information. In June I took fifty thousand dollars and established the Image Foundation, to serve as a clearinghouse of information regarding breast implants. Denis moved to Chicago and donated over a year of his life to running the foundation for me, and he talked patiently to many women who were looking for information.

The number of calls we received was overwhelming, so we hired some help. We provided a list of government, medical, and consumer organizations, plus attorney and physician references and national and local support groups. Sometimes women called just to have someone to talk to.

We still provide information, although the number of requests has subsided considerably. If you need help, write to:

> The Image Foundation
> P.O. Box 3630
> Chicago, IL 60654

35

Sink or Swim

Finding an experienced executive producer for our second season wasn't easy, because talk shows had mushroomed so fast there were more jobs than people to fill them. But after an extensive search, we found a package deal: Debby Harwick, an Emmy Award–winning producer on *Donahue*, and her Emmy Award–winning *Donahue* fellow producer and fiancé, Ed Glavin. They had my vote from the first time I met them; they lived and breathed talk shows, had tons of energy, and seemed like they'd be fun to work with. They had come on board in August of 1992, ready to drag us from the bottom of the ratings heap. "I don't mind competing against everyone," Ed said. "It's a knock-down drag-out battle every time. I roll around in the mud over this stuff."

As a team, they're unbeatable. Debby has amazing instincts, an almost mystical sense of what viewers want to see. I think that's something you either have or you don't—and she has it. As you might expect from his quote, Ed is the competitive one. He's a numbers guy who can tell you about any show, what its ratings are and were, what topics they covered, and how those topics rated. He follows every competitor's ratings. And he loves to win. He'll call up close friends who produce other shows and say, "Ah, ha! We kicked your butt!"

We're all very close now, but it was a bumpy ride in the beginning. Debby and Ed were used to Phil Donahue coming in an hour before the show. With his years of experience, Phil didn't feel the need to hang around the office all day like I did, so it took awhile before my new producers understood that, although I wanted to be involved, I didn't pose a threat to their position. Not only did they understand that I wasn't questioning their authority, I was pleasantly surprised to learn that they believed me competent to host the show on my own. It was almost time to tape our first show of the new season, and since I had not seen any sign of a script, I mentioned it to Ed.

"There is no script," Ed said. "You're on your own. Sink or swim."

I didn't know how to react. I'd always had to work with a script and I always hated it, but, like I said, I had nothing to compare it to and assumed that's how it was done. I was excited about my new freedom but a little scared too.

"You can do it," Debby said. "We watched you all last year, and we always said that you were good but the show was wrong for you."

"Trust yourself; we trust you," Ed said. "You're going to have a lot more freedom than you've ever had. You can go to commercial break when you want to, ask whatever questions you want to, and if you don't like the TelePrompTer material, change it."

I wanted to cry, but I was so used to disappointing people I was terrified they were wrong about me and I really couldn't do it. As we began taping the new shows, people started noticing a change for the better, and at a staff party held at Chicago's North Pier the next month, Ed was asked if they'd "reinvented" Jenny Jones. "No, we didn't reinvent Jenny," he said. "We just set her free."

A few weeks after Debby and Ed arrived, the *New York Times* said:

> *With two* Donahue *producers in charge and a year of daily talk shows under her belt, Jenny Jones feels she should be taken seriously. That's why her syndicator, Warner Bros. Domestic Television Distribution, has announced this season Jenny will tackle subjects that have long been associated with Donahue, Sally Jessy Raphael and Oprah.*

Wanted: Executive assistant
(must be able to work under pressure!)

Debby and Ed were a critical professional addition to the team that summer, but on a personal level there was an even more important hiring. I had recently lost my assistant and was hunting for another, so I ran an advertisement in the *Chicago Tribune*: *Executive assistant for busy executive. Must be detail oriented and able to work under pressure.*

The people applying for the job had no idea who their employer would be. I interviewed several candidates, but no one struck me as just the right person. Then one afternoon my future assistant, a young woman named Dana Lasker, strolled into my office wearing a long granny-style skirt, T-shirt, and sandals.

Dana hadn't expected to be interviewed that day. Along with many others, she'd sent in her résumé expecting several days' notice. But I needed to make a decision about the assistant position, and while Dana didn't have as much experience as the others, I wanted to meet with her. We called to see if she could come in that very day.

"Couldn't I come in tomorrow, so I can dress up a little?" Dana asked.

"Today would be much better," our staff person said. "And don't worry about what you're wearing. We have no dress code."

Weeks later, Dana told me that at the time she thought, if it's meant to be, it's meant to be.

Not only did Dana and I like each other immediately, we had some things in common. For starters, she was a high school dropout who got her GED, and I was a high school dropout who had been thinking about getting a GED. (In fact, Dana was the one who coached me when I was preparing to take the test. Every time I said I was nervous, she'd say, "If I could pass it, so can you.")

We have something else in common—an appreciation of Italian men. One of the things I do as a "thank you" for Dana is give her a trip every year, because she's much more than an assistant, she's a true and loyal friend. She gets to pick any place in the world and I send her there, all expenses paid. She's gone to England, Greece, France, and Spain. I've also invited her to join me on trips. She vacationed with me on an African safari and she joined me in Hawaii. She was on the beach when I caught a wave, and she said it was "gnarly."

The place Dana's come to love most is Italy. She says she agrees with me: There *is* something about those Italian men. They are only surpassed by Irish men, now that I know and love Denis.

Whenever we can, we combine work and play. One thing we work on for weeks every year is the staff Christmas party. We start in late summer shopping for gifts ranging from Caribbean cruises to large-screen TVs to camcorders to vacation getaways, even fine jewelry, which are all put on display in the backstage area. On the day of our party, each staff member puts his or her name in a bowl. Dana and I turn the subsequent drawing into *Let's Make a Deal* by adding a box of envelopes containing varying amounts of cash up to $1,000. Each person has to decide whether to take a gift or draw an envelope, while the rest of the staff cheers.

"Go for the money!"

"Take the cruise and take me with you!"

As much fun as we have, it takes immense planning and organization for a staff of seventy-five, and thanks to Dana it's run smoothly every year. I'm always looking for new ways to surprise Dana, so this year I've decided to reveal her Christmas 1997 present right here in this book. Hey, Dana? Are you sitting down? This year I'm paying off your condo for Christmas! Thanks for everything! (If anyone who knows her reads this before she does, please don't tell.)

Dana also helped inspire me to go ahead and get my GED. Throughout my adult life, I had skirted around the fact that I was a high school dropout. I was ashamed to admit it, so during interviews, if someone asked me when I graduated from high school, I'd say, "Oh, I left in 1964." I never actually lied and said I graduated, but I definitely gave the impression that I had. It was something that embarrassed me and left me feeling inadequate and inferior. So in 1996, I decided to get a GED. I got a book that explained how to prepare for the test and called on Dana a few times to help me prepare. After a few months, I made an appointment to go and take the test.

Waiting for the results was grueling. I worried that I might have flunked because the science and history tests were harder than I expected and I just guessed at some of the answers. I finally got a notice in the mail and called Dana in before I opened it. I couldn't believe how nervous I was, opening the envelope. I passed! Not only that, I aced it! Dana and I hugged and I cried. My GED now hangs proudly framed in my office.

Having my new diploma has given me a new confidence. Although I've landed a great job in television, a day doesn't go by that I don't remind myself how lucky I was to get it. When I needed a regular job, I had no qualifications to get a good one. It was only because I learned how to type in high school that I was hired for the office jobs I'd had. So other than typing, what could I put on a résumé?

Times have changed drastically since the days when my high school typing skills could get me in an office. Companies require more than that now, and I worry that many teens aren't preparing themselves to compete in today's job market. Gangs and teen pregnancies are a sad part of our lives today too, and we all need to do whatever we can to help keep kids in school, pregnancy-free, and drug-free.

Getting my GED served to remind me of the importance of an education and of the responsibility we all share in encouraging young people to stay in school. I wanted to give back some of my good fortune to my community, so over the next few months I established a scholarship fund, one based not solely on grades but on character, need, and potential. There are four of us involved—Denis, Dana, Laurie Bartholomew, and myself, and we donate whatever time we can. There are no salaries. We're all personally involved in every stage from the initial interview to staying in touch with the students. We've gone to the schools several times to meet with counselors and students.

The first time I visited some of the schools was an eye-opening experience, because of the security guards and metal detectors, things that were unheard of in my days as a student. Schools in low-income neighborhoods are in desperate need of more professionals; in some cases, not only are they understaffed, but the counselors are apathetic and uninvolved. We've experienced times when no one would even return our calls, and we were trying to give them money!

We are now in our second year of providing scholarship money, and it's been an extremely rewarding experience. We've stuck by the students who were having problems, because I believe that emotional support is just as important as financial. (If anyone can understand the need for emotional support, I can.) If everybody hangs in, it looks like in a few years we'll have some accountants, veterinarians, computer engineers, a mortician, doctors, school-teachers, dentists, an artist, nurses, lawyers, and, yes, a few "undecided." That's OK too.

If you want to feel really good, do something for your community. If you can't give money, give your time. You can volunteer or be a Big Brother or Sister. Or just be a good role model. If you make a difference in one person's life, it's worth it.

What so proudly we hail

Having co-workers who are trusted friends is important for anyone, but especially for an individual like me, who had very little family support. I wasn't seeing Mother as often as when I was on the road doing comedy, but she did come to Chicago on two occasions. (The second time, she brought along her "boyfriend" Roland. I was so happy that their friendship had developed into a love affair. Mother sounded like a teenager when she told me how they loved to cuddle. For the first time in her life she had unconditional love.)

I wasn't sure if she enjoyed her visits to Chicago. She seemed a bit lost amid all the activity surrounding the show. When we'd walk past my portrait in the lobby of the NBC Tower, she never seemed to see it. Even though it felt like I'd arrived, her confidence in me seemed to sink to an all-time low.

In August, I excitedly phoned her with the news that I'd be singing the national anthem at a White Sox game.

"But don't you have to have a good voice to do that?" she asked.

I told her there was an offer on the table to do a television movie about my life.

"What's so exciting about your life story?"

I didn't have any comeback for either comment, so I told her I'd call later.

"I want to know something," she said.

"Yes?" I asked, interested to see what information could top a White Sox game and a made-for-television movie.

"After your surgery, are you gonna wear a padded bra or just be flat?"

"I'll just be flat, Mother."

I did sing the national anthem at the White Sox game. In addition to my usual lack of confidence and attack of nerves, I had received a death threat that morning—just another celebrity perk they don't tell you about. So the whole time I sang, I kept wondering whether the threat was for real and if he was out there in the crowd. Also, there's a sound delay in a stadium, and because I couldn't hear well, I sang painfully slowly.

Mother was right. I think I disappointed everyone.

36

Poetry with a Mission

The man who decides the future of all the Warner Bros. shows, including mine, was Barry Meyer, executive vice president and chief operating officer of Warner Bros. If you think show business is full of phonies, knowing Barry will quickly change your mind. He is as gracious as he is genuine and has always treated me fairly. He really showed me his caring nature when, in our second season, we were again waiting for word on the show's renewal.

It was almost Christmas and we still had not heard. Barry called me at home and said, "I didn't want your Christmas holiday to be spent worrying about your job. Just between you and me, the show will be renewed. We just won't be announcing it until January. Have a great Christmas." Barry is a gentleman and a class act.

Before that magic phone call, I was getting anxious about not yet being renewed, so I decided to have a little fun with Barry and some of the other executives and started faxing them a poem a day. It was a way to let them know how anxious we all were in Chicago and to make them laugh at the same time. So I got out my rhyming dictionary and got back to my comedy roots.

DAILY POEM
Jenny Jones is sweet and kind,
As a talk show host she's really a find.
If you know what's good for you,
You'll renew for another.

Yours very truly,
Jenny's mother.

A LOW BLOW

Perhaps you're not sure if I'm worth renewing.
   Perhaps there's talking where there should be doing.
Perhaps this decision which looms so large
   Might already be made, were a woman in charge.

Some of the guys called and said they really enjoyed the poems. My favorite one was the one I sent after the show was renewed, thanking everyone from Bob Daly, chairman of the board, to Jim Paratore.

GRATITUDE

I've tried to find a way to express
My gratitude for "bringing it home."
A basket of flowers seemed just too mundane
So I decided on . . . a poem.

But this poem is different as you'll soon discover,
It's sung to the tune of "Fifty Ways to Leave Your Lover."

Thanks for the job, Bob,
Some butt you did kick, Dick,
I owe you a lot, Scott,
I'm grateful to you.

You went out on a limb, Jim,
Your brilliance you gave, Dave,
We'll be around longer than *Little House On The Prairie*, Barry,
And I owe it all to you.

The changes Debby and Ed made when we switched to a single-topic format caused me some anxiety that season, since the new shows featured personal stories and some guests were extremely emotional. I grew up in a household teeming with conflict, and it's caused me to run from confrontation my entire life. But with the new format, I was compelled to deal with my fear of friction, and as the guests spoke their minds I slowly learned to do the same.

Debby and Ed said one deciding factor in their wanting this job was that *The Jenny Jones Show* had a great lineup of stations. What they didn't realize when they accepted their executive producer jobs was that due to low ratings we'd been dropped from two-thirds of those original stations.

Ed says he looked at our first ratings of the new season, and it was like "Where's Waldo?" *The Jenny Jones Show* was almost nowhere to be seen! He picked up the phone and called Jim Paratore.

"Uh, Jim, we don't appear to be on a lot of the stations we were on a year ago," he said.

"Oh, yeah," Jim said. "We've been downgraded because of low ratings."

Ed hung up and told Debby, "Man, this is gonna be a taller order than we thought."

Since we were now doing shows more like our competitors, competing for guests became an occasional issue. At one point, one of Sally Jessy's people even called up a guest we'd booked, claimed to be representing *Jenny Jones*, and told the guest he'd been canceled. Then they called back and attempted to book him on Sally's show.

Our ratings slowly started to climb—not as quickly as we had hoped, because we'd lost a lot of key stations, but we made steady progress. And although it was rumored in the industry that we'd be canceled, I knew, of course, that we'd be on the air for another year, thanks to that phone call from Barry Meyer. I'm also well aware that this show would not have remained on the air had it not been for the support and commitment of certain other Warner Bros. executives, as well, especially Sandy Reisenbach, Dick Robertson, Scott Carlin, and Mark Robbins. Mark, who headquarters in Chicago, has been our biggest cheerleader since day one. Whenever we got discouraged, Mark was always there to show us the bright side.

Hosting a talk show has afforded me opportunities I would never have otherwise had. In February 1993, I was invited to Washington to introduce the new members of Congress along with Cokie Roberts. A few months later I was a guest on *The John and Leeza Show* and got to play the drums with John Tesh. As brilliant a musician as he is, he graciously invited me to play "Wipe Out," a cheesy rock 'n' roll relic, so I could be featured on the drums. And last year I was invited to introduce the entertainment at a fund-raiser for the grand opening of the Michael Jordan Boys and Girls Club in Chicago, created in honor of Michael Jordan's father. The entertainment? Boys II Men! I even judged a meatball contest with Donny Osmond.

I've also been afforded a much improved lifestyle. It wasn't so long ago that I was traveling from one roach-infested condo to another on the comedy club circuit. I now own a weekend cabin away from the city. It was there that I drew my revolver for the second time.

I was alone in the house one night just drifting off to sleep when I heard a crashing sound of glass breaking in the next room. I didn't know what to do, but I knew I had to move fast. I always kept my .38 by the bed so I grabbed it with one hand and grabbed the phone with the other. By now I expected someone to come crashing into the bedroom and I quickly dialed 911.

"Please, send somebody right away." I gave the address and hoped I was coherent because my adrenaline was pumping.

"What's the problem?" the officer asked, sounding a bit too calm.

"I think someone's in the house and I'm alone. I have a gun and I'll use it if he comes in the bedroom."

"The police are on the way," he said.

"Please hurry," I said, "and thank you." I started to hang up.

"Don't hang up! Is your gun loaded?"

"Yes it is. I'm crouched behind the bed and it's aimed at the door. If anyone comes in I'm going to shoot." My hand was shaking but still aimed at the door. I couldn't understand why the intruder had not found me yet.

"Before you shoot that gun, you'd better be sure it's not some-one you know," he cautioned.

"Don't worry," I said. "It won't be anyone I know." Denis was in Los Angeles so I knew it wasn't him.

The officer told me to stay on the line until the squad car arrived. The three or four minutes it took for them to get there seemed like an hour. When I saw the car coming up the driveway, I told my phone partner that I was afraid to go to the door and let them in.

"Just stay where you are," he said, "and they'll walk around the house first." The man on the phone was talking to them on their radios and then to me so I knew what was going on.

Even when he told me it was OK to let them in I was still afraid.

"Put the gun down first. And then let the officers in," he said. That was probably a good idea. Even the good guys don't want to face a panicked woman with a gun.

I held the gun at my side and made my way slowly to the door. When I saw two officers at the door, I laid the gun on the table and let them in. They went through the house and found where a heavy book had fallen over onto a glass vase, shattering it on the floor.

I was happy to get back to Chicago until I learned that a *Sun-Times* column had trashed me again, saying that by rights *Jenny Jones* should have been canceled after its first "abysmal" year. "Ratings stunk, stations were bailing out, and Jones wasn't cutting it as a feminist comic turned fluffy talk show host," it continued. Then, they said, I'd been repackaged as a "finger-pointing busybody," and they called the show "an ugly hour."

I thought the negative local press might turn around when *Chicago Magazine* approached our publicity department saying they wanted to write a positive feature article about me. A reporter visited me at the office, came to some shows, and I thought we got along very well. We welcomed her to every area of our offices and studio and then waited for the story to come out.

At least somebody in Chicago likes me, I thought.

I couldn't have been more wrong.

She's a perk-crazed, demanding prima donna

The issue of *Chicago Magazine* that contained my profile came out in April 1993, and the first I heard about it was when Mark Robbins called.

"Have you seen it?" he demanded to know.

I had to admit I hadn't.

"Well, you better read it, because it's very negative toward you."

I hung up and rushed to the publicist's office to see if someone could get a copy. There it was, lying on her desk, open to the article on me. She said it was so bad she didn't know how to tell me about it and felt responsible for suggesting I do the interview in the first place. I took it back to my office to see the extent of the slur.

The title of the article was "Talking Trash." The first part of the story was an indictment of single-topic talk shows; then the writer put me, personally, on trial.

Among the choice morsels on the show and the host:

> *She was a Teflon talk-show host; perhaps in part because of her comedy background, she seemed to be thinking about the next thing she would say rather than listening to her guests. . . .*
>
> *She was haughty and indifferent to the local NBC talent. She refused to push the buttons in the elevator herself. She was perk-crazed, demanding limos and bragging about how she got to keep the wardrobe for her show. The* Tribune's *"Inc." column printed rumors that Jones had fired up to fourteen hairdressers in just over two months.*

I sat there in a fog, unable to think of one thing I'd done during the interview that would make this woman believe I was such a diva that I wouldn't even push an elevator button. I walked to work almost every day and made it a point to say hello to everyone, from security to the cleaning people to the guy who polishes the floor in the evening. I took cabs most places and rode in limos only for special appearances.

I still don't know why the magazine did the scathing piece on me. My first reaction was to call the editors and issue a complaint that the article was nothing but a bunch of lies and to challenge them to prove any one of the ridiculous accusations. I was advised by our head of publicity not to contact the magazine, so, as always, even when I disagreed, I complied.

Two years later the same magazine printed more garbage about me and reprinted some of the same lies about my being such a prima donna I wouldn't push my own elevator buttons. This time I didn't ask the bosses, I called the editor myself and invited him and the writer who initially interviewed me to lunch.

The editor showed up, but not surprisingly the writer couldn't make it.

"Wasn't once enough?" I asked him. "Why would you print that stuff again?"

"Nobody called to complain, " he said. "We figured if it wasn't true somebody would have called us."

It seemed to me that the more successful the show was becoming, the more often I was attacked by the press, and I began to wonder if this was people's way of "keying the car." You know how some people see a great car and scrape a key along its side as they walk past it, resentful that someone else has something really nice? They damage the car, never knowing what it took to finally own that beautiful piece of machinery. Sure, it could have been a gift from a wealthy parent to a spoiled child, but it could just as easily have been the result of twenty-five years of hard work and commitment to succeed. I didn't have a car to damage, but I did have a reputation that took twenty-five years of hard work and commitment to build.

Not only did I not keep the show wardrobe, I didn't even like the show wardrobe.

I don't care much about fashion and only dress up when I have to; if you stop by the office you'll probably find me in sneakers and a sweater. In fact, I didn't even know any designers' names until I started dressing up for the talk show.

At first I thought I was supposed to wear everything the show's wardrobe stylist handed me, whether it felt right for me or not. After all, who was I to question? The wardrobe supervisor the first year had put me in lots of pastels and casual clothes, and while I love soft colors, I don't like wearing them every day. Then we started receiving mail that indicated people thought the repetition was boring, so a new wardrobe woman came in and dressed me in expensive high-end fashion suits and jackets by frou-frou designers. The wardrobe supervisor loved this designer stuff, but it was her style, not mine.

I kept telling people it didn't feel like me, but they loved the chic look and paid no attention. Finally I made a stand and demanded to be part of wardrobe decisions. Now I wear what I like.

(Just for the record, I sometimes compromise. For example, when I wore a bunny suit on one of our Halloween shows, it wasn't my first choice. I wanted to go as a chicken, but Ed Glavin got the chicken suit.)

37

A Day in My Panty Hose

The life of a daytime TV talk show host is an unforgiving blur of constant motion: two shows usually taped back-to-back three days each week, two hundred shows each season, with the rest of the week set aside for preproduction. One day runs into the next with barely time for even a breath in between. While we're taping one show, another waits in the wings, while the show after that is on its way to being assembled. The past seven years have been a nonstop marathon of show titles: Makeovers, Reunions, Out-of-Control Teens, My In-Laws Are Ruining My Marriage, My Husband's a Slob, My Mom Dresses Too Sexy, People Who Think They're All That! . . . shows about every conceivable subject.

But I share one important characteristic with every guest and every audience member. We're all from the same world.

I'm not a former actress, journalist, or beauty queen. I come from the world of hard work. My jobs as a waitress, movie theater ticket taker, receptionist, office manager, musician, caterer, accounts payable clerk, and housewife and stepmother gave me all the talk show experience I've ever needed. I understand my guests because we come from the same world, where everyday life is filled with drama.

The Jenny Jones Show is a platform for everyday people, and I'm proud to give them a place to be seen and heard. Our show is both entertaining and informative, but, most importantly, it fills a gigantic void. Just because some of our guests are not rich or beautiful or well-educated doesn't mean they don't deserve to be on national TV, no matter what the critics say. It's clear from their inaccurate reporting that most critics never watch talk shows anyway.

I'd like to take you behind the scenes into our production offices to see how a typical show gets made. For me, the process begins when one day's taping has ended and preparations for the next day have already begun. It's probably five o'clock in the afternoon and the office has been bustling all day long.

The area you'd probably notice first is our "PA Row," where a bank of a half dozen computers is manned by production assistants (PAs) striving to keep pace with a flood of incoming calls, letters, and E-mail messages. When people want to appear on *The Jenny Jones Show*, their first contact with our show is usually PA Row. Each of our seven production assistants gets twenty-five to thirty calls an hour, about everything from show ideas to ticket requests to responses to our in-show plugs. ("If your family disapproves of your mate, call 312-832-4180.")

Shows like *The Tonight Show* and *Letterman* can find their guests through agents and publicists, but most of our guests have to find us. They contact the show through the phone numbers we flash on the television screen. Some people think the talk show host does everything, including book the guests. While I'm finally involved in most aspects of the show, I don't book the guests. Booking two thousand to three thousand guests per year requires a sizable staff working countless hours. People who know me joke that if I had the time, I'd probably want to do that, too. But it would be impossible.

Most of the people who call our offices feel like they know me, which, of course, they do. Each morning, our PA Row phone lines are clogged with hundreds of messages, from people in every corner of America. Something in our show has struck a chord with them, and they've dropped what they're doing to call us.

"Hey, Jenny, my life is better than fiction. . . ."

"Hi, Jenny, I have a story to tell you. . . ."

"Good morning, Jenny, I have a great show idea!"

I can still hardly believe that I host a national talk show. But it's not about recognition, much less celebrity or fame. It's about the satisfaction of making a difference in somebody's life, whether it's a teenager who changes her behavior after seeing herself on the show or a battered wife who finally leaves her abusive husband with our help and support after the show is over.

In spite of what you might have heard from the critics, many people really do come on talk shows seeking assistance. And our help doesn't stop once the cameras are off. We're constantly supporting people after they appear on our show, whether it's paying for counseling for a troubled family or getting someone hospitalized for an eating disorder. It might be a mother who disowned her son because he had AIDS, reentering his life after being reunited with him on our show. Or it could be the woman who cringed after watching herself being taken to task by our audience for her blatant racism toward her Hispanic son-in-law. She returned less than six months later to declare her radical change of heart in the same place she had declared her prejudice. Those kinds of stories, however, never make the headlines.

I think interracial shows are important and feel compelled to do them. Racism exists throughout America, but where else is it really exposed for its ugliness? I realize that you can't change every guest in one hour of television, but it's just amazing how much impact an audience of 250 people can have when every single one of them disagrees with your way of thinking.

Every so often we reach somebody. Those are the shows that make my job worthwhile. But, of course, our show isn't just about providing information; we're also about entertainment. As a stand-up comic, I've always tried to take the lighter approach, to use humor to help make people comfortable. I get a thrill every time the audience explodes in laughter. If you're a regular viewer of the show, you know that happens a lot.

We're always trying to come up with new show ideas, especially when we're starting a new taping season—which runs on a schedule similar to a school year, from August to May, with a summer hiatus. Show topics are assigned by the executive producers, but all of the members of our staff suggest their own ideas. I always know which topics are in the works, but on days that are more hectic than usual, or if I've been traveling, I sometimes don't know which topic we're taping until the night before. Other times, I'm expecting to tape a show about one topic, but due to last-minute cancellations, it turns out to be a topic we'd originally scheduled for another day. You'd be surprised how many shows are not finalized until the last minute.

I'm always excited to try something new. I'm even more grati-fied when it's a new idea of mine, like the Positive Self-Image Week, or a children's talent show. We often repeat our most popular top-ics, always looking for new ways to do them. When we come up with a topic that has not been done before, we guard and protect it like a military secret to keep the competition from doing it first. It's a bit like my days in stand-up, when we were afraid to do new ma-terial with certain other comics around.

At 5 P.M., PA Row is buzzing with callers. Since it's the end of the taping day, you would find me in my office overlooking the Chicago River. You probably wouldn't recognize me. I am out of my show outfit and back in my street clothes, preparing for the tap-ing of tomorrow's two shows. Generally when we tape, the day runs from early morning until 4 or 5 P.M. While Debby, Ed, and I, along with that day's producers, associate producers, production assistants, and others are in the studio with the crew, the rest of the staff is busy working in the offices on the next day's shows. As I've said, we usually tape two shows a day, three days a week, sometimes taping two days in a row. Those back-to-back days are the hardest, because we usually work about thirty-two out of forty-eight hours.

A homework night

The blueprint for every show is assembled in what we call the fold-ers, standard file folders prepared by our segment producers. I call it my homework, and it's one of the hardest parts of my job. But I've never been afraid of hard work. I pride myself on always being prepared. I owe it to my guests to know their stories when they come on my show and to help them feel more comfortable on the air.

At approximately 7 P.M., I head home to my Chicago condominium, grab a bite of the home-cooked dinner I prepare ahead on the weekends, and immediately settle in for a full night's work. First, I slip into my "work clothes," a pair of sweatpants and a denim shirt. I slide on a pair of socks—never shoes—and lie back on the sofa with my feet propped up on the armrest. I'll remain in this position, with only brief recesses for stretching, for the next four or five hours. I take a deep breath, mostly from the thought of the workload to follow, then open the first folder and begin reading.

Pretty soon, a mountain of paperwork builds up around me. With the first folder on my lap and assorted pencils and pens under my chin, I soon become literally buried by my work. I'm so trapped beneath the papers that I have to use a cordless phone for outside communication; otherwise, it would take an eternity to dig out from under and get to the phone. Some nights I might be able to read uninterrupted, but on others the phone will ring ten or fifteen different times, with members of the staff calling about guest cancellations or other crises.

The first thing in every folder is the "Dear Jenny" letter, which is the introductory note from the segment producer describing the overall nature of the show. It usually begins the same way: "Dear Jenny, today's morning show is . . . " and then the title of the segment—"My Sister Can't Stand My Sexy Clothes" or "I'm the King and She's My Slave." The letter is an introductory element Ed and Debby created to add a personal touch to the paperwork to follow. It's a chance for the segment producer to convey last-minute information and to give personal thoughts about the guests. Even though the segment producer and I may have already discussed the show together in person, he or she always includes the "Dear Jenny" letter.

Next, it's time to read the blue cards. Remember those blue cards I was straining to see when I sneaked into *The Phil Donahue*

Show? I'll never know what was written on Phil's blue cards, but mine simply contain the highlights of each guest's pre-interview. The blue cards are my Cliffs Notes: Some people think there are questions on them, but my cards contain only a series of one-line "bullet points" designed to trigger my memory about the basics on each guest. It's a way for me to recall quickly the guest's name, age, marital status, and story. When I'm finished reading the blue cards, I have an understanding of the story, but it's only a synopsis. For the full story, I turn next to each guest's pre-interview.

If the blue cards are the Cliffs Notes, the pre-interview is the book. The pre-interview gives me the essence of a guest's personality, as well as his or her story. Every guest who appears on our show is interviewed first by phone, and the pre-interview is an edited transcript of that interview. There are usually eight to twelve pre-interviews, depending on the number of guests on the show. The most we've had so far is twenty-five! I've probably read close to twenty thousand pre-interviews in the last seven years.

Next comes the script. This is nothing like the forty-to-fifty-page scripts from year one, which included exhaustive questions and lengthy answers. It's simply a series of introductions for each guest and "teases" ("When we come back, we'll meet Bob, who has another version of the story."), along with dialogue to open the show. During my first year on the air, I read every script on camera exactly as written, afraid even to ask if it could be changed. But from season one to season two, the script was reduced from fifty pages to a handful, thanks to producers who believe in my judgment and my ability to ad lib. At night, I rewrite many of the scripts, which usually adds an hour or so of homework. But I'm willing to take the time to find fresh and creative ideas, especially new ways to open the show.

Then I scan several pages of "chyrons," the names and descriptions that will flash across the bottom of the television screen during the show, identifying each guest and giving a brief description of the topic at hand, such as: SUSAN: ABOUT TO MEET HER LONG-LOST LOVE, immediately followed by SUSAN: JUST MET HER LONG-LOST LOVE.

The production rundown comes next. It details every entrance, exit, prop, musical cue, lighting, special effect, and so on in the upcoming show. Since we make so many last-minute changes, I often end up creating a handwritten revised rundown during the morning briefing. The rundown is crucial information. Which of our set's nine different entrances is the guest going to be using? I need to know. Is anyone going to get up and dance or sing, recite poetry or propose marriage? I need to know when and where. Since we do more elaborate production than the average daytime show, I always have to know what's happening on the technical side: when to call for music, when to call for tape, when to call for photos. It's a lot of information to process. Without the production rundown, the show would be chaotic. Even then our shows may not go as planned, and halfway through we sometimes wind up totally winging it anyway.

Once I have made my own abbreviated version of the production rundown on yellow cards, I'm ready for the research packet. Some topics don't require research. On a makeover show, for instance, there's no need to know how many people changed their looks in 1996. But other stories require background. How many teenagers get pregnant in America each year? Shows about AIDS, domestic abuse, interracial relationships, promiscuous teens—I have to be up on the latest information and statistics. All of this is included in the research packet, which can be substantial, especially for shows about topics in the news like the O.J. Simpson trial.

Then it's time to look at the photos. How can I even begin to describe the photos? They're like postcards from America. You'd be amazed at what potential guests send us. Naked pictures? Yes, it's happened. But most of them are just plain fun. If we put out a plug on the show—"If your husband's a slob and needs a makeover"—we get envelope after envelope full of photographs that more than prove the point. The photographs are vital. We have to know the guy is truly in need of a Jenny Jones makeover.

Finally, I get to the seating chart. It indicates where each guest will be sitting onstage. It's crucial to know who's sitting where, in order to direct the questions to the right person.

Finished with the first folder in two or three hours, I begin to work through the second. When I'm done with that it's usually past midnight. I take a quick bath—since I'm not willing to sacrifice the sleep time a shower would steal from me in the morning—and collapse into bed.

Everyday people

The alarm clock goes off at 7:30 A.M., making an unwelcome series of electronic bleeps. I'm out of bed in a flash, washing my face, getting dressed, gulping green tea, and grabbing my briefcase— packed with the two complete folders and my lunch of home-cooked soup, turkey chili, or leftovers. I walk or drive the short distance to work, arriving less than thirty minutes after the alarm clock's ring.

By the time I swing into the NBC Tower, audience members are already waiting in line for the show. Our studio audience is enormous. It numbers 250 people per show, for two shows a day, three days each week—which means half of a million people will have attended a taping of *The Jenny Jones Show* by the millenium. But almost none of the audience members recognizes me in the morning, not even when I say hello. With no makeup and my hair hidden under a baseball cap, I'm just another working girl arriving for yet another day. I have one of those faces that disappears without makeup; I could be anybody. That's why I can do my own grocery shopping and freely walk the streets of Chicago. I get a radical makeover every morning before I go on camera. I never wear makeup when I go out, because I'd be recognized. I do my job and then go home, and if I go out at all I go quietly.

Our staff includes seventy-five people—executive producers, segment producers, associate producers, production assistants, technical crew—and sometimes it seems everybody urgently needs something from me at once. Early on taping day mornings, they can find me in my second-floor makeup and wardrobe room.

From 8 to 10:30 A.M. on taping days, the makeup chair is my command center. Immediately upon arriving, I'll undress, wash my hair in the bathroom sink, and slip on a bathrobe. The makeup area is actually like a tiny studio apartment, consisting of the makeup and wardrobe room, a briefing room, a bathroom, and a makeshift kitchen, where I usually cook my own breakfast and lunch. Five minutes after arriving, I'm in the makeup chair, and the transformation begins: It takes two and a half hours, with interruptions. All the while I'm talking and writing or rewriting material. Sometimes our director, Tom Maguire, will pop in to discuss that morning's show, or a segment producer will have an issue requiring my immediate attention. My makeup artist, Earl Nicholson, has become adept at applying makeup to whatever parts of my face are not moving.

Beside the makeup mirror, a monitor with a live feed from one of our cameras lets me keep up with what's going on in the studio. It's always bustling. Equipment is being checked and set up: cameras, audio, lighting, TelePrompTer, chyron, tape machines, monitors, control boards, headphones, and props, if required. The stage is being set for the morning show. That work could include, depending on the topic, erecting walls, setting up band equipment, building ramps, and installing special spotlights. If the stage requires extra preparation or decorating (for our Christmas show, for example), or if we are performing weddings on the air (and we've done several), then the crew stays late the night before to get the job done. I constantly check out the monitor to stay abreast of the progress. And there's a steady stream of phone calls, so a cordless phone is always at my side.

Sometimes the director needs me on the set, so I'll leave the makeup chair, still in my robe, slippers, and hair rollers, and try to sneak down the hall, where I invariably run into a stray audience member. I have a hot line to Debby and Ed; we're reviewing show details throughout the morning. Liz Chevrie, our TelePrompTer operator, comes in to get my revised version of the script to enter the material into her prompter. (If there's a lot of material, I will have faxed it to her the night before; I don't read anything on camera that I haven't personally reviewed.) Megan Anderson, our booth coordinator, comes by to check on any changes we may have made in the guests' seating arrangements.

That's the first hour. It's now 9:00 A.M.

Ed, Debby, and the segment producer arrive in the makeup room, and we all go into the small briefing room next door.

"So, Jenny, how do you want to open?" Ed might say.

"Well, here's my idea," I'll answer, then begin to lay it out for the group.

The briefing is supposed to take fifteen minutes, but it's seldom that short, and occasionally it runs closer to an hour. The segment producer offers any last-minute information that was not included in the folder, since by now he or she has met all the guests in person. There are photos to pass around and videotapes to screen. These tapes are the "field pieces" each producer has created prior to his or her show, usually staying up late the night before editing the clips. We sometimes make drastic changes in the entire show during this briefing, in which case I do another handwritten set of rundown cards on the spot, which I then have photocopied for everyone who needs it.

When the briefing is over, Debby and Ed might then want to discuss something that's totally unrelated to the day's show but requires my immediate attention, like an employee problem or a decision on a graphic design. Then it's back to the makeup chair. Sometimes I find things that were placed on my chair during briefing, like some on-air promo spots I'll need to read on-camera after the second show. ("She lost one hundred pounds and gets a makeover: Next *Jenny Jones!*") I'll review the material, edit if necessary, and call Kim Raymonds, our promotions director, if I have any questions.

On the days when I do a live radio interview on a morning drive show, it's done from the makeup chair. We just shut the door and put a Do Not Disturb—Live Radio sign on it while I go on the air. Between all of this, I continue to sip green tea and try to review the materials in my folders, awaiting the additional changes that will invariably come. Just when I think we're finally set, a producer might rush in and say the entire order of the show is being changed, requiring a total overhaul of the script and production rundown. All the changes have to come to me, because I do the final script and final production rundown.

Around 10:30, Liz brings in a printout of the script from her TelePrompTer and I give it one last read, while the stage manager, Kat Lysek, begins asking about my estimated time of arrival. There's so much to do that often we're barely able to fit it all in without running late. I've been on the phone with Dana, who might need my response on a scholarship question, or our publicist may have needed an immediate quote to meet a press deadline. By now, I should be getting into wardrobe, but my hair and makeup aren't finished, and I'm starving. No time to make oatmeal. I eat a piece of toast and gulp down a glass of skim milk and then, once hair and makeup are done, put on whatever Earl, who is also my wardrobe supervisor, is holding up for me to wear. I grab the blue cards and begin the race toward the studio for the 11 A.M. taping. Earl is usually chasing after me, frantically fixing a sleeve or tucking something in, while my personal assistant, Brian L'Heureux, chases me down with whatever I've forgotten.

My first stop is the two or three green rooms (which are never green, by the way), where the guests for the day's shows are waiting. Sometimes while walking to the green rooms, especially when we're doing shows involving mothers and daughters, I think about my own mother. What would she say if she could see how hard I work and how much I've grown? She was able to attend two tapings before she passed away. She appeared to enjoy being there but never seemed impressed by how much I was contributing behind the scenes. I guess she just tuned out. If ever she were going to tell me she noticed, it would have been then. It never happened. But that's another story.

Right now, I'm getting ready to welcome two or three green rooms full of guests. They arrived in Chicago the night before, if everything went smoothly, from all corners of the country. When I open the door, it's always a rush, a revelation. Some have their luggage with them; some have brought along their babies. For some guests this trip is their first time ever in a big city, and for some their first ride in an airplane. They come from big cities and small towns, from Griffin, Georgia, and Janesville, Wisconsin, and Maryville, Tennessee, all eager to tell their stories on national television.

They're all excited to see me, someone they consider a celebrity. Many of them actually gasp when I walk into the room. But they're not always starstruck. "You look a lot taller on TV," they'll say. I'll just smile, answer their questions, and try and help them feel comfortable about their impending television debut. Not surprisingly, the most often asked question is "What are you going to ask me?" My answer is usually the same: "I don't know yet, except that my questions will be based on your interview. I don't have any particular questions planned." I believe that's what keeps our show spontaneous.

We'll take some pictures if they ask, and after I've met all of the guests I head for the control room, which by now will be bustling with activity. I give Debby and Ed my impressions of the guests I've just met. Sometimes, I feel strongly about making changes in the order of their appearance. The crew might grumble a bit, but they trust my instincts and we make yet another change. Finally, the last of a morning's changes are made, just as guests leave the green rooms and are taken backstage to get their microphones checked.

Then Ed and I head backstage, where he'll say something like, "All right, we're going out!"

Finally it's show time, and the culmination of all of our efforts is about to begin. The cameramen take their places, and the guests prepare to go onstage. By now our resident comedian is warming up the audience. I get a last-minute hair, wardrobe, and makeup check. Then I walk up three steps to a tiny alcove at the side of the stage, where Ed is waiting. I pause a moment for any last-minute conferences and, perhaps, a quick sip of water. Then the audio technician hands me a mike, and I step out onto the stage.

It is the closest I've ever come to experiencing magic. The audience immediately erupts. Applause! Screams! Hoots! Whistles!

It's so over the top that I keep looking over my shoulder to see if someone's behind me telling them to stand and cheer. I'm always amazed to discover that there never is. Walking onto the set always makes me feel like I've come home. The new set was designed with my input, so it's exactly how I'd furnish my house. It's modern and comfortable, painted in all of my favorite colors, with the Chicago skyline in the background. Best of all, just like home, my family is waiting for me there: my audience. We're a team, my audience and I. They're opinionated, smart, and passionate. And they never hold back from letting me know exactly how they feel.

I chat with the audience from the stage for a moment, answer a few questions, then walk down to a spot in the middle of the crowd and begin the show. It's never dull, never ordinary. Except for the opening, the introductions, and the teases, our show is totally spontaneous. That's what makes it fun to do and fun to watch. What the viewers don't see is the continuous communication I have with Ed on the sidelines. He reminds me of last-minute changes by flashing hastily scrawled cue cards, while keeping an eye out for equally urgent signals from me. (By the way, I should get some kind of award for being able to read his cue cards.)

Hosting a talk show is the ultimate balancing act: keeping the audience involved, the guests telling their stories, the production aspects running as smoothly as possible . . . all with twenty hands being raised in the air around you and three people talking at once onstage.

We tape seven segments for each show, with seven or eight minutes allotted for each. It can all take as little as an hour or, if it's a makeover show, two hours or more. When we stop taping to actually do the makeovers, I spend a little time with the studio audience, just chatting and answering questions, and then I spend the rest of the time in the green room where the makeovers are being done. I've already seen and approved all the makeover clothes, but I want to make sure the guests are happy with their new looks. If they're not, I ask the stylists to try something different. Many times I've loaned a pair of my shoes or a belt or jewelry to a guest who needs it. If we're running behind, I'll help dress the guests.

The show is over in a flash. While the audience is still applauding and the cameras are still rolling, Ed and I are already discussing when to brief for the second show. The producers and guests leave the studio, but I sometimes stay on the set to take pictures with fans or to tape a prearranged interview with one of our affiliate stations. Then Dana accompanies me back to the dressing room, updating me as we walk on any calls or business that took place that morning. Back in the dressing room, I slip out of my show clothes and get back into the robe.

Upstairs, a thousand details await my attention. There's mail, and phone messages, stacks of photographs to autograph, requests for personal appearances, T-shirts to sign for fundraisers, publicity requests to review, calls to return to women with breast implant concerns, viewer mail to answer, and constant administrative duties. I'm continually meeting with Debby and Ed about the staff and crew, and we're always passing production ideas back and forth. I try to catch up with these things on the two days we don't tape.

Later in the day, there will be special promotional spots to tape for any of our close to two hundred affiliate stations that request them. ("Hi, I'm Jenny Jones, and you're watching WWOR in New York.") Or maybe there's a field shoot on location in a restaurant or a movie theater. I even went to an airstrip for our skydiving piece. I do special vignettes shot in the studio, like when we did "Jenny and her twin" or "Jenny skiing down the slopes." There are always wardrobe fittings, and ideas to discuss with individual producers, and production elements to review with the show's director. I'm also very involved in our office management, whether it's helping to set up organizational systems or making sure our kitchen is clean. I participate in the planning of every staff party, right down to the menu, and I plan my own treats for the staff, like lunches, in-house manicures, massages, yogurt sundaes, and Christmas gifts. I'm told not every host is as involved as that, but it's what I choose—and love— to do.

But right now all I can think about is the second show. Thirty minutes after the first show ends, we're briefing for the second, and the entire process is repeated again.

38

Talk Show Topics

Since our shows cover a lot of topics, I know we can't please everyone. What we can do is try and provide a balance. For instance,
we'll do a show on women who think they are too beautiful to get
a date, then two days later air a serious show on AIDS. We bring ex-
perts on when we deal with people in emotional trauma. We've provided therapy and treatment for girls with anorexia and safe houses
for battered wives; we've helped gang members move and assisted
with the expense of having their gang-related tattoos removed. We
continually provide information about AIDS and promote safe sex.
We even got a doctor to donate time for someone's needed surgery
and have provided countless guests with follow-up counseling, sometimes with our staff psychologist, sometimes with someone in their
own area. The best letters we get from viewers are the ones that say,
"I watched your show and decided to leave my abusive boyfriend"
or "If that lady on your show could lose a hundred pounds, so can I."

A May-December marriage

One of our best post-show developments involved neither a medical nor a psychological remedy. In this case, the show made a very
personal commitment to the growth of one of our guests.

When Ed Glavin was still a segment producer on *Donahue*,
he received a letter from a woman named Jan, who started dating

her husband, Tyler, when he was sixteen and she was thirty-six. After he became our executive producer, Ed put together a show featuring several May-December couples, but none of them had a story to tell like Jan and Tyler.

They began their affair when Tyler was dating Jan's daughter. Back then, Jan was married and Tyler was a virgin. Now they made quite a pair—the handsome young man and the blonde bombshell—their every emotion played out in the open.

Jan was Ed's idea of the perfect guest. She was attractive, camera savvy, and outspoken. She knew when she agreed to come on the show that the audience would chastise her for the marriage, and she didn't seem to mind their disapproval a bit. Tyler was a handsome, personable young man who looked younger than his nineteen years. He was more nervous than Jan before the show, but he too seemed to enjoy the attention. His mother, Marilyn, had been matron of honor at Jan and Tyler's wedding, and she also appeared on the show. The audience loved their story.

This one booking might have been the end of it. But the following year, Ed learned that Jan and Tyler were divorcing and wanted to make a return appearance. Their on-again off-again relationship finally ended, but not before they had been back to the show four times. Not only did their marriage fall apart, their personal lives had disintegrated by their final appearance. I knew Tyler had suffered from drug problems, while Jan was trying to market her own X-rated videos.

Several months after the last Jan and Tyler show, Ed stopped by my office and totally floored me with what he said. "I'd like to hire Tyler Thomas to work here."

I was stunned. "Why?" I asked. I only knew Tyler as a guest—and a volatile, unstable, former drug-using guest at that. "I have a hard time picturing Tyler in this office," I went on. "I don't know what to say."

"Well, think about it," Ed said. "I just feel he should do something with his life. I see something good in him. I see potential."

I didn't go back to Ed with an answer because I didn't have one. A few weeks later, he broached the subject again.

"Jenny, I was serious about wanting to hire Tyler," he said, indicating that he meant to have a serious conversation by closing the door to my office behind him.

"Why?" I asked. "What do you see in him that I don't see?"

"I see myself at that age," he said. "I see a kid who is smart and talented but has never had any direction. I think, with a little help, he could do well. But if he doesn't get some guidance—well, I don't know what will happen to him." I respected Ed's judgment. Even if I didn't share it, his vision was good enough for me.

"Go ahead," I said. "I don't want to stand in the way of whatever it is you see in him."

Ed phoned Tyler, offered him a job as a production assistant on the show, and then laid down the law. He said Tyler could come to work for us, but if he messed up, he was out the door. "I plan to hold you to a higher standard than anyone else in this office," Ed said.

Since Tyler had his GED, Ed decided the next step should be college and suggested classes in television and business writing as a good start down a long but important road. Ed held up his own father, who went to school at night for nine years to get a college degree, as an example. Tyler was hesitant, fearing his dyslexia set him up for failure. Fortunately for Tyler, failure is a concept Ed never accepts. Tyler has more than lived up to Ed's faith in him, having successfully completed a television course, and just as this book was in its final stages he got his final English grade, a B. He says bringing in that grade was one of his proudest moments; it taught him that in the long run having dyslexia doesn't have to ruin his hopes for a career. In the short run, he says, it just meant staying home and studying when his friends went out partying.

Today, Tyler is one of the hardest working employees we have. He's dependable, loyal, and honest. He's been promoted from production assistant to guest coordinator and has already filled in as an associate producer.

When Tyler learned that he was going to be a part of this memoir, he asked for the opportunity to say something about his mentor. "At times Ed's been like a big brother, and at others he's like a father," Tyler told me. "I feel comfortable joking around with him, but at the same time he commands respect, and I want to live up to his trust and belief in me. When he gives me additional responsibilities, he always says, 'OK, Tyler, I'm givin' you the rope — don't hang yourself with it.' That always makes me sweat, and that's good, because I just work harder to prove him right about me."

I'm proud of Tyler and even prouder of Ed's commitment to someone in whom he truly believed.

Mothers and daughters

Some people think talk-show hosts just do their shows and go home. Not always. I've kept in touch with some guests personally after their shows were taped. Other guests simply leave indelible memories. One time we had a woman who asked to confront her brother's killer, who'd just been released from prison. I was surprised that he agreed to come on the show, and I was nervous, never having faced a killer before. As the victim's sister vented her anger, it was clear to me that a part of her had died with her brother. All she wanted was an apology.

At first the man said coldly he would make no apologies for the murder; he'd done his time, and that was the end of it as far as he was concerned. "I just felt like killing somebody," he said. I asked him if he was sorry, hoping to see some remorse. When he replied with an emotionless "No," I felt I'd failed the woman who had requested the confrontation. Then, when the show was over, the cameras were off, and he'd started to leave the set, the killer turned back to me and said, "Tell her I'm sorry about her brother." It was a small victory.

Another time a convicted rapist agreed to come on the show to give women advice on how to avoid at-risk situations. It was a difficult show for me to do, since even though I hadn't been raped, I'd certainly been beaten. I talked about the feelings I experienced, the terror of being afraid for my life. The man kept looking at me intently, and I saw tears in his eyes. When I asked him why he was crying, he said, "I've never looked into the eyes of a victim before."

Those segments touched me deeply, but I never fell completely apart on a show until a taping we did in April of 1993. "Mothers and Daughters" was part of a week-long series we did on self-esteem. Both the panel and the entire studio audience were made up of mothers and daughters, and we invited Dr. Victoria Secunda, the author of *When You and Your Mother Can't Be Friends*, to be our expert. Victoria's daughter, Jennifer, was also a guest. Victoria spoke about her own mother, an aloof woman who seldom showed Victoria affection, and said that when Jennifer was born she'd vowed to do the opposite.

I began to feel uneasy, reminded that I couldn't recall any affection from my own mother.

As other women told their stories one by one, I started praying no one would ask about mine. I didn't want to talk about something this painful in front of millions of viewers. I knew for certain that I couldn't hold back the tears. It was just too painful.

The audience got very involved in the show, and at one point a woman stood and said something that went straight to my heart. "I wish my mother would call me more often. Come and visit. She has time, just not time for me."

I couldn't help myself. "My own mother never calls," I said. "Never. If I don't call, we don't talk." Tears started rolling down my face. "Why is this so difficult?" I said, trying desperately not to fall apart.

Victoria spoke up: "When my writing career took off I was constantly trying to be successful, yet never getting my mother's approval, no matter what I did. It just wasn't going to happen. Did you ever feel that way, Jenny?"

"Yes," I said, still crying.

"It hurts, doesn't it?" Victoria asked. "If one could say to one's mother as I did to mine — I wrote the last part of this book to my mother, and it was really a love letter to her — if one could say, 'Could we just start over, because I always thought I was doing what I thought you wanted. Why is this never enough?'"

"My mother does the best she can," I said, "but our relationship is never going to be what I wanted it to be. It's never going to get better, and I've accepted that. Or maybe I haven't, and that's why I'm crying."

After the show, I often thought about the letter Victoria had written to her mother, but I didn't know if I could make a similar gesture. I wouldn't know where to start. I didn't mention the show to Mother and hoped she wouldn't see it.

Not long after the show aired, the *National Enquirer* called and wanted to interview me about that segment. What was wrong with the relationship between me and my mother? Why had I broken down on the show? I told them I did not want to talk about it.

They didn't give up. They sent reporters to Canada, searching for my family. They located my sister, my aunt, and my uncle, and finally they got past the security at my mother's apartment and knocked on her door. Mother was very ill by this time and answered the door in her housecoat, with disheveled hair, wearing no makeup. They told her they needed a photo of her holding a photo of me and refused to leave without it. She finally agreed and posed for the picture, thinking they'd never go unless she did as they said.

When she told me about it I was furious. I told her she had every right to hang up on people or slam the door in their faces if they tried to bully her. She said she didn't want to be rude. It struck me as strange that she could say the most horrible, hateful things to me but didn't want to offend the *National Enquirer*. My lawyer contacted the tabloid immediately, and the photo was never published.

Oddly, Mother never once asked me—or anyone else, that I know of—what had prompted the *Enquirer* to show up at her door. Maybe she sensed that asking about the incident would lead to a conversation that she didn't want to have. She wouldn't have been able to deny the true state of our relationship.

39

Good-bye, Mother

There wouldn't be much time left to repair our relationship. Mother was slowly fading away. About a month after the mother-daughter show, Liz called to say she thought Mother was dying and should be in a nursing home or a hospital. I phoned Mother to see if I could get a feel for her true condition, but she made light of Liz's concerns, saying, "Liz thinks she is God and that she can cure me."

I knew, as did Liz, that Mother never believed she was sick—she still denied ever having lung cancer, even after they removed part of her lung! Both my sister and I knew Mother's condition had worsened, that while the cancer was in remission, other problems were becoming more serious. Her kidneys were failing, her circulatory problems were so severe she might lose a foot, and she was becoming more forgetful, even talking of being places and having no idea how she got there.

I didn't know how bad it was and needed to find out for myself. But when I tried to push Mother for more information, she got irate and said, "I'm not a guest on your talk show! It's you who are making me sick!" By now you'd think I'd have been numb to her hateful comments, but I wasn't.

When I phoned her again a few days later, she must have been very depressed, because she finally admitted that she wanted Liz to visit from her new home in Thunder Bay. She didn't say anything about wanting me to come, so I bought Liz a ticket, and Liz went to see her for a few days. It did little good. Mother was still smoking and drinking

The next time I called, I woke her at 7 P.M. She was groggy, speaking in a slurred voice, and said she didn't know how long she'd been asleep; she slept most days. Her left hand and arm were numb and just hung by her side due to a minor stroke. Her vision was so weak she had trouble reading. She told me everybody was bothering her and to stop calling. If I wanted to know about her, she said, "Call Liz."

"I'll come soon, too," I promised.

"Just don't expect me to entertain you," she said.

The next time I spoke with Mother, she cried and told me the doctor had said there was nothing he could do for her. I thought that was an awful thing for a doctor to tell someone, but I let it pass.

"I'm losing my memory, I've forgotten how to take my blood pressure, and I walk like a turtle," she said.

She wasn't trying to be funny. She saw herself as an old turtle, stuck in its shell, barely able to get across the room. She asked me to get Liz another ticket to visit her, and while I promised I would do it, Liz didn't want to go, saying, "Mother always does this. Then when I get there she says she doesn't want to see anyone."

I didn't know what to do. I kept thinking I should visit her, yet I kept putting it off, never knowing if she sounded groggy from being weak or being drunk. A part of me believed I should go and make arrangements for her to enter a nursing home, where she could get proper care. But the times I'd mentioned that idea to Mother, she had let me know very clearly that she planned to die in her apartment, not among strangers. So I stayed in Chicago and threw myself into the show, thinking if she wanted me to come she would ask.

It wasn't difficult to insulate myself with work, because the show was undergoing a great deal of change in 1994. For one thing, my five-year contract was almost up and it was time to renegotiate. I hired attorney Jim Jackoway and signed on for another five years, through the year 2000. But I was most gratified to finally get the level of involvement I'd always wanted, the opportunity to participate in whichever areas I chose. I happily took on the increased responsibilities and was soon juggling not only added duties but additional guests as well.

We've made many changes in the past several years, one of the biggest being the sheer number of guests. For example, a typical show used to have an average of seven guests, and that number shot up to seventeen. It's the evolution of the genre; viewers like to hear from all parties involved in any given story and to see more stories. Every year we study the ratings as they relate to specific topics, and it's easy to see the different trends. Viewers' tastes are constantly changing. We also upped the level of production; I don't think any other talk show is as well produced and directed. Ed had the idea to book musical groups on our show; that gave us an added dimension while also giving some up-and-coming bands national exposure.

One area where I think we've been a trendsetter is with our production of field pieces. On many shows we will fly a cameraman out to a guest's hometown to shoot footage in the home, especially on makeover shows where we sometimes look through the guest's closet. Other times the pieces are shot in Chicago at landmarks like Navy Pier or on the shores of Lake Michigan. The tapes are then edited by the producers into little mini-movies and add a very popular visual element to our shows. Another evolution on a more technical level is the use of handheld cameras, which are constantly moving, as opposed to the traditional stationary ones.

I'm very proud of the quality of our production and our staff. And I'm also proud to say there are many people on staff today who have been with the show since its inception, so it truly feels like a family. A few staff members who got their training on our show have moved on, with our blessing, to other ventures, including Fox News, MSNBC, *Oprah*, and even the Home Shopping Network. One producer left us and is now a director of programming and development at a major television syndicator.

Beginning to let go

Toward the end of September, 1993, Mother's health had deteriorated to the point where she was admitted to the hospital. Within days she decided that a nice peaceful nursing home was a far better alternative. I flew to London and made the arrangements, even though by the time I arrived she had talked to her heartsick love Roland and changed her mind about the move. But the doctors assured us there was no alternative. Liz's daughter Lisa and I moved her belongings, and I bought her fresh fruit and flowers. She actually seemed to like her new home. We had agreed on a small room but there was only a large one available, and they gave us that until a small one became available.

I went home to Chicago the next day. (Every time I went to Canada I would fly to Detroit, rent a car, and drive for two hours; I preferred that to the small planes that flew into London.) I got back just in time to start my homework for the next day's shows. While I was reading, the phone rang. It was Mother, saying she hated the nursing home and wanted me to rent her an apartment and sign her up for Meals on Wheels. The next day she changed her mind.

When the smaller room became available, I went back to London to get her moved in. She complained about having to move again and said she wanted to stay in the big room, but the rent was an additional $500 per month for a room that was only three feet wider, which we all agreed was exorbitant. So we sent her to the smoking lounge, and her granddaughter, Lisa, and Lisa's husband, Duff, and I switched rooms.

She hated it. She told me she was embarrassed to tell people that Jenny Jones, who was on TV, was her daughter and wouldn't put her in the nicest room the home had to offer. I said, "Mother, they are charging five hundred dollars a month extra for three feet of space! It's outrageous." I bought her some new things for the room, deposited money in her account, and went back to Chicago. True to form, the next time we spoke she said her room was too big.

Roland was devastated. I wasn't aware how much until I found a letter from him addressed to Mother at the nursing home. His penmanship was shaky and his grammar bad (he was French-Canadian) but his love for Sophie was very clear. This is exactly how it read:

> Hi Sophie. I am sic to se you sic. To day I call your place de toll me you was O.K., you look the TV — I was appy to no dat. Sophie I stell love you. Wan you call me I was appy to eard your voiss in a telepnone. I remember the trip in Nort we sleep in a motel. I was appy to sleep wit you I lak you kep me warm. The time change to day not the same.
>
> I dont forget the pass eff I can doo someting for you let me no. I was appy to elp you Sophie. Eff you dont like tha place I ca elp I si a loyer e toll me i ave more otorety on you dan your family.
>
> Your family nevver care for you like me. I nevver live you a lonne for the lase 5 yers. I never go to my brather wit out you. On September 25 I live to get your birhday kake on the 27 you did not come to my place to have piss of kake. Liz toll you dont go.
>
> Dont forget tha Sophie I love you the same. I dont rite good I nevver go to scool. By By Sophie. I love you. I nevver forget you.
>
> Love, Roland

My heart broke for Roland as I read his letter. I knew he loved Mother and he always looked out for her. They had lived right across the hall from each other and they left their doors open all day long so it was like one big apartment. They spent every day together and I suspect that he was part of Mother's reason for finally letting me buy her a car. They went on trips together. Mother provided the car and Roland paid for the gas and hotels.

I couldn't understand why she wouldn't talk to him. She'd never known love like this in her life and I knew she cared for him deeply. They had even talked about getting married.

I called Roland myself to find him very angry. In his desperate broken English he said, "Sophie and I said we would never leave each other. I would never have left her like this. We said we would die together." He told me he would not stay at the apartment without her.

Most of his anger had been directed at Liz. They had had a big confrontation one day because he felt Liz was not acting in Mother's best interest. After Liz and Roland's big fight, Mother was caught in the middle. She chose her daughter. The next time I called Roland, his phone was disconnected.

I went back again in a couple of weeks and found Mother so depressed that the doctors had prescribed Prozac. "If I had a gun I would shoot myself," she said grimly. She feared she was losing her mind. I told her I didn't think she was losing her mind at all. "Mother, you've had to move away from your home and away from Roland, and you're sick. Of course you'll get depressed from time to time. That doesn't mean you're crazy!" I told her that, in my opinion, the best thing she could do was stay as active as possible. In a move that took me by surprise, she agreed to let me take her to Covent Garden Market, a wonderful mixture of farmers' fruit and vegetable stands and bakeries where I loved going as a child. We got a wheelchair, and I took her all around.

Over the months to come I tried to find things to keep Mother's mind alert. I brought her new jigsaw puzzles, magazines, and anything else I could find that might hold her interest. Once when I spoke with her on the phone, she said, "You know, Jenny, today I feel pretty good. I did a couple of pieces of the jigsaw, and I even smiled and said hello to someone!" I couldn't stop myself from smiling, even knowing that her time was short. Then she said something I didn't expect. "I'm gonna take care of myself and get better, Jenny. I miss you. When can you come back?"

"I miss you too, and I'll be there soon," I said.

The closeness vanished as quickly as it had come, and by the next time I spoke to her she didn't want me to visit. So I didn't.

In February of 1994, Mother decided to move to Thunder Bay and live with Liz. She said she'd been unhappy with the lack of privacy at the nursing home for several months and she wanted to spend what time she had left with her daughter.

She continued to get weaker throughout the rest of that winter, and in April she was admitted to the hospital, where she could undergo dialysis. The doctors didn't think she would ever leave the hospital. I kept up with her progress and wrote daily dispatches in my diary.

> *May 28: Liz called to say Mother isn't doing well. Don't know whether to fly up or not. I started getting a headache and threw up. Don't know why.*
>
> *May 29: I called Mother, and she sounded awful. She went in and out. I asked if she wanted me to come and she said she couldn't have any visitors. Then I said I could come up and she said, "I've heard that so many times before." Then she drifted off.*
>
> *May 30: Not much change except the doctor has to have Mother tell him to stop the dialysis and she didn't. She just drifts in and out, it's so sad. For a while I made reservations and was going, then got frustrated 'cause I don't want to go. What if she says something horrible to me and then dies? I cried. I even hoped she'd die right away so I wouldn't have to go.*
>
> *May 31: Vacillated all morning about going. Finally decided to go tomorrow.*
>
> *June 1: Finally flew to Minneapolis and changed to a nineteen-seater twin engine prop to Thunder Bay. It was late, but I got a taxi right to the hospital to see what she looked like. Her face was puffy and her arms were bruised and thin. Checked into hotel and didn't sleep much: 3:00 A.M. to 7:30 A.M.*
>
> *June 2: It was so sad to see Mother. She had no response to anything. I talked to her and told her we'd all miss her, told her I was glad she stopped the dialysis and that it would be OK. Told her hello from Roula and Denis. She seemed restless, especially in the afternoon. I believe she knew I was*

there. She looked right at me once. It seemed like she wanted to say something. The nurses kept coming in to move her but I couldn't watch. Everyone assured us she was not in pain. I watched them give her morphine in a syringe in her mouth because she was too weak to swallow.

I brushed her hair a couple of times and held her hand, but she didn't squeeze back. It was just a matter of time.

I didn't want to stay so I flew back to LA. I couldn't stop thinking about her, so I decided to call the hospital about 11:30 P.M. The nurse said she was resting soundly. About ten minutes later the phone rang and it was Liz. The hospital had just called her to say Mother had stopped breathing. Much as we all wanted it, it was still hard to take. Denis thinks that's why I had the urge to call. It seems that was exactly when she died.

I will always believe that she went tonight because we all said good-bye. I still haven't cried.

I didn't cry that night or the next day, when Liz called to say Mother was being cremated even as we spoke. I didn't cry for a long time. My unfulfilled relationship with my mother had wiped me out emotionally. I had cried so much for so long, there were no more tears left. These days it seems like I cry about her on a regular basis, but not about her death. The times I cry are when I think of her life.

I returned to work with the shadow of Mother's death and my unresolved grief stalking me. But as we worked hard to produce even better shows over the following months, little did I know that another tragedy was right around the corner.

40

Secret Crush

We were running down the home stretch of our fifth season: dead tired but nonetheless on a high. Our Neilsen numbers were better than ever. The *Today* show was about to tape an interview; *USA Today* was scheduling a positive piece. We were finally reaching our stride. We even thought we had a fighting chance to win an Emmy nomination for best daytime talk show.

Then, on Monday, March 6, 1995, we taped the same-sex secret crush show.

It was a fun show, it really was. Secret crush shows are always fun. It's always about somebody thinking someone else is cute or sexy or somehow desirable. Revealing the attraction on national TV makes it all the more exciting.

Secret crush shows are, of course, a staple of daytime TV talk shows. Between 1992 and early 1997 there were more than fifty secret crush shows on the air. The appeal is simple: *We've all been there.* Who hasn't had a secret crush? Secret crush shows have been done by Donahue, Maury, Montel, Sally, Ricki Lake, even Vicki Lawrence, in every possible variation, from "Guests Reveal Feelings for Others of the Same Sex" (Maury) to "Montel Plays Matchmaker by Uniting Secret Crushes." In my opinion, if a secret crush show is OK., then a same-sex secret crush show is OK, too. I loved the "same-sex" angle and I'm always looking for ways to include gay people in our shows. After all, gay people have crushes just like straight people.

By March of 1995, we had done several secret crush shows, one involving same sex crushes, which had aired with great success the prior November. Everybody always had a great time. The audience loved it, and, more often than not, our crush shows ended with what we call a "love connection," both parties declaring their interest in each other on the air.

Three of the guests were from Orion Township, Michigan, a Detroit suburb. Scott Amedure, thirty-two, a gay army veteran and bartender, lived in a trailer home on a street called Blue Bird Hill. Jonathan Schmitz, twenty-six, lived in the Lake Orion Apartments. A former roofer and furniture restorer, Jon worked as a waiter in a local restaurant called the Fox and Hounds Inn. His upstairs neighbor, Donna Riley, a probate court clerk and single mother, introduced him to Scott one day in the apartment parking lot. Jon and Donna were friends; they liked to talk, play backgammon, and listen to their favorite band, the Cars. They were trying to fix a broken brake light on Donna's car when Scott, whose brother, Wayne, also lived in the apartment complex, walked over, looking for Wayne.

Donna let Scott borrow her phone to try and locate his brother. On the way up to the apartment, Scott asked her if Jon was her boyfriend. Donna later said the following in her deposition: "I said no, and he said, 'Oh, he's a nice looking guy. . . .'" Donna had a strong feeling that Scott was gay, a fact he readily admitted. In fact, in her pre-interview she said she was trying to get Scott and Jon together. She invited both of them over to her apartment for dinner. During their first evening together, Jon discovered that Scott was gay and began asking questions on the subject. Pretty soon, the two men began joking. "They were mimicking like somebody that would be overtly gay, like talking with a lisp and stuff, and they were both doing it and laughing," Donna said in her deposition.

When we ran the guest plug seeking viewers who had same-sex secret crushes, Scott was watching and called the show, saying he had a crush on a young man named Jon. One of our segment producers called him right back and scheduled a pre-interview for later that night. Scott told the producer to call him at Donna's apartment, then, according to depositions, he called

Donna's answering machine and left a long, detailed message. It was a dramatic way to break the big news and ask her to join him on an all-expenses-paid trip to Chicago, where they would go on *The Jenny Jones Show* together to meet his secret crush. Then Scott called Donna at work and told her to check her answering machine.

Donna got very excited about the prospect of a free trip to Chicago. That night, Scott met her at her apartment, where they were contacted by one of our segment producers for their pre-interviews. From the beginning, Donna said later, she knew Scott's secret crush was on Jonathan Schmitz.

"Do you think Jon is gay?" the producer asked, according to Donna's pre-interview.

"He says his family and friends think he's gay, that they've confronted him about it," Donna replied. "I'm not a hundred percent positive about his preference."

"Do you and Scott discuss Jon?" the producer was quoted as saying.

"Oh, yeah, every day," said Donna. "Scott wants to take him skinny dipping. I'm trying to set it up this summer."

"Are you trying to help Scott get together with Jon?" the producer asked.

"I have them over together for dinner and stuff. . . ." said Donna. "Jon knows Scott's gay and he's fine with it."

"How do you think he'll react when he finds out Scott has a crush on him?"

"I have no idea," said Donna. "I think he's pretty open-minded, so he may be into it. I hope so for Scott's sake."

Since Jon didn't have a phone, Donna gave the producer Jon's work number. The next day, the producer called Jon at work, telling him that someone had a crush on him, that it could be a man or a woman, and that he was invited on the show to discover the identity of his admirer. Jon said he wasn't sure if he wanted "a guy saying that to him on the air" and wanted time to think about it. He thought about it for thirty minutes, then called the producer back and said he'd be "fine" with it.

According to Jon's pre-interview, it was clear that he was made aware that the person who had a crush on him could be a man.

"What if it isn't a woman?" was the question posed by the segment producer.

"I'm not into it, but I'll say, 'Thanks, but no thanks,'" Jon replied. "It would be a disappointment. Don't worry, I'll be OK."

He also told our producer that even if the crush was a man, he would "go with the flow."

When he got off work, Jon drove home and immediately went over to Donna's apartment. Scott was there.

"He came and confronted us about it," Donna said in her deposition. "He was really nervous and everything. He came in and said he had gotten a call from the—and he screwed up the name—*The Jenny Mitchell Show* I think he said—and we were laughing, and then he's like, 'What?' Because right then I think he suspected, you know?"

"Is it you, Scott?" Jon asked, according to Donna's deposition, wondering whether it was Scott who had the secret crush.

"Well, what if it is?" Scott asked Jon.

"No big deal," Jon said. "I'm going to go for it. I don't care what anybody says."

But Donna said Jon still had strong suspicions. In the same conversation, he pulled out a bracelet he had found on his car. "He asked Scott if he put it on his car, and Scott had said . . . 'Yeah, I did,' and he (Jon) said, 'What does it mean?' And Scott told him it was just a friendship bracelet."

Jon put the bracelet on his wrist.

According to what Donna later told police, Jon told her that same evening, "I feel it's a guy," because "that's all that are attracted to him," and that ". . . the last three people that hit on him were men." Also, two friends of Jon's, Michelle Wright and Jean Ratchford, each gave statements to the police saying they had spoken to Jon prior to the taping about the show's being a "same-sex" secret crush show. According to the police report, Ms. Ratchford told Jon explicitly that she had seen the "plug" for the show and it was definitely a same-sex secret crush show. Ms. Wright asked Jon how he would react having a male be his crush, and he replied, according to police reports, ". . . he would be polite about it but would say he was 100 percent heterosexual."

Jon bought some new clothes and flew to Chicago to tape the show. Scott and Donna flew to Chicago together on a different flight, and we put them up in a different hotel from Jon's, which is always the way we keep our guests separated on secret crush shows.

On the day of the taping, Jon was picked up by a staff member, brought to the studio, and taken to the green room to join the other "crushees," as we call them. Scott and Donna were picked up at the same time at their hotel and taken to a separate green room to join the people with the crushes. No one knew it then, but we learned later from court testimony that on the way to the taping Scott had gone to a drug store and bought a bottle of vodka and had apparently smuggled it into the green room.

While all of this was happening, I was in the makeup room, looking forward to doing a show about one of my favorite topics. As usual, I stopped in both green rooms and greeted the guests, then headed for the control room. I imagine it was bustling as always with last-minute preparations. Then I headed for the studio and walked onto the stage.

Secret crush shows are always produced pretty much the same way: The person with the crush goes on first. In this case, I interviewed Scott first, with Donna at his side.

"Now, Jon, he knows you're gay, right?" I asked Scott.

"Yeah," Scott said.

"Do you know that he is?" I asked.

"Anything's possible," he replied.

"Do you have any reason to think he is, Donna?" I asked.

". . . He says his family has questioned him on it," she said. "He's a very open person. So it really wouldn't surprise me."

After Scott described a fantasy he had that involved Jon, I invited Jon to walk onto the stage. He came out, smiling, hugged Donna, then was embraced by Scott and sat down beside Scott.

Suddenly, something occurred to me: Maybe he thought it was

Donna who had the crush. So I asked him, "Did you think Donna had the crush on you?"

"Did I?" he asked. "No, we're good friends."

"Well, guess what, it's Scott that has the crush on you." I said.

He laughed, clapped his hands, then turned to Scott and, still laughing, said, "You lied to me."

The comment was not unusual, because most people in Jon's position attempt to find out before the show who has the crush on them. They question all of their friends, and if they guess correctly the person with the crush usually denies it. In many cases, all the crushee's friends know the identity of the crush. But they'll deny it, too, just like people don't tell the guest of honor about an impending surprise birthday party. So when someone is surprised with a party, they commonly respond by saying, "You lied to me." I've said that the "lying" comment is fairly common on secret crush shows, and I know it's true. But that statement would soon come back to haunt me.

Throughout the show, Jon showed no sign of embarrassment and seemed to be having a good time. If any of our guests seem upset during a taping, I will approach them during a break to find out if there's a problem. Sometimes they don't feel like they've had a chance to say everything they wanted, or sometimes they feel misunderstood by the audience. In this case, I felt no need to approach the guests.

After Scott revealed his crush, I asked Jon on the air if he was interested.

"Can you tell us what your status is?" I asked. "Are you involved with anybody?"

"No," Jon said. "But I am definitely heterosexual, I guess you could say."

The audience applauded. Jon added that he was "flattered" by Scott's attention, and Scott didn't seem disappointed.

"If nothing else it's a nice compliment to pay somebody," I said.

Before the show ended, I reviewed each of the same-sex secret crush couples with the audience to see who we thought might have made a love connection that day. When I came to Scott and Jon,

I said, on camera, "Scott and Jon? I don't think so. Jon's straight, so that's the end of that."

It was a good show. We all felt like it was a big success. The guests were great. The audience loved it. It was fun, and we thought we'd made some love connections. Everybody seemed to leave happy. I left the studio for my office, filed show folder number 4138 in the filing cabinet, and started tackling the never-ending stack of "to do" stuff on my desk.

The week was starting well. I headed home later that evening, looking forward to telling Denis about how much fun the show had been. I never dreamed that by week's end the reputation I had worked twenty-five years to establish would almost be destroyed.

On the next Jenny Jones: Rush to Judgment

While I was headed home for another ordinary night in Chicago, little did I know that Jonathan Schmitz was taking Scott Amedure out for drinks in a bar.

After the taping, Jon, Scott, and Donna all rode together with some of the other secret crush guests from our studio to the airport in the same limousine. During the ride, Jon was asking the other guests questions about "the gay lifestyle," Donna recalled in her deposition. "Like what occupation are you in. . . . Does it affect your job. . . . He was just real inquisitive about gay topics." According to Donna's deposition, Jon didn't seem remotely upset, angry, or humiliated about the show.

When they got to the Chicago airport, Jon offered to give Scott and Donna a ride home to Orion Township after they arrived in Detroit. Since Scott and Donna were on a different flight from Jon's, they changed their flight at Jon's request so they could all fly back together. Jon bought Scott's drinks in the airport lounge, according to testimony, and he "high-fived" him when he walked past him on the plane.

An ice storm was hitting Detroit when they landed. On the way out of the airport they passed through a construction site, and Scott stole a flashing street signal and some yellow construction tape from the site as a prank. Once they got to Scott's place, Jon wanted to go out for more drinks at a neighborhood bar called Brewski's. According to courtroom testimony, Scott said he wanted to stay home. But Jon was persistent. He finally persuaded Scott to go out with him for more drinks. Pulling off the icy streets into the bar's parking lot, Jon missed the turn and hit a guardrail. He nonetheless drove on into the lot, and the trio walked into Brewski's, where Jon bought Scott more drinks and they talked about the day.

"Jon did tell me at one point during the evening that he kind of knew it was going to be us when he was back in the green room because . . . he heard Jenny Jones say my name," Donna said in her deposition.

Brewski's closed early because of the ice storm, so the party moved on to Donna's apartment.

"They (Scott and Jon) drank and listened to music and danced around. . . ." Donna said in her deposition. "(Jon) came up behind me and he was playing with my hair, and I was like really uncomfortable, you know, and Scott was sitting across from me at the table and I kind of looked at him, and he (Jon) said let's go for it. My impression was he wanted a threesome. . . . I said, "It's late . . . you have to get going. I have to get a couple hours' sleep."

Jon left around 4 A.M., and Scott spent the night on Donna's couch. The next day, Scott asked Donna to go check on how Jon was doing after she got off from work. She found him asleep in a chair in his apartment. According to Donna's deposition, they talked about Scott, about how Jon "didn't think Scott was an honest person." Nonetheless, Jon told her he wanted Scott to go shopping with him over the upcoming weekend to pick out ceiling fans and, according to Donna, to help install them in Jon's bedroom and living room.

We'll never know exactly what happened between Scott and

Jon. I was surprised, however, when I learned that Jon had asked for Scott's help shopping after he told me on the air he wasn't interested. It seemed that Jon was pursuing the relationship.

The next day, two days after returning home from Chicago, Scott and Donna went by Jon's apartment. Jon wasn't home, but the street signal stolen from the construction site was sitting on Jon's window ledge. Scott took the light, fixed it so it would blink on and off, then returned it to Jon's apartment. He tied a strip of yellow construction tape onto the door handle, wedged the now-blinking light between the screen and the apartment door, and left a note scrawled on a paper towel. "If you want it off, you have to ask me," the note read. "It takes a special tool. Guess who?"

Scott Amedure, I later learned through court testimony, could be extremely persistent when it came to romance. Scott's mother later would say on WXYZ TV in Detroit that Scott had told her that he and Jon "had an affair," and Scott's brother told reporters that Scott told the brother's wife and sister that he had gotten together with Jon after the taping. Scott's former live-in lover told the court that Scott was "known for fighting . . . when he was drunk, and when he was on drugs he was just abusive." He added that Scott had "outed" him in front of his mother, brothers, and sisters without his consent, "saying he wasn't my buddy, he was my lover." He went on to say he had been beaten up by Scott on several occasions, once spending two days in the hospital because of the beatings, and had been warned by more than one of Scott's former lovers that he "beat them up. . . . He wasn't afraid of anything." According to testimony, Scott Amedure had a reputation for being relentless in his pursuit of lovers.

"This guy wouldn't leave me alone," Jon was quoted during the trial as saying. "He was persistent on this stuff."

"At that point," Jon told the Oakland County sheriff's detective assigned to the case, referring to the moment he found the blinking light and the sexually suggestive note, "I decided I was going to kill him."

Scott's note, according to one of the psychiatrists who testified at the trial, enraged Jonathan Schmitz and pushed him over the edge. He found the note when he returned to his apartment at 9 A.M. the next morning, three days after returning from Chicago. He had worked a double shift the night before, then gone out drinking and spent the night at a co-worker's house.

Jon left his apartment and withdrew $350 from his savings account. He bought a twelve-gauge pump-action Mossburg shotgun with a camouflage finish at a local gun store. He then purchased a box of Remington shotgun shells—designed for hunting deer and black bear—at a hardware store. He drove back to his apartment and sat in the parking lot, thinking "this would be the last time he saw it," the Oakland County sheriff's detective testified. Jon then drove to Scott's trailer, parked, and assembled and loaded the shotgun. But when he walked up to the trailer, he left his car running and the shotgun on the front seat. He opened the trailer door and was met by Scott's roommate, who testified later that he didn't hear the ensuing conversation. Scott came out of the bathroom, where he had been flossing his teeth. Seeing Jon, he went back to the bathroom. Jon followed.

"I just remember seeing his face," the testifying psychiatrist quoted Jon as saying. "I looked at him really seriously. I was serious. I asked him if he had written the note, and he smiled and shrugged his shoulders." During a previous interview, the psychiatrist testified, Jon described the smile as a smirk.

"I got angry because he didn't care how I felt," Jon told the psychiatrist. ". . . He just didn't give a shit. . . . I went back to the car and got the gun. I came back and knocked on the door. I was standing there and the door opened a little bit. I pushed it open."

"What are you doing?" Scott screamed when he saw Jon return with the shotgun. Seeing the gun, Scott picked up a wicker chair as a shield. Jon fired the shotgun once at point-blank range. The buckshot hit Scott on the left side of the chest. As Scott fell to the floor, Jon racked the gun and shot him again.

"Ed says to come into his office right away," Dana told me. "It's important."

I dropped what I was doing and headed down the hall. It was

midmorning on a Thursday, March 9, 1995. We had two tapings scheduled for the next day, and I was about to treat the staff to lunch. It wasn't the first time I'd been urgently called to Ed's office. I wondered if one of our staff members had given unexpected notice, or if perhaps we had landed a big booking. Maybe Debby was pregnant again! Nothing prepared me for what I was about to hear.

"We've just heard that one of our guests has murdered another guest," Ed said.

"What guests?" I said, absolutely stunned, my mind racing to recall any recent emotional topics. "What show?"

"It was the same-sex secret crush," he said.

I couldn't believe it. It just had to be a terrible mistake.

"But it was a fun show!" I said. "It's not possible!"

I tried to recall the guests on the show. Ed said the rumor was that Jon Schmitz had shot Scott Amedure, claiming we humiliated him on national television.

"But we didn't!" I couldn't even make sense of what I was hearing. I vaguely remembered Jon's smile and laughter as he walked out on stage. "He was fine. How can he say he was humiliated? We have it on tape. He was fine."

Thus began the worst day followed by the worst month followed by the worst year of all of our lives. From the moment I heard the news, as the rumor evolved into horrible fact, I was caught in a maelstrom. I just couldn't accept it. I kept thinking it had to be a mistake. I remember people coming in and out of the office between constant back-and-forth calls with our executives in Los Angeles.

Then the news reports began: a slowly escalating, unrelenting barrage of blame. We would never air that secret crush episode, but the story about the murder led every TV prime-time news report in America, even preempting the on-going O.J. Simpson murder saga, a major feat back in 1995. The press descended upon us in a swarm. Within an hour, the networks, newspapers, radio, wire services, and supermarket tabloids were tying up our phones. They hovered in packs outside the building. Our staff members were forced to sneak out back exits. We heard that one tabloid TV show even offered one of our staff members $100,000 for a copy of the show. By nightfall, some of them were reportedly trying to break into our offices, while others rummaged through the trash. Then they went to my apartment building, looking for me.

Usually, I would walk the block and a half home, but that night Denis arrived to drive me. We took the elevator down to the NBC basement and drove out through the garage, right past the assembled knot of newspaper reporters and TV cameras. In my everyday clothes and usual baseball cap, I wasn't recognized by any of the reporters. It was like they were looking past our car for the TV image of Jenny Jones, and they didn't see me slipping by under their noses.

We pulled into my apartment's secured parking garage, going unrecognized there, too. I don't remember much about the rest of the evening. But I know I had to do homework for the next day's shows. The first few days after the murder are still enveloped in a fog. It was just an endless episode of finger-pointing—all directed squarely at me. There I was on each and every newscast, my face sandwiched between footage of Jon Schmitz being led away in shackles and Scott Amedure being wheeled from his trailer in a body bag. All three networks led with the story, and the news spread like a grass fire.

"In a crime that stunned the world of TV . . ." Nancy Glass said on *American Journal.*

"Daytime television drove him to kill," *Hard Copy* declared.

The media immediately branded the case "The Jenny Jones Murder."

The made-for-TV movie was soon to come. But first came the lawyers in a dirty parade of scorn and twisted legal strategy.

On the day after the murder, I turned on the television and saw the Oakland County prosecutor, Richard Thompson, sounding like a defense attorney. *"The Jenny Jones Show* ambushed this defendant with humiliation, and in retaliation, this defendant ambushed the victim with a shotgun," he said.

I couldn't believe it. This was a prosecutor speaking! His job was to prosecute Jonathan Schmitz for murder. But he was, in effect, taking the blame off the confessed killer and putting it on my show and me. There hadn't been time to gather all of the evidence—in fact, the investigation had barely begun. But that didn't stop this obviously irresponsible prosecutor from using his golden moment in the media spotlight to appear on national television and blast television talk shows.

Even the *Detroit News* took Thompson to task, saying he "sounded less like a prosecutor than a televangelist posing as Schmitz' defense attorney."

When Richard Jewell was charged, and convicted by press and public opinion, in the 1996 Olympic bombing, I knew exactly how he felt. What right did Thompson have, without fully examining the facts, to go in front of the country and blame me? I assumed he wasn't just a confused county prosecutor but a media-hungry politician who thought this diatribe would get him reelected. (If that was the case, it didn't work. Thompson lost his bid for reelection the following year.)

But it was his choice of one particular word that was like a knife in my heart: *ambushed.*

I must have heard it a thousand times, and every time I wanted to scream. I wanted to grab the TV and shake it and say, "It wasn't an ambush!" I couldn't believe this many supposedly responsible reporters, who hadn't even seen the tape of the show, who had no evidence and no information about the circumstances regarding the show or what transpired between Scott and Jon, were merely aping the words of a irresponsible prosecutor. It wasn't an ambush.

Yes, we would later learn, Jonathan Schmitz allegedly suffered from manic depression and alcoholism and had twice attempted suicide. Yes, his father had once, upon catching Jon skipping school, punished him in an incident that would haunt Jon the rest of his life. According to the father's testimony, the father had taken "him back to the school. And I took off my belt, and I walked him into the class. I pulled his hair and I strapped him on the butt . . . and I told (the teacher) that my son wasn't raised to be a liar or a cheat." But we didn't force Jon Schmitz onto our show, and we certainly didn't hand him a shotgun. Scott Amedure called us and suggested we call Jon. We issued an invitation, gave him every opportunity to think about it, and he accepted, knowing fully well in advance that his secret admirer could be a man. He even suspected that it could be Scott, we would discover later. It was a terrible tragedy, that's for sure. But it wasn't an ambush.

In the first hours after the killing, Ed's father, an industrial engineer, called him from Philadelphia, saying he'd heard we'd "lied" to a guest, and because of that lie, one guest was now dead and another arrested for murder. Ed was devastated. "My reaction was, "Dad, that's not what happened,'" Ed remembered. "I was shocked. Even my *father* believed the story he'd heard on the radio. And if he believed it, I knew the whole country did."

From the *New York Times* to the *National Enquirer,* they all said we lied, repeating the phrase as incessantly as the crowd that soon began to form in Chicago, calling for television reform, chanting, "Stop the killing!"

Most everywhere, the story was the same . . . *Trash TV, Ambush, Murder, Lied.* When it came to presenting our side of the story, I never saw evidence of balanced reporting. Everybody just repeated everybody else. And the fine line between tabloid and mainstream journalism seemed to vanish altogether. Ted Koppel opened *Nightline* by comparing us to pornography. *Larry King Live* devoted an entire hour to the story. Donna Riley related details of the secret crush show taping, its prelude and aftermath, in paid interviews on *Hard Copy* and *A Current Affair.* Everyone hung us out to dry, except, oddly enough, the gay and lesbian advocacy leader Jeffrey Montgomery. He called the murder a "hate crime," an outright instance of national "homophobia."

"Say Schmitz goes on a show and instead of meeting Scott he meets a girl and she's Jewish," Montgomery said in an interview. "Say he kills her because he was humiliated because she was Jewish. Would the world have trouble understanding the motive of this crime? We wouldn't be saying, 'Gee, *The Jenny Jones Show* is horrible. They should have known this man was humiliated!'"

The gay community has followed this story closely, as the crime appears to have more to do with homophobia than anything else.

How tragic that Jon would rather have been labeled a murderer than a homosexual.

I was amazed that while saying Schmitz was "humiliated" came easy for most critics, no one bothered to question why being found attractive by someone of the same sex would be considered even remotely humiliating, particularly to someone who had been hit on by men before. What if someone was humiliated because his admirer was fat? Some men are embarrassed by fat women. I know it's true. I once did a show on it.

I was the star of the media scandal of the moment. I didn't watch television; I couldn't stand to see my name dragged through the mud. I didn't turn on the radio; I led the news on every station. I didn't read the newspapers; too often I made the headlines. Hearing about the murder again and again was in itself just too painful, regardless of how I was portrayed. I tossed each day's newspaper articles onto a stack that soon stood two and a half feet high. For the first time, I was actually grateful for homework. After all, we still had six shows to tape a week, and work became my salvation.

For six months, my routine was the same: home to studio; studio to home. I was terrified to go out in public. Afraid that people would blame me. I was already being called a liar in the media; I just couldn't bear for somebody to call me a liar to my face.

We came in to work the morning after the murder, all of us literally sick to our stomachs, both from the pain of a senseless murder and the pressure of being blamed. Our world was crumbling around us as we tried to focus on that morning's show. But the studio audience had filed in as usual. The guests were miked and eager to go onstage. For one anxious moment, I waited in the stage-left alcove before heading out to start the show, every thought focused on one thing: *It's one day after a horrible murder. How will the audience respond?* I always take time to talk to the audience before each show begins and to answer questions. Their reaction to the incident would be the most important thing to me personally. I expected a few probing questions: *Was it your fault? Did you lie?*

Taking a deep breath as the microphone was handed to me, I stepped from the backstage shadows into the bright TV studio lights. I'll never forget the feeling: It was the loudest, sweetest applause I'd ever heard. I walked down into the crowd and chatted with the audience, and without one question being asked about the case or one person even raising an eyebrow, I began the show.

From that moment on, I knew I would survive.

Going public

Within two hours of hearing of the murder, I desperately wanted to talk to the media, to tell people the facts about what really happened on the show. We were not merely being associated with a murder, we were being *blamed* for it—and I knew we hadn't done anything wrong. I felt that people needed to hear from me directly, and I desperately wanted to tell them the truth.

But our attorneys had different ideas. First of all, there was an ongoing criminal investigation and the possibility that potential testimony could be tainted if it came out in the press before the trial. Second, they didn't think the media would give me even a fighting chance to tell my story. They felt that anything I said would be reduced to sound bites that would only feed the media frenzy. Now I understand their position, but back then I felt our silence made us look like we had something to hide.

I wanted to call Scott Amedure's family and express our condolences.

The attorneys asked me not to contact the family.

I'd fought long and hard to have a voice in my own show and not just be "hired talent," and now, once again, I was being shut out. I felt that continuing to stay quiet just gave reporters one more chance to print another headline calling "The Jenny Jones Murder" an "ambush." Meanwhile, death threats began arriving in the mail, along with hate mail, mostly from homophobics. There was a bomb threat, too. For a few days, I was under twenty-four-hour protection. Our crew stopped wearing *Jenny Jones Show* jackets and T-shirts for fear they would be accosted. Our staff members got unlisted phone numbers to stop the unrelenting calls from the media and producers trying to book them as guests on other talk shows.

I thought speaking publicly would stop all of this madness. Every major news anchor was competing for an interview with me. But the attorneys still said no. Then I suggested a second option: I wanted to air the show so people could see, first, that Jon wasn't humiliated, and second, that everyone left happy.

"Let's air the show and let people judge for themselves," I said.

But the attorneys still said no.

"We have to at least make a statement," I said. "I have to go on the air. I have to tell people what really happened."

"No statement," came word from the attorneys.

"If we don't say anything, it looks like we're hiding something," I argued, "and we have nothing to hide."

I suggested doing an interview with Diane Sawyer of *Primetime Live*. She had flown to Chicago and was camped out at the Four Seasons, urging me to talk, insisting that people needed to hear from me personally. Ed suggested Phil Donahue. Someone else suggested asking another anchor, possibly Jane Pauley, to host my show, and I could be a guest.

By now, the "suits" who oversee our show were in Chicago. I told them I was going to talk to Diane Sawyer on *Primetime*, with or without their blessing. I wondered if it was already too late, as the critics continued to voice their bitter disdain for talk shows—and for me personally.

All I could think about was getting the real story out. Our attorneys, however, kept urging me to consider the more likely possibility of the interview focusing on "trash talk" instead of what really happened between Scott and Jon. The show's advisers and I sat down together and discussed the most likely line of questioning. They threw some possible questions at me:

"Have you ever done an ambush on your show?" one attorney asked.

"Yes," I said, "but it was a makeov—"

"Then you admit to using ambush tactics."

"Yes . . . No . . . I . . ."

I didn't know what to say.

"Are you still lying to your guests?"

They had made their point. It was a no-win situation. I was exhausted, running on no sleep and little food and the most intense stress I'd ever experienced, and I still had the unceasing workload that comes with taping six shows a week. I called Diane and declined the interview. I was convinced the interview would only feed the media frenzy.

Even though it was my decision not to talk to Diane Sawyer, and even though I now agreed with the lawyers that the media had only one agenda, I still wanted to make a statement. They contended that whatever I said would be edited and presented for maximum negative effect. But they finally agreed, and I prepared to go on camera. The statement took most of the day to draft and redraft, getting passed between all of the attorneys for final approval.

On March 15, 1995, six days after the murder, I went before the cameras in our studio and issued the followed statement:

> *Before we air our regularly scheduled show today, I'd like to take a moment to address an issue that is very important to me. As I'm sure most of you know,* The Jenny Jones Show *has been in the news lately because of a tragic incident involving two guests. They appeared on a program we taped about secret admirers.*
>
> *More than anybody, I want all the facts to come out. Because of the ongoing investigation, up until now I've been instructed not to make any comments. However, because of the tremendous number of misstatements and allegations that have been made, I want to set the record straight.*
>
> *First, as much as we all regret what happened, the fact is that this tragedy is about the actions of one individual. He was a guest on that show, and he, like every other guest on that show, was told before he agreed to appear that he'd be meeting a secret admirer and it could be a person of the same*

sex or the opposite sex. In fact, when I read his pre-interview, one of the questions was, "How would he react if his secret admirer was a man?" There was no question he knew it could have been a man.

The show was in no way confrontational. In fact the show was lighthearted and the guests were clearly at ease through the entire taping. One of the guests involved actually called us the next day and told us they all went out socially when they got home and they had a good time together. That's why this was so much of a shock to me.

On a personal level, I feel very sad about what happened last week. My show staff and I want to extend our deepest sympathy to Scott Amedure's family and friends. In the meantime I cannot thank you enough for the calls and the letters of support and encouragement to our show. We're really having a hard time getting through this, and your thoughts mean a lot to us.

Thank you.

I'd said exactly what I wanted to say, and it didn't matter who drafted the final statement.

Then, immediately after releasing the public statement, I stepped further into the fray. We heard that *People* magazine was planning a cover story on the murder. I still wanted a chance to tell my side of the story and felt that *People* would be fair in its coverage. Since it was a magazine and not a television news show, I felt safe from the risk of being edited into negative sound bites. I told the attorneys I was going to do it. They insisted on having someone from the legal department present during the interview, and the magazine at least didn't misquote me.

"(Schmitz) was not misled," I said. "All the guests knew it could be a man or a woman—it's very clear (from phone logs and producer's notes) that he did know. This was not an ambush show."

According to the *People* article, Scott's mother "later claimed her son told her he slept with Schmitz that night," referring to the night they had returned from Chicago and gone to Brewski's for drinks.

People also reported that Morton Downey Jr., whom it dubbed "king of the sludge heap," was now trashing tabloid talk shows.

But one line in the story haunted me. Scott Amedure's mother was quoted as saying, "I'm very angry, and nobody from the show has called to express their sorrow." I hope Mrs. Amedure will some-day know that I did want to call her and that I still share in her sorrow.

My comments in *People*, however, went largely ignored. Typ-ical of the reporting in the weeks following the murder was a story in *USA Today*: "Jenny Jones finally demonstrated the high price of daytime TV's sensation-seeking junk talk when her show ambushed a guest with his secret gay admirer, who was then killed a few days later by the embarrassed guest. There's no excusing this crime."

It was ironic that amid all of this bashing, *The Jenny Jones Show* won the prestigious 1995 Nancy Susan Reynolds Award in the day-time talk show category for a show we did on AIDS. We would win again in 1996. But few in the media noticed. The critics obviously had an agenda that did not include my being innocent until proven guilty. Knowing that, and in light of the ongoing investigation, I de-cided to comply with our attorneys' wishes to make no further state-ments.

Little did I know that the next time I would speak publicly about the case would be in court.

Going to the circus

"You've got blood on your hands."

The letter came from an anonymous writer soon after the mur-der, and I couldn't get it out of my mind. There were other hate-ful letters, too, all from people who believed everything they read in the newspapers.

Jonathan Schmitz's murder trial was slated to begin on Octo-ber 7, 1996, in the Oakland County Courthouse in Pontiac, Michi-gan. From the time of the murder, Jon's attorneys had been loudly demanding in the media that I testify in the case. Their strategy was obvious: blame *The Jenny Jones Show* for the death of Scott Amedure in an attempt to distract the jury and get a lighter sentence for Jonathan Schmitz. Having me testify would certainly qualify as a major distraction. That's all it could be. I had no information relevant to the case. I didn't have any recollection of specifically talking to Scott, Donna, or Jon in the green rooms. As I've said, my green room visits are more of a group welcome. The entire sum of my interaction with the guests could be seen on the videotape of the show, which by now was being played in the media.

My deposition was taken on December 11, 1995, nine months after the murder. After the deposition, the judge made it official: My testimony wasn't relevant to the case, and I wouldn't be called to the court. The judge reiterated that ruling six months later. But when the trial began on October 7, 1996, the attorneys were still unrelenting in their mission to get me into the courtroom. So in the middle of the trial, on October 30, the judge changed his mind.

I was ordered to appear the next day.

I was angry. I knew I had nothing to say that would make a bit of difference in the murder case. Jonathan Schmitz's lawyers were only looking for publicity. It was just a big, tawdry show, a blatant attempt to shift blame. I had already been though seven months of attacks; this was going to be the climax.

Immediately, of course, it was headline news: JENNY JONES FORCED TO TESTIFY IN TRASH TV MURDER CASE! We canceled our tapings for the following day, and I prepared to head to the Oakland County Courthouse. But how could I get there without running into the media? Reporters and paparazzi were staking out the airports in both Chicago and Detroit, waiting for me. I refused to give them the pleasure of using my picture with their nasty negative headlines. So what to do? We discussed chartering a plane, but the media were staking out the private airports, too. And the sight of me emerging from a private jet would be like pouring gasoline on a bonfire.

"I know what to do," I finally told Ed. "I'll drive."

"You can't drive," Ed replied. "It'll take you five hours."

"But it's the only way to get into Michigan without being tailed," I said. "Besides, you know I hate to fly anyway. Denis will drive me."

Denis wanted to come with me, of course, and to ensure we wouldn't be tailed he rented a nondescript four-door Oldsmobile from Budget Rent-a-Car. I dressed as if I were headed to work—no makeup, hair under a baseball cap, and everyday clothes. I packed an overnight bag, and in the dark of night we slipped out of the apartment building's parking garage, headed toward Detroit. Five hours later, at 1:30 in the morning, we checked into a motel on the highway about ten minutes from the courthouse in Pontiac, Michigan.

I waited in the car while Denis checked in under an assumed name and paid the bill, upfront, in cash. I didn't sleep at all that night. Even after a good day I had insomnia, and this had not been a good day. The morning dawned like a bad movie, and the movie kept running all day long. First thing, I met with our attorneys. With less than twenty-four hours to prepare, their instructions were simple:

"Tell the truth."

"Keep your answers short, preferably 'Yes,' 'No,' or 'I don't know.'"

"Give answers only about the episode in question."

I'm glad they kept it simple, because simplicity was all I could handle. I was absolutely exhausted from taping two shows the day before, then driving all night.

The courthouse was a circus, not a setting for a murder trial. The small, office-style building was ringed with reporters and photographers and video crews—at least sixty cameras, all anxiously awaiting my arrival. We slipped right past the mob in a passenger van, with me in the backseat. Luckily, there was a back entrance into the courthouse. Later, I heard the paparazzi had complained that using the back entrance wasn't "fair."

Inside the courthouse, we were led into a cramped waiting room. It was too small for all of us even to sit comfortably, but I still found room to pace. Down the hall, the trial continued with steadily increasing intensity. I could be called in at any moment. It seemed like we waited an eternity, even though I was later told it was just under an hour. My stomach was in a knot. My palms were sweaty. My throat was dry, and my eyes were red from lack of sleep. Someone drew a map for me so I would know what direction to go when I entered the courtroom. I stared and stared at the map, but it didn't register. All I could remember was to go right.

I kept sipping water, more out of nervousness than thirst. When the court took a recess, I heard a sound outside the waiting room's closed door, a passing jangling, the sound of chains. It was a shackled Jonathan Schmitz being led down the hall for the break. I thought I'd be sick to my stomach.

Then I was told I'd be summoned after the break. After a few minutes, I heard the jangling of chains again, and knew that Jon was being led back to the courtroom. My time on the stand was about to begin, and CNN, Court TV, and news stations across the country prepared to go live.

. . . *so help me God*

A guard entered the tiny room and said, "Miss Jones," then led me down the hallway. The courtroom door opened, and I stepped inside. I felt the heat of flashbulbs exploding in my face and, struggling to maintain my composure, headed right toward the witness stand and managed to sit down without stumbling. The scrutiny I was under at that moment made me absolutely numb with fear. I glanced at the jury, then looked straight ahead, hoping the microphone wasn't picking up the sound of my pounding heart.

Then I was sworn in.

I felt like a lamb being led to slaughter, realizing that I was brought into the courtroom not to provide pertinent information, but merely to distract the jury. Apparently I wasn't the only one who was nervous, because many of defense attorney Fred Gibson's questions were so convoluted the judge had to intervene no less than fifty times to clarify or rephrase them. At one point Gibson himself admitted he didn't understand his own question.

Bumbling as he was, he used my earlier deposition to serve his purposes exceedingly well; it gave him a blueprint of everything I didn't know. He asked me questions he knew I couldn't answer. Each "I don't know" from me was worth a hundred headlines for him. In the end, it wasn't what I said, but how nervous I looked, that made headlines.

Gibson's questioning was over. Finally, I thought, I'll have an opportunity to present my side of the story! But the prosecutor said, "No further questions, your honor."

I was devastated.

I assumed the prosecutor didn't cross-examine me for a very simple reason: My testimony was irrelevant to his case. He already had a confession from the suspect and an eyewitness. I had been used as a prop, a decoy, to distract the jury from the facts. My time on the stand was finally over. I had answered all of the questions. I had told the truth.

We left the courthouse the way we came in, but now the photographers found us. We did some evasive driving to lose any tails, then drove back to the motel, checked out, and headed back to Chicago. I felt better on the way home, relieved that it was over and satisfied that I had told the truth, even when it was manipulated to make me look incompetent.

But any feeling of satisfaction vanished by morning. Once again, the headline news was not about the murder trial; it was about Jenny Jones.

• Associated Press wire service: "Jones, usually smiling and gossipy on the show, became guarded and appeared nervous on the witness stand." Sharp observation. Maybe it's because this was a murder trial!

• *Washington Post:* ". . . she looked tired, serious and subdued." News-flash: I *was* tired, serious, and subdued.

• *Newsweek:* "Her face was strained and puffy." I'll keep this simple. Stress = strained. No sleep = puffy.

• *Newsweek:* "She . . . doesn't talk to guests before they are on-stage." That's just not true. I always talk to guests in the green rooms. I just couldn't remember ten thousand conversations. I was most disappointed in *Newsweek,* a publication I considered reputable, for printing total misinformation.

The media even attacked what I was wearing—a conservative winter-white suit—saying the suit had a plunging neckline. Once again, it was obvious that everyone was still more interested in bashing me than in reporting the facts of what really occurred between Scott and Jon.

We hadn't lied. But in response to a question about Jon's saying "You lied to me" to Scott, I said that the lying comment is fairly common on secret crush shows; everyone who's asked if he's the crush denies it. For a critic with an agenda, that statement, taken out of context, was enough to vilify me. The press seemed happy to do it. Nice big letters, top of the page: "THE LYING COMMENT IS FAIRLY COMMON"—JENNY JONES.

As horrible as the criminal trial was, it still wasn't the end. The Amedure family filed a fifty-million-dollar wrongful death civil action against the show, and just five months after appearing at the criminal trial I had to be deposed once again for the civil case. When I walked into the lobby of the "private" office where I was to be deposed, a news crew was waiting for me. I shouldn't have been surprised, because this time I was up against attorney Geoffrey Fieger of Southfield, Michigan. He had been hired by the Amedure family to represent them in their civil suit.

He's a poster boy for attorney misconduct: fined thousands of dollars by various judges; accused of lying in court documents; even singled out in an August 6, 1997, *USA Today* article about "an outbreak of rude, crude and downright uncivil behavior by lawyers in the nation's courts." The article featured a photo of Fieger, quoting him as saying, "I grossly exaggerate to make a point. . . . I try to be an equal-opportunity offender."

Fieger is absolutely obsessed with the media. He was all over the news shows after the murder. You should have heard him blasting me on *Larry King Live;* he snarled into the camera like a World Wrestling Federation match promoter. *"Jenny Jones Show* better be ready for this!" Fieger bellowed. (Hey, he'd be make a great talk show guest. I can already see the show title: "Confessions of a Media

Addict: Next *Jenny Jones!*") In fact, I heard he was trying to get his own talk show. If it were up to Fieger, this case would drag on for-ever, keeping him bathing in media coverage. He once raised the issue of settlement with our attorney, John Schulman, but then told him that he had problems settling the case because he didn't think he could give up a month of being on national TV. Two months later he had a similar conversation with another one of our attor-neys, Jim George.

"This is a ridiculous case," George said. "You're never going to get any money from it. You can't get punitive damages, so what are you doing it for?"

"So I can be on national television for four weeks," Fieger grinned.

When it came time for my deposition in the civil case, Fieger kept me waiting while he held a press conference in the lobby down-stairs. When my deposition was completed, he headed back down-stairs for yet another press conference, keeping the next witness waiting as well. And when he finished deposing that witness, he ran to yet another press conference, incessantly repeating the line that would make the best sound bite: "Jenny is a liar."

But Fieger wasn't finished. After my two-hour videotaped dep-osition, which I had been led to believe was intended only for the courts, he edited together, MTV-style, all of the times I said "I don't know" and released a two-minute tape to the media. This time I was more than hurt; I was disgusted.

Then came the final straw. It happened on the nationally syn-dicated *Judge Judy Show*, the court TV program whose star, Judge Judy Sheindlin, tries cases on national TV. The show opened with its usual flair. The court deputy entered the courtroom and an-nounced gravely, "All parties in Fieger versus Downey step forward please."

Then, in a solemn voice, the announcer did the opening: "Is *The Jenny Jones Show* to blame for the death of one of her guests, Scott Amedure?"

Once again, I was back in the courtroom.

The announcer continued: "The two sides: Amedure family

lawyer Geoffrey Fieger says, 'Yes, and they should pay!' Talk show host Morton Downey Jr. speaks out for the producers." (Morton Downey Jr.!? He has absolutely no association with our show and no firsthand knowledge of what happened!)

"All rise," the deputy said.

Judge Judy entered the courtroom, and Fieger started spouting garbage.

That the show was being aired at all was insulting enough. But to be defended by Morton Downey Jr. was absolutely insane. What right did he have to "speak out for the producers"? What followed was an affront to the memory of Scott Amedure and a travesty of the judicial process. Even worse, after listening to Fieger's distortions, Downey switched sides and threw in the towel.

"There is no way I can defend the activity of Jenny Jones in this manner because she knew what was going on," said Downey. "That (conduct) is not only criminal, your honor, that's mean—that stinks!"

It would have been funny if it hadn't been so pathetic.

On November 12, 1996, the jury found Jonathan Schmitz guilty of second-degree murder. The vote had been ten to two for first-degree murder. The judge imposed the maximum sentence, twenty-seven to fifty years, with no chance for parole for at least twenty-five years. Jon is currently appealing his conviction.

There isn't a day I don't think about the murder. It was a senseless crime, and my heart aches for the families involved and the lives ravaged. As for me personally, I know I'll be forever branded. The backlash will never be undone, and it probably won't be forgotten. But you know what? I can live with that. I can live with the media that slammed me, the attorneys who called me a "liar," and all of the critics who sat in judgment without bothering to learn the facts. I can live with all of that because none of these people know me.

My audience, however, does know me. They watch the show and see a caring, honest, compassionate woman, and they have steadfastly stuck by my side. If they had turned their backs on me, I would have been devastated. Because my audience is my family. I'll be forever grateful to them for seeing me through the last two years.

Epilogue

There is no way to adequately describe what it's like to be attacked in public and branded both a liar and a fool. It has been devastating. You become more distrustful, more reclusive, relying on a tight group of friends and colleagues for emotional support. You start to fear saying anything, writing anything, because it will be taken out of context, twisted, and somehow used against you. That fear stalked me throughout the writing of this book, and while I know it still may happen, at least this time I won't be caught off guard.

I've often wondered how my parents would have reacted had they been alive when I was under such an aggressive and negative media attack. My father would probably have pushed me to talk publicly. I think he would have thought that if I just told the press the facts, everyone would understand. Knowing his hardheaded nature he might even have gone to the media himself to defend me; after all, this would have been a terrible reflection on him.

I could also hear him saying, "See, I told you this show business was bad. You should have listened to me."

As for Mother, I can only guess what she would have said to me. Since she seemed to celebrate any occasion to put me down, I wonder if this might not have been her golden opportunity. I lie awake at night sometimes, hearing her voice in my mind. *I hope you're happy now that someone is dead. You always thought you were better than everybody else. Now everybody knows you're not.*

On the other hand, she might have surprised me with unqualified emotional support, but that's something I'll never know.

In the same way that I hope this book may help someone else overcome adversities, the one person I believe it *will* help more than anyone else is me. I know that I never properly grieved for my mother, and maybe I never will. But spending this much time thinking about my life, so tied to hers, has brought all the old issues to the surface again, reopening every wound and reminding me of every cut. It brought to mind all the times Mother lacked compassion and I lacked understanding.

In the years since Dr. Secunda appeared on the show discussing mothers and daughters, I've thought a great deal about what she had to say. One thing stuck out in my mind: She said that in one of her books she wrote a letter to her mother. I think she said that for a reason, and I've decided to take her advice and write a letter too.

Whether or not my mother hears me, I need to do it for me.

Dear Mother,

I'm sorry. Sorry for so many things, starting with our lost relationship. I'm not so much sorry for your death as for your life, one that seemed to be lived with little hope. I wonder, did you ever have dreams and aspirations, and, if so, what were they? I realize now that I never knew much about your childhood, your youth. And the older we got the less I felt I knew you. By the time you died it seemed as though we were strangers. Now there are so many questions I wish I could ask. Where did you come from, and what was your life like before war broke out in Europe? What kind of little girl were you? Were you like me? Did you have any toys or friends? What did you want to be when you grew up? Were you happy then, or was your childhood full of pain and hardship?

You never talked about your life. Maybe you wanted to forget your past, but I wish you had talked more about yourself. Well, not as much as Father did. Remember how he talked and talked? Hey, could you see me making faces at

Liz and rolling my eyes? I'd happily sit through any of those long speeches of his just to have one day with you now. There is so much I wish I could say.

I forgive you. Not for the way things turned out between us, because I know that was all you knew how to do, but for a mistake that you made when you were very young. How tragic that one mistake, a wartime affair, could change so much. Father could never forgive you, but I understand that people make mistakes. You were only twenty-three years old, the same age I was when I was racing blindly into adulthood, making one mistake after another.

As for all the hurtful things that you said, I forgive you for that too. After you died, I went through a box of your things and found every postcard and letter I'd ever sent you, and every newspaper clipping and article, all painstakingly put in scrapbooks. You saved everything. Then I found a slip of paper folded over with a picture of us inside. On the paper you had written down everything I ever gave you, from the car right down to the new can opener. I hope those things made your life a little better. I wish I could have done more. If I could have helped you recover from your disease, there was so much more we could have done together, like taken trips and cruises, or gone for long walks in Springbank Park.

I found something else among your things, your Canadian citizenship papers ripped to shreds. I wonder if you hated everything about life in the new world.

Please don't blame yourself or put yourself down for drinking. Alcoholism ran in your family, and being an alcoholic doesn't make you a bad person. There are many people with the same illness. Some recover, some do not. I understand now, and I hope you forgive me if I ever seemed judgmental. I never meant to be. I see now that I could have become an alcoholic very easily myself.

I know that much of what I remember about our relationship is negative. In your own way, perhaps without meaning to, you made me a stronger person. I'm going to think of *the good things now, because I know you are no longer in a negative place. I hope you are somewhere playing your guitar and singing Polish folk songs, or maybe sitting on a blanket in the sun, making a crown of dandelions like you used to make for me. Maybe you're still doing puzzles, but this time I hope you've finally put all the pieces together.*

Hey, guess what? My talk show is more successful than ever, and this is my seventh year on the air. And because of that, somebody even wanted to publish a book about my life. Now I know that at one time you didn't think I'd done anything interesting, but in looking back I think I have. And my life, whatever it is, is tied to yours, so I'm writing about you too. I hope you understand that I had to tell the truth. But I think people will come to know you in a way I only understood too late.

I even put your picture in the book, and in this one family picture you look so beautiful. That's how I'll remember you. You were a hot-looking woman. A hot momma!

I miss you, Mom.

Love,
Janina

After writing the letter, I thought about a question I'm often asked: "What would your ultimate dream show topic be?"

I really hadn't given it much thought before. But after writing the letter to my mother, a show idea came to me in such vivid detail I felt like it was scheduled to be taped tomorrow. I could even see the title on the show folder: "Mothers and Daughters: Finally Friends." But once I opened the folder and began doing my homework, it became clear that this would be no ordinary show. In this fantasy I'd get to be not only the show's host but also its first guest.

I laid the show folder on my lap, closed my eyes, and watched the show unfold on a television screen in my mind.

I walk out from backstage, as usual. The audience applauds, as usual. I answer a few of their questions, as usual, then walk to my mark in the middle of the crowd. But from this point on, nothing about this show happens as usual.

I introduce the first guest and it's me, sitting alone onstage beside an empty chair.

Then the camera cuts to me as talk show host, standing in the audience. "Welcome to today's show, which we're calling 'Mothers and Daughters: Finally Friends,'" I say. "I'd like to introduce my first guest, Janina. She says she has spent her entire life trying to please her mother, only to be criticized and put down. She says she can barely remember any sign of affection from her mother. And even though her mother passed away in 1994, Janina still feels that no matter what she does it's never good enough."

I barely begin to interview myself about my relationship with my mother when a dozen hands shoot up around me. I walk over to a well-dressed woman in the middle row and hold out the microphone.

"Did you ever think that maybe there were things in your mother's past that prevented her from showing you affection?" she asks.

The camera cuts to me onstage, and my words pour out with barely choked-back emotion.

"I never thought about her childhood until I wrote my book," I say. "I know now that she lived the only way she knew how, but I still can't help wishing things could've been different. Somehow, I still blame myself for not being able to help her, just as I blame her for just checking out of life, instead of grabbing and embracing it the way I did. I wish I could've been more tolerant and understanding. If I could do things over again I would urge her to talk to a therapist to help her understand herself. Then maybe she could have been able to tell me more about her life and her feelings. I don't think she was ever in touch with her emotions."

Back on the floor, another woman has her hand up. I hold out the microphone and, as our audience members always do, she immediately gets to the heart of the matter.

"Who knows what was going on in your mother's past?" she asks. "Was there sexual abuse? Physical abuse? You say her father was an alcoholic. Who knows, and finally, what does any of this matter now? You have two choices: continue feeling the pain, or choose to believe that your mother really did love you, but she just didn't know how to show it. Seems to me you ought to let your mother's memory be just that—a memory—and get on with your own life. That's the best way to honor your mother—and yourself."

The audience applauds in a strong show of support.

By now tears are streaming down my face.

"There's nothing you can do now to change anything that has happened," I say. "So where do you go from here, Janina?"

I finally have my answer. "Only forward," I say from the stage. "Never back anymore."

Now dozens of other hands are rising up, mothers and daughters eager to relate their own unique experiences, in hopes of helping me. I sit on the stage, anxiously waiting to reunite with my mother. Since this is my fantasy, I get to have her with me one more time. Only now she comes walking out from the wings not as I saw her last, but as the beautiful young woman I always remembered her to be. She's wearing a big, luminous smile and a gorgeous crown of freshly cut dandelions. She hugs me, then reaches up and takes the flowers from around her head and puts them on mine.

We stand embracing before the audience with tears streaming down our faces. Pretty soon the audience is on its feet and crying too. Even the cameramen and crew members begin to cry, as we fade into the break. When the segment is over, Mother and I, still embracing and still crying, stand triumphantly in this one perfect moment of absolute clarity and understanding. Because it's only through understanding, even if it's gained through the medium of a daytime talk show, that we can finally begin the journey toward a new tomorrow.

When I open my eyes, the show is over, but the enlightenment remains.

What does it all mean? Maybe I've been afforded yet another chance to reinvent myself. One thing is certain. Wherever the road leads me next, at least I won't be looking back anymore.

The Susan Love Breast Cancer Research Program at UCLA

I am very grateful to Jenny Jones for her generous support of breast cancer research. Breast cancer has reached epidemic proportions, affecting one in eight women. We still do not know the cause of this disease nor how to prevent it. Early detection can sometimes find a tumor at a curable stage, but one-third of women who are diagnosed with breast cancer still die of the disease. All these facts would be very gloomy if it were not for the enormous wave of innovative research under way, which promises to change the way we think about breast cancer forever. I am very optimistic that we can turn the tide of this disease.

At the Susan Love Breast Cancer Research Program, we are excited to be pursuing research interests on many fronts. Funding such as that provided by Jenny allows us to pursue new ideas and take risks. The answers to this disease are not going to come from following the same old path, but from daring to go down new paths with courage and determination. We are grateful to Jenny for her support.

Dr. Susan Love
Pacific Palisades, California
August 14, 1997